Mitchell College Library
New London, Conn.

PSYCHOLOGICAL STUDIES

OF

FAMOUS AMERICANS

PSYCHOLOGICAL STUDIES

OF

FAMOUS AMERICANS

The Civil War Era

Edited by

NORMAN KIELL

TWAYNE PUBLISHERS, INC.

NEW YORK

© *Copyright 1964 by Twayne Publishers, Inc.*

ALL RIGHTS RESERVED

Library of Congress Catalog Card Number: 63-19366

MANUFACTURED IN THE UNITED STATES OF AMERICA

973.7
K-54

20118

Mitchell College Library
New London, Conn.

For

MATTHEW

ACKNOWLEDGMENTS

The compiler of this volume is genuinely grateful to the following individuals and publishers who so generously gave their permission to use the following materials, and wishes to express his thanks in this necessarily inadequate fashion.

To the American Psychological Association for D. A. Hartman's "The Psychological Point of View in History: Some Phases of the Slavery Struggle," originally published in the *Journal of Abnormal Psychology*, 1922-23, 17:261-273.

To Alfred A. Knopf, Inc., for the chapters by C. Vann Woodward and David Donald. Professor Woodward's "John Brown's Private War" originally appeared in *America in Crisis; Fourteen Critical Episodes in American History*, edited by Daniel Aaron in 1952, pp. 109-130. Professor Donald's "The Vacant Chair" comes from his *Charles Sumner and the Coming of the Civil War*, published in 1960, pp. 323-342.

To Edward J. Kempf, M.D., and the American Medical Association for "Abraham Lincoln's Organic and Emotional Neurosis," first published in the *AMA Archives of Neurology and Psychiatry*, 1952, 67:419-433.

To Dr. A. Bronson Feldman, Ezra G. Benedict Fox and the Editor of *Psychoanalysis and the Psychoanalytic Review* for the following three articles: A. Bronson Feldman, "Abe Lincoln: the Psychology of a Cult, *Psychoanalysis*, 1952, 1:7-24;

Ezra G. Benedict Fox, "Was General Lee a Victim of Group Psychology?" *Psychoanalysis and the Psychoanalytic Review,* 1961, 48:62-68; and L. Pierce Clark, "Unconscious Motives Underlying the Personalities of Great Statesmen and Their Relation to Epoch-Making Events. A Psychological Study of Abraham Lincoln," *Psychoanalytic Review,* 1921, 8:1-21.

To the Editor of *American Imago* for George W. Wilson's "A Prophetic Dream Reported by Abraham Lincoln," which appeared in that journal in 1940, 1:42-48; and for Paul Lauter's "Walt Whitman: Lover and Comrade," which came out in the same journal, 1959, 16:407-435.

To W. W. Norton, Inc., for "The Tyrant Father," a chapter from Fawn M. Brodie's book, *Thaddeus Stevens. Scourge of the South,* published in 1959, pages 94-102.

To Professor William B. Hesseltine for the chapter from his *Ulysses S. Grant: Politician,* "Forty Years of Failure," published by Frederick Ungar in 1957, pages 1-8.

To Philip Weissman, M.D., for his "Why Booth Killed Lincoln. A Psychoanalytic Study of a Historical Tragedy," which first saw print in *Psychoanalysis and the Social Sciences,* Vol. V, edited by Warner Muensterberger and Sidney Axelrad, and published by International Universities Press in 1958.

To *Surgery, Gynecology, & Obstetrics,* Copyright, 1948, by the Franklin H. Martin Memorial Foundation, for Josiah C. Trent's "Walt Whitman—A Case History," originally published in *Surgery, Gynecology, & Obstetrics,* 1948, 87:113-121.

The selection by John Aldington Symonds comes from his work, *Walt Whitman, A Study,* published in London by J. C. Nimmo in 1893. The excerpt, "The Religion of Healthy-Mindedness" by William James is abstracted from *The Varieties of Religious Experience,* pages 76 to 84 in the New American Library edition of 1958.

Table of Contents

Introduction

IN NORMAN O. BROWN's stimulating book, *Life Against Death,
the Psychoanalytic Meaning of History*, there appears the provocative chapter, "Neurosis and History." In it, Brown states flatly, "The
necessity of a psychoanalytic approach to history is pressed upon
the historian by one question: Why does man, alone of all animals,
have a history (3, p. 15)?"

And he presents the arguments of what psychoanalysis has to
offer. "Psychoanalysis offers a theoretical framework for exploring
the possibility of a way out of the nightmare of endless 'progress'
and endless Faustian discontent, a way out of the human neurosis,
a way out of history. In the case of the neurotic individual, the
goal of psychoanalytic therapy is to free him from the burden of
his past, from the burden of his history, the burden which compels
him to go on having (and being) a case history. And the method
of psychoanalytic therapy is to deepen the historical consciousness
of the individual ('fill up the memory gaps') till he awakens from
his own history as from a nightmare. Psychoanalytic consciousness,
as a higher stage in the general consciousness of mankind, may be
likewise the fulfillment of the historical consciousness, that ever
widening and deepening search for origins which has obsessed
Western thought ever since the Renaissance. If historical consciousness is finally transformed into psychoanalytic consciousness, the
grip of the dead hand of the past on life in the present would be
lessened, and man would be ready to live instead of making history, to enjoy instead of paying back old scores and debts, and to
enter that state of Being which was the goal of his Becoming
(3, p. 19)."

William M. Langer, in his presidential address before the
American Historical Association in 1957, also vigorously called for

11

the application of psychoanalysis to historical studies. Preceding him, near the turn of the present century, were such other eminent historians as James Harvey Robinson (20), Preserved Smith (21), and Harry Elmer Barnes (2), and, subsequently, a number of others.

It was clear to them that the relationship between history, biography and psychology was clearly established, although not always recognized. The historian, it was felt, needed fundamental ideas of human behavior; he needed knowledge of the character patterns of specific individuals and groups and how such patterns have been produced, and he needed to understand the intellectual and emotional background of personality. All these psychology could furnish. Psychology, the argument continued, is related to the historical approach and as such is valuable to the historian and biographer because (1) it is microscopic and macroscopic; (2) it is interested in concrete cases and events as well as in the general character of experiences; and (3) it studies causes and effects.

In about 1890, the first systematic attempt to correlate history and psychology was postulated by the Leipzig historian, Karl Lamprecht, who based his doctrines on the psychological investigations of his fellow townsman, Wilhelm Wundt. Lamprecht's thesis, that history is a socio-psychological science, exerted "a deep influence on many European historians, as well as upon progressive historians in America, by boldly staking out a relatively new field. To Lamprecht, history was the collective psychology of the past rather than the collective biography, as had been the opinion of the typical historian who had generally followed Carlyle's view on historical causation (1)."

At about the same time Lamprecht was working out his theories, the Italian psychiatrist Lombroso and the German investigator P. J. Möbius were producing a number of case studies detailing the clinical histories of geniuses who showed abnormal symptoms. Möbius originated the term "pathography," and his work is a forerunner of the numerous German studies, and subsequently English, French and American, in this field. The historical importance of Möbius' work is attested to by Lange-Eichbaum who stated, "It is to him that we owe the fact that psychopathography attained the rank of science in Germany." The terms, psychograph, pathography, and psychobiography, never caught on, although works in this area were published profusely in the early decades of the nineteen hundreds. Some examples are: "Hector Berlioz, eine pathographische Studie (10)"; "La Psychographie de Marcel Proust (4)"; "The Art of Psychography (6)"; "Les methodes de pathographie historique et biographique (8)."

In Great Britain and the United States, in the late nineteenth and early twentieth centuries, the new science of psychology interacted with biography in ways stimulating to both disciplines. The controversy, according to Garraty, which raged in the profession over the relative roles of heredity and environment in controlling human nature led to the study of biographies of great men by the proponents of the two sides and resulted in a recognition of the importance of both factors in the life of the individual. "The psychologists who turned to biographies for evidence were usually willing to assume the factual accuracy of the average life, but they were appalled by the prudishness and psychological ignorance of Victorian biographers. . . . In working on his *Study of British Genius* (1904) which drew evidence from the *Dictionary of National Biography,* Havelock Ellis was shocked by the lack of psychological understanding in most lives. Indeed, as early as 1896 he had decried the unscientific nature of most biographical writing. Biography, he said, was really a branch of applied psychology, yet few biographers knew anything of the theories of men like Wilhelm Wundt, G. Stanley Hall, Hugo Münsterberg, and Joseph Jastrow . . . (14)."

This was almost to be expected, for in the tradition of biographical writing up to this time, little of the personal life of the subject was dwelt on. There is an unexpectedly abundant number of autobiographical documents, dating back to the second and third millennia B.C., to be found among the ancient civilized peoples of the Middle East. "But," Misch tells us, "in all this abundance of material there is an infinite poverty of individual character. In all these documents we scarcely ever find any personal touch (19)." This is similarly true for the personal documents of the Greeks and Romans, for these people were "unable to conceive an individual man in the full reality of his existence (23)." It is not until St. Augustine that we have the intimate revelation of the whole course of an individual life. There followed but a handful of works which approximate our modern idea of history, such as the autobiographies of Cellini, Cardan, and Guibert, Abbot de Nogent Sous Coucy.

In his study of English biography before 1700, Stauffer writes, "During the period here studied, biographers based their works upon the seldom-questioned assumption that the life of an individual might be expressed as the sum of his separate acts. With such models in the sixteenth and seventeenth-century life-writing before them, the autobiographers themselves also produced objective accounts—impersonal annals of *res gestae* . . . (22)."

This almost unbroken tradition of sterile and restricted biographical material, reaching its apogee in the Victorian period, was pierced with the publication of Sigmund Freud's *Interpretation of Dreams* in 1900. It rocked the whole intellectual world with its emphasis on unconscious motivation and sex. "By the outbreak of the First World War the master himself had applied his theories to biography, and together with a few disciples had produced the first really important new development in the writing of lives since the eighteenth century. To demonstrate the applicability of psychoanalysis to biography Freud chose a subject for whom a conventional approach was seriously handicapped by the shortage of evidence: Leonardo da Vinci (14, p.112)." Freud ingeniously took a single childhood memory of Leonardo's, together with the known facts of the artist's trial and acquittal for homosexuality, and masterfully reconstructed the whole unconscious psychic life of the most inscrutable, the most fascinating personage of the Renaissance.

Its mark on biography is still felt. The psychoanalytic technique for understanding personality and for acquiring new insights into the meaning of documents was of paramount importance. Garraty ascribes five reasons for the importance of Freud's life of Leonardo: (1) Its assumptions and generalizations behind the specific conclusions about a specific case; (2) Its explanation why seemingly petty details supply "the clearest descriptions of virtue or vice in men. . . . All the great biographers had recognized intuitively the relationship among chance expressions, casual mannerisms, oddities of behavior, and a man's underlying character; only with Freud was this relationship given a theoretical basis"; (3) Its comments on the overly biased biographer and the pitfalls inherent therein; (4) Its dry, scholarly, yet completely candid exposition of the role of sex, which compelled people to recognize that sex could not be ignored; and (5) Its reconciliation of science's tendency to generalize with biography's tendency to particularize. "The rise of the social sciences had harmed biography because the scientists had insisted that the individual was worthy of study only as a means of determining the 'laws' of human behavior. Freud's own study of many individuals had led him to the 'laws' of psychoanalysis. In his *Leonardo* he had turned the process back on itself, using the 'laws' to throw light on the individual. But . . . he did not insist that the 'laws' *determined* the actions of the single case (14, p. 118)."

Freud himself wrote in his *Leonardo*, "In general, we must fix the limits of what psychoanalysis can accomplish in biography in order that every omitted explanation should not be held up to us as a failure. Psychoanalytic investigation has at its disposal the data of the history of the person's life, which, on the one hand, consists of accidental events and environmental influences, and, on the other hand, of the reported reactions of the individual. Based on the knowledge of the psychic mechanisms, psychoanalysis then seeks to investigate dynamically the character of the individual from his reactions, and to lay bare his earliest psychic motive forces as well as their latest transformations and developments. If this succeeds, then the behavior of the personality is explained through the co-operation of constitutional and accidental factors, or through inner and outer forces (12)."

Freud's humility, in confessing frankly that he could not demonstrate Leonardo's case beyond argument, was unhappily not matched by many of his followers. Even as late as 1956, Edward Hitschmann, one of Freud's earliest disciples, pompously wrote, "Only a psychoanalyst is completely competent to write biographies of great men, for their greatness is rooted in the conflicts and stresses of the oedipal drama (16)." The dogma of orthodox psychoanalysis was also objected to because it was felt to be totalitarian in form, tending to imprison man in the strait jacket of its own excesses. The unrestrained certitude of many psychoanalysts in positing the new theories provoked the traditionalists into obdurate resistance. In addition, the shock of the daring Freudian theses created massive personal resistances to acceptance. When Freud's theories seeped down to the popularizers of biography in the nineteen-twenties, the "pseudo-Freudians titillated the public with jargon-filled analyses of the psyches and psychoses of great men, and debunkers flailed about wildly demolishing reputations. Imagination was substituted freely for research, fact was subordinated to effect, rumor replaced reason. . . . The result, in the hands of experts like Strachey, André Maurois and Emil Ludwig, was great fun to read. But these 'new' biographies failed to treat adequately the serious side of their subjects' lives . . . [Then in the thirties] a far more important, if less noticed, trend appeared. It was spearheaded by scholars who saw in the excesses of the 'new' biographers the germ of a method that could produce books important as well as interesting, reliable as well as readable (13)."

What is important about the competent biographer's use of psychoanalysis and the psychoanalyst's use of personal documents and history is that it is not a mere matching of roughly corresponding elements from each of these areas but a true integration of scientific facts and hypotheses with the material of the study. What is still more important is that the biographical subject stands in the center of focus while psychoanalytic insights are used not as ends in themselves but only as a means to bring the subject into clear definition.

It was early recognized that the difficulty with biographies is that they do not fulfill the conditions of exact laboratory observation; there is no adequate guarantee of their authenticity. Screen memories, deliberate distortion, unconscious bias and omissions, preclude it. But nevertheless, "to the psychiatrist, biography is of particular interest, as it gives him a broader view of what the possibilities of human life are; it shows him that outside the clinical field there are a great many experiences which form part and parcel of the varied texture of human life and which are not monopolized by the patients of the psychiatrist (7)." Similarly, Marie Bonaparte, in her defense of biography, wrote, "Biography . . . has another and higher function than the mere satisfying of an idle or unhealthy curiosity. For those who understand . . . biography becomes a means of communing with a wider humanity (5)."

Despite such opportunities to study human nature, the social scientist and the literary writer, as well as the psychologist and psychiatrist, still have doubts about applying psychological principles to biography and history. What Goldenweiser wrote in 1940 is still fundamentally true today. "The psychological findings and theories of the psychoanalysts, although no longer ignored or merely scoffed at as they were at the beginning, are not by any means accepted by more than a fraction of psychiatrists, psychologists, or social students (15, p. 391)." He warned that "It is tempting to apply the insights of psychoanalysis to a speculative interpretation of historical characters. . . . But the procedure is hazardous in the extreme. . . . If psychoanalysis is to maintain its status as a system of individual psychology, using a minutely controlled biographical method, then historical characters and literary figures represent but poor material for its application. After all, what psychoanalysis, at its best, is attempting to do is to reveal new facts and processes of psychic life and to illumine them by the light of its theoretical constructs, not to project speculative possibilities such as interpretations of historical characters. . . (15, pp. 416, 417)."

But no one should object to the use of Freudian techniques, says Garraty, "if they are explicitly described as speculations, and if known facts are not twisted or ignored in order to bring the subject into a preconceived pattern. We cannot get our Luthers, Wagners, and Napoleons on the couch, but we know some of the things they could have revealed there and no harm can come from considering the available facts in the light of Freud's insights. Much of the criticism that has been aimed at psychoanalytical biography has arisen from the dogmatic way in which the authors of such works have stated their cases. . . . If the psychoanalytic writers would confess the speculative nature of their conclusions, their critics would be less bitter. With a measure of tolerance and co-operation, historians and biographers could learn a great deal from the psychologists, but they seldom have been willing to try . . . (14, p. 220)." Complementing this statement, two psychologists, Cantril and Bumstead, in writing about the value of personal documents, say, "We should pay attention to what is revealed through other avenues to 'truth,' to modes of inquiry that differ from those of science. Most human beings carry on their living, their learning, their observing, outside the scope of the scientist's laboratory or constructs (8)."

It is my belief that in the course of recent years, psychology and biography have become almost inseparable. Psychoanalysis, together with anthropology, history, biology, sociology and literature, plays an essential part in the science of man. The unconscious processes of an individual are indispensable for the understanding of his character and personality. Psychoanalysis has given a new dimension to understanding in the problems of human behavior; and the essence of biography today, like the psychoanalytic method, is to uncover the unconscious and to demonstrate the modes by means of which the unconscious retains its content, while powerfully determining behavior. "In the psychoanalytic process the analyst has constant access to the symbol life of his subject—dreams; modes of expression (such as slips of the tongue and the pen); association; the interconnection of experience; rationalization; involuntary memory; the events of everyday life. A biographer also deals in such materials . . . (9)."

The biographer, too, has access, albeit not constant, to the symbol life of his subject. The larger armamentarium of the psychologist today enables the biographer to pursue mutual goals. Some of the tools include the analysis of handwriting, paintings, drawings, dreams, projective techniques and a content analysis of the subject's written works. This implies a thorough-going knowledge of psychoanalytic theory and psychological techniques on the part of the biographer-social scientist (and on the other hand, the psychoanalyst must become a deep student of history and literature).

This is assuredly within the realm of possibility. Leon Edel, Lionel Trilling, Alfred Kazin, Edmund Wilson, Floyd Dell, Leslie Fiedler, William Ellery Leonard, Stefan Zweig, Romain Rolland, and Ludwig Lewisohn, to name a few creative writers and critics, and Freud, Ernest Jones, Mark Kanzer, David Beres, Charles Kligerman, Ernst Kris and Gustav Bychowski, all psychoanalysts, have combined their knowledge in their respective competencies with other disciplines to produce some of the greatest insights and illuminate areas which were heretofore impenetrable. Louis

Fraiberg, an outstanding literary critic, states, "If we are to derive the greatest benefit from psychoanalysis in our study of the creative process—or any other literary problem for which it has relevance— we must always keep before us the difference between our way of looking at literature and the psychoanalyst's. Since they are not the same, this means that in order to make intelligent use of psychoanalytic findings and theories we need to understand where they came from and how they were arrived at. To put it bluntly, we must know psychoanalysis as well as we know literature and criticism (11)."

Extensive use of psychoanalytic principles by literary writers and historians is now being made. The biographer today rightly feels that his work becomes meaningful only in relation to personality and to his interpretation of personality. Biography, writes Kanzer, "is not to be approached merely in terms of external events; inner motivation must always be stressed, and this must be deduced by the biographer according to the facts and insight that he has at his disposal. We may well assume that analysis is a justified, indeed the most justified, tool that a biographer can use for this purpose. Our problem is to define not whether psychoanalysis is applicable to biography, but how and with what limitations (17)."

I have tried, in bringing together this collection of psychologically oriented biographical studies, to use an orthopsychiatric approach. The writings represented come from the pens of psychoanalysts, psychologists, general medical practitioners, medical specialists, historians with an intuitive understanding of the psyche, as well as other, more psychologically-sophisticated historians, and lastly, literary critics, with equally perceptive psychological insights.

The nine troubled men in this volume were all central figures in the drama played out during the Civil War. My interest in this period was aroused as I read the psychological literature on personalities of the Civil War days which was scattered in a number of professional journals. It was only natural, it seemed to me, to bring these pieces together not only for the new insights they convey but also for the enjoyment they provide. From a reading of these essays, it will be seen that man is so complex that no simple determinism can explain him. This is perhaps the great point that Freud has contributed to human understanding. It has occurred to the editor and publisher that because man's behavior is not always explainable by outward manifestations, a series of similar volumes, dealing with the unconscious motivations of famous poets, playwrights, novelists, religious leaders and other historical personalities, might serve a useful function.

The orthopsychiatric approach used in this book will give rise, it is hoped, to greater understanding of the personalities discussed. For example, the section on Lincoln consists of four parts. The first is concerned with the organicity of Lincoln's neurosis. Dr. Kempf reaches the conclusion that Lincoln was shackled to his melancholy by virtue of the interaction of an organic visual neurosis (consequent to a severe head injury at the age of ten) and a specifically functional neurosis (mother fixation) that worked in a repetitive circle. For protection, Lincoln developed his well-known philosophy and humor. The second article, by Dr. Clark, relates the unconscious mechanisms which were operative in Lincoln's personality, dwelling primarily on his oedipal conflict and ensuing depression. In the third article, Dr. Wilson analyzes a dream reported by Lincoln, to which the latter attributed prophetic significance. Lincoln's carelessness in exposing himself to physical attack contrasted with his many presentiments and his pessimistic attitude regarding his own fate. The manifest content of a dream shortly before his death depicts his exhibitionistic and self-destructive impulses as well as the omniscience and denial of actual death by the dreamer. The concluding article, by Dr. Feldman, is concerned with the myths and the cult that have developed about the personality of Lincoln. To American mythology, the Lincoln legend offers unrivalled raw material for study, social illusion and social and national dreams. Lincoln is shown as standing in strong psychic consanguinity with his country, although he was not always seen as representing fatherhood. Lincoln's loss was so great because he so perfectly exemplified the ego-ideal of the common man, the anonymous, the mass; and his magnetism consisted of the craving of the masses for a paternal, a Mosaic liberation from their dull and deadly servitude. For John Wilkes Booth, at least, Lincoln represented so completely a father image that, as Dr. Weissman shows us in a later section, his assassination of Lincoln represents the physical expression of an overwhelming, repressed, patricidal impulse. In his reconstruction of the personality of Booth, Dr. Weissman indicates the paranoid personality of the assassin and shows that Booth's act not only constituted patricide but represented fratricide as well.

Not every personality included in this book has been the subject of so much psychological interest. Thus, with the other exception of Walt Whitman, the reader will find only single chapters on Civil War personalities of the seven remaining. But the diversity of approaches here too will enable one to read the subject with new insights. The application of psychology to biography, it is hoped, will add to the reading public's interest in these areas. The truly significant facts of human behavior illuminate the behavior of the historical personality, make him come alive, and provide the leavening for the historian's factual data. It is with this prospect that the reader can turn these pages for reconstructions of some of the outstanding personalities of the most fascinating era in United States history.

Kgs. Lyngby, Denmark,
March 29, 1963.

Notes

1 Barnes, H. E. Psychology and history. *Amer. J. Psychol.*, 1919, 30:348.
2 Barnes, H. E. Some reflections on the possible services of analytic psychology to history. *Psychol. Rev.*, 1921, 8:22-37.
3 Brown, N. O. *Life Against Death. The Psychoanalytical Meaning of History.* NY: Random House, 1959.
4 Blondell, C. *La Psychographie de Marcel Proust.* Paris: Vrin, 1932,
5 Bonaparte, M. A defense of biography. *Int. J. Psycho-Anal.*, 1939, 20:239.
6 Bradford, G. The art of psychography. *New York Post Lit. Rev.*, 1923, 3:641-642.

7 Campbell, C. M. Psychology and biography. *Amer. J. Psychiat.*, 1931, 10:855.

8 Cantril, H., & Bumstead, C. H. *Reflections on the Human Venture*. NY: New York University Press, 1960, p. 6.

9 Edel, L. *Literary Biography*. Garden City, NY: Doubleday Anchor Books, 1959, p. 92.

10 Feis, O. *Hector Berlioz, eine pathographische Studie*. Wiesbaden: Bergmann, 1911.

11 Fraiberg, L. Literature and psychology: a question of significant form. *Lit. & Psychol.*, 1955, 5:77.

12 Freud, S. *Leonardo Da Vinci. A Study in Psychosexuality*. NY: Vintage, 1961, p. 117.

13 Garraty, J. A. How should you tell a man's story? *New York Times Book Rev.*, July 5, 1959, p. 1.

14 Garraty, J. A. *The Nature of Biography*. NY: Alfred A. Knopf, 1957.

15 Goldenweiser, A. Some contributions of psychoanalysis to the interpretation of social facts. In Barnes, H. E., Becker, H., & Becker, F. B. (eds.), *Contemporary Social Theory*. NY: Appleton-Century Co., 1940.

16 Hitschmann, E. Some psycho-analytic aspects of biography. *Int. J. Psycho-Anal.*, 1956, 37:265.

17 Kanzer, M. Autobiographical aspects of the writer's imagery. *Int. J. Psycho-Anal.*, 1959, 40:52.

18 Ley, A. Les methodes de pathographie historique et biographique. *J. belge Neurol. Psychiat.*, 1934, 34:438–444.

19 Misch, G. *A History of Autobiography in Antiquity*. Cambridge, Mass.: Harvard University Press, 1951, Vol. 1, p. 19.

20 Robinson, J. H. *The New History*. NY: Macmillan, 1912.

21 Smith, P. Luther's early development in the light of psychoanalysis. *Amer. J. Psychol.*, 1913, 24:260.

22 Stauffer, D. *English Biography before 1700*. Cambridge, Mas.: Harvard University Press, 1930, p. 175.

23 Wilamowitz-Moellendorff, U. von. Die Autobiographie im Altertum. *Int. Wochenschrift für Wissenschaft*, 1907. 1:1105.

PSYCHOLOGICAL STUDIES
OF
FAMOUS AMERICANS

1

WILLIAM LLOYD GARRISON

HARTMAN, IN THE FOLLOWING CHAPTER, ATTEMPTS TO INTERPRET THE
struggle over slavery on a psychological basis. He analyzes the
techniques of abolitionist propaganda literature in terms of likening the cause which one espouses to causes concerning which
there is no doubt, and likening the cause of one's opponents to
lost, unpopular and detested movements. He then traces the development of the attitude of the South toward slavery from 1830 until
the Civil War.

Hartman finds the conflict to be primarily between the profit
motive of the growing cotton industry and the dawning realization of the moral evil and danger of slavery. The moral issue was
ignored by the South, thus making necessary a defense mechanism.
This took the form of various rationalizations: (1) slavery was
sanctioned by God; (2) the Negro was better off economically;
(3) slavery protected the "honor" of the white women of the South
(that which was lost in the moral behavior of the white men was
compensated for by the chastity of the Southern women); and (4)
the terrible nature of white prostitution in the North.

The author deals not only with the psychology of slavery but
also writes about the reformer and abolitionist William Lloyd

Garrison. Hartman raises the question and tries to answer it: What were the unconscious drives behind Garrison's interests and work as the noted editor of the *Liberator?* He points up the significant factors in the editor's youth which illuminate his behavior and will perhaps surprise the reader.

In addition, Hartman demonstrates how pre-bellum citizens committed to anti-slavery were labelled by slave owners as socialists and communists; that not only was slavery believed to be approved by God but evidence for it was also readily available in the Bible; and that rather than an evil, slavery was a humanitarian institution and a boon to mankind. It is rather startling to discover that some of these century-old defenses are still being used today to justify the segregation of the Negro, whether in the South or the North.

The Psychological Point of View in History: Some Phases of the Slavery Struggle

D. A. HARTMAN

THERE HAS DEVELOPED within recent years an increased interest in the application of psychology to history,[1] a demand for a greater co-operation voiced by both the historian and the psychologist. Psychology offers the historian the modern scientific concept of human behavior to take the place of the antiquated theories of human nature. The psychologist, on the other hand, borrows from the historian the results of researches. The extent to which this has been carried on is striking when one recalls how replete with examples from history have been recent books on social psychology. The historian, however, has been much slower in making use of psychology. The psychological interpretation of history, it must be granted, is in its initial stage. A considerable resistance must be overcome, for the average historian shares with all people the inertia of custom and self-satisfaction.

I have heard many historians lament the fact that the reading public has lost interest in history. Is it not possible that the intelligent reader with a scientific understanding of human behavior finds the history written from the point of view of some antiquated conception of human nature rather unreal and, consequently, uninteresting? Perhaps some historians have given too much time to the digging up of past facts of human conduct, and too little time to the recognition of the real significance of those facts. The historical problem is fundamentally a psychological problem. The modern science of human conduct offers a tool for the solution of the problem. "The historian needs his psychology as the physicist needs his mathematics." [2]

The writer of history is dealing with human behavior in the

past. Before he writes about a given period he must find all the
facts that the record of the times can give him. But the great
number of details that he discovers cannot be placed before the
reader. The historian must select the significant facts. But if he
approaches his task with some antiquated notion of human nature,
he will be blind to the truly significant facts of human behavior.
To the intelligent reader his history will be unreal.

The reformer of 1830 had a "psychology" as well as has the
reformer of today. The historian, to give a true estimate of the
work of William Lloyd Garrison, the Abolitionist, should understand the nature of the reformer. Was the realization of the evil
of slavery the driving force behind Garrison's efforts, or was Abolition merely one means of expressing a far more general drive? In
this connection it is interesting to note that Garrison was a "reformer" before he became an abolitionist. In 1828 he was editor of
one of the first "prohibition" papers in the United States, *The
Philanthropist.*[3] As late as 1829 Garrison said: "I acknowledge that
immediate and complete emancipation is not desirable. . . . No
rational man cherishes so wild a vision." [4] Two years later, in the
first number of his abolition paper, the *Liberator,* we read: "I shall
strenuously contend for the immediate enfranchisement of our
slave population—I will be as harsh as truth and as uncompromising as justice on this subject—I do not wish to think, or speak, or
write with moderation—I am in earnest—I will not equivocate—I
will not retreat a single inch, and I *will be heard!*" [5] Did the fact
that few people cared to read *The Philanthropist,* that a prohibi-
tionist in 1830 would not be "*heard*," account to a certain degree
for this change?

As editor of *The Philanthropist,* in 1828, Garrison advocated, in
addition to temperance, many other reforms. He fought lotteries,
imprisonment for debt, and particularly "the desecration of the
Sabbath." [6] Universal peace was another cause to which he was
devoted at this time, and of which he never lost sight during all
of his later abolition agitation.

From evidence such as this it would seem reasonable to conclude that Garrison was primarily a reformer, an agitator, and that
the abolition of slavery was merely one method of expression for
this more fundamental drive.

A study of the factors beneath this drive for social reformation is still more interesting. It is fitting here to submit for the reader's consideration two seemingly significant instances in Garrison's youth.

I. In July, 1827, Garrison, who was then a young man of but twenty-two years, attended a nominating caucus at Boston. Although he had been in the city not more than six months, and knew very few people, he came to the political meeting with a memorized speech in behalf of a man he admired. During the course of the evening, he seized an opportunity to deliver his address. Before he had concluded, however, his memory failed him, forcing him to read from the manuscript the remainder of the eulogy.

A man who had been present at this caucus, a well-known local politician, considered the bold interruption as rather presumptuous on the part of an unknown young workingman, and expressed himself quite freely in the *Boston Courier,* July 12, 1827. Two days later the same paper published young Garrison's reply. The nature of the conclusion of this reply is significant: "It is true my acquaintance in this city is limited—I have sought for none. Let me assure him, however, that if my life be spared, my name shall one day be known to the world—at least to such an extent that common inquiry shall be unnecessary. This, I know, will be deemed excessive vanity—but time shall prove it prophetic." [7]

II.   A year later (1828) Garrison wrote the following "prophecy" to a newspaper editor who professed to ignore him: "I have only to repeat without vanity, what I declared publicly to another opponent—a political one (and I think he will never forget me)— that, if my life be spared, my name shall one day be known so extensively as to render private enquiry unnecessary, and known, too, in a praiseworthy manner. I speak in the spirit of prophecy, not of vainglory—with a strong pulse, a flashing eye, and a glow of the heart. *The task may be yours to write my biography.*" [8]

A close study, from the psychological point of view, of the life of this famous reformer may be able to show us that the recognition of the evil of slavery was not the primary cause that led to his agitation for abolition. As has been pointed out, Garrison had tried other reform activities; prohibition, anti-lottery, universal peace, and the old opposition against "the desecration of the Sabbath." It may be that the desire that his name should "one day be known so extensively as to render private enquiry unnecessary" was a factor of far from minor importance in the character of the man who played a leading part in the struggle that led up to our Civil War. Whether or not the "desire to be heard" was a potent factor in the career of this reformer can be answered by the historian who brings to his aid the results of modern psychology.

The forces behind other individuals in the abolition movement require the same study. How much truth is there in the suggestion that the abolitionist zeal of the New England deacons pleasantly obscured the fact that they and their fathers had gained their fortunes from the rum trade with the Negroes of the West Indies? [9] Was hatred toward the "aristocrat" of the South, the slave-owner whose "delicate hands" [10] did not have to "take hold of the plough, and cultivate lands" as did his brother of the North, a more powerful force than pity for the poor slave? [11] Hate is a common response against injury or a threatened injury. Man experiences this emotion "when he hears of injury or has reason to believe that injury is to be suffered." "His sufferings are largely mental and his responses are to imagined or foreseen injuries rather than to real injuries." [12] This appeal to hate by suggesting possible injuries to the northern workingman by the South was made use of in political campaigns. [13] It is also to be found in early, as well as later, anti-slavery literature. One campaign document used in 1856 alleges the following quotation from "a South Carolina paper."

The great evil of Northern *free* society is that it is burdened with a *servile* class of *mechanics* and *laborers unfit for self-government,* and yet clothed with the attributes and powers of *citizens.* Master and Slave is a relation as necessary as that of parent and child; and the Northern States will yet have to introduce it. Slavery is the natural and normal condition of the *laboring man,* whether *white* or black.

The same document quotes the *Richmond Enquirer* as saying that the principle of slavery "does not depend on *difference of complexion.*"

We find a similar quotation in an anti-slavery magazine of 1836.

Let Christian freemen awake to their political responsibilities. The penalty of a little more slumber will come upon them like "an armed man," and it may be to wear on their own necks the yokes they would not break from the necks of others, *when they had the power.* [14]

Pity for the slave was not the strong force. It was not until hate and fear entered the situation that the movement had the power to bring results. The growing class of wage earners in the North came to feel that slavery was a menace to the white workers individually and as a class. [15] To this class were added the small business men and farmers. [16] When the slave interests began to thwart the westward extension of the North into the territories, the real power of the movement against the South was developed. Hate and fear, the common response to the thwarting of the economic drives of various classes in the North, made ready that section for the conflict. Pity for the slave furnished a happy rationalization. "The Republican party was not an anti-slavery party. It was a homestead party. On this point its position was identical with that of the workingman. . . . Only because slavery could not live on one-hundred-and-sixty-acre farms did the Republican party come into conflict with slavery." [17]

We have already seen one way in which hate for the South was developed in the northern workingmen. There was another method used which is of interest here. Angell has made the observation that the crowd leader continually "likens the issues he desires to defend to other issues, whose merits are entirely beyond doubt. If he can thus identify his cause in the minds of his hearers with another cause already enjoying their cherished confidence, his victory is easily won." [18] There can be no doubt that this is an effective means of establishing a favorable attitude. It is necessary, however, to recognize a corollary of this; i. e., by likening the cause of the opposition to lost, unpopular, or detested movements, an unfavorable attitude toward the opponent's cause may be established. In this study it has seemed that the latter method has been used more than the former.

From the South we have the statement that men committed to anti-slavery ". . . are, in effect, committed to Socialism, and Communism, to the most ultra doctrines of Garrison, Goodell, Smith and Andrews—to no private property, no church, no laws, no government—to free love, free lands, free women and free churches." [19]

We find the same method again used in this form:

. . . the great movement in society, known under various names, as Communism, Socialism, Abolitionism, Red Republicanism and Black Republicanism, has one common object: the breaking up of all law and government, and . . . the destruction of the family is one of the means in which they all concur to attain a common end.[20]

A northern author employs the principle observed by Angell, as well as the corollary suggested above, by comparing the northern people with the Puritans and the people of the South with the Cavaliers. The Puritans were the men ". . . who overturned the throne of Charles I, reared a Commonwealth out of the chaos of civil war, and engendered among the English people a republican spirit . . ." On the other hand, the Cavaliers were "of that effeminate and supercilious nobility" who tried to support the tyrant king.[21] In this connection, the title of the author's book, *Barons of the South,* is of equal significance.

Closely related to this method is the giving of only the extreme cases on the opponent's side, and thus creating the impression that such deplorable conditions were universal. Garrison, in the *Liberator,* made constant use of this illusion. One historian has remarked that a person "reading the abolitionist literature . . . would come to the conclusion that the people of the South were all man-stealers and kidnappers, and that the swish of the lash was constantly heard south of the Mason and Dixon line from the beginning of the year to the end thereof. Many good people, thousands of them, hundreds of thousands of them, believed this word picture to be true." [22]

The title of the *Liberator,* and its motto, "Our Country is the World—Our Countrymen are Mankind," and titles of books, such as *Barons of the South* and *Cannibals All, or Slaves without Masters,* tend to show what wide use was made of connecting one's own cause with all that was good and one's opponent's cause with all that was bad.

It would be difficult to find in history a problem more interesting from the psychological point of view than the development of the attitude of the South toward slavery from 1830 to the outbreak of the war. Down to 1830 the South was open to discussion on the slavery question: "churches, the missionary societies, and individuals urged moderate treatment." [23] Benjamin Lundy, a northern anti-slavery man, founder of the abolition paper, *The Genius of*

Universal Emancipation, was able to organize anti-slavery societies in the South as well as in the North. [24] But about 1830 a change came in the attitude of the South toward slavery discussions; "the denunciation of slavery slacked, the efforts at amelioration hesitated, and eventually ceased," arguments against the institution changed to excuses, then to justification, "then to positive praise of slavery, then to a state of mind in which the admission that any part of its 'Peculiar Institution' ought to be reformed was regarded as disloyal." [25] Calhoun said in the Senate, February 6, 1837: "But let me not be misunderstood as admitting even by implication that the existing relations between the two races in the slave-holding states is an evil; far otherwise, I hold it to be a good, as it has thus far proved to be to both." [26] This came to be the view of practically the entire South.

The change in attitude was reflected in Congress, resulting in the House rule of 1836 by which all papers and petitions relating to slavery were held to be laid on the table without the possibility of further action. Not until December, 1844, was this "gag rule" rescinded.

About 1830 the slave-holder faced a dilemma. On the one hand was the growing belief that slavery was "the *heaviest* calamity which has ever befallen any portion of the human race," "a curse upon him who inflicts as upon him who suffers it." [27] On the other hand was the fact that cotton culture by slaves was becoming profitable. [28] The conflict between these two forces, the economic drive of the growing profit of cotton and the dawning realization of the moral evil and danger of slavery, demanded a solution. The economic pressure proved the stronger, but the moral phase could not be ignored. The solution of this conflict by the South was the building up of a *defence mechanism,* a social phenomenon worthy of the study of both the historian and the psychologist. To one who does not recognize the significance of the *defence mechanism,* a great part of the speeches and publications coming from the South after 1830 will seem to be a mass of glaring inconsistencies, worthless excuses, and pure hypocrisy.

A common form of defence mechanism is termed *rationalization.* This serves as a method of escape from "facing the facts." The individual cannot bring himself to look upon the true causes of his conduct. His escape is to replace these real causes by reasons, invented unconsciously, but accepted with the full belief that they are true explanations of his behavior and feelings.

The mechanism would seem to be similar in the case of a large social group. The "reasons" replacing the true causes come from individuals. The group as a whole is limited to accepting or rejecting these suggestions.[29] Once accepted, they are tenaciously held, impervious to all logic. We shall now examine various rationalizations accepted by the South from 1830 to 1860.

Could a man enjoy the increasing profits of slavery and at the same time be a Christian? The abolitionists incessantly hurled this question at the South. The slave-holder could not retain slavery and at the same time admit that the institution was sinful. For his own peace of mind a defence must be constructed. The attitude that slavery was sanctioned by God was gradually developed. The following quotation, taken from the writings of a pro-slavery man, shows how this was done. The author points out that "St. Paul actually apprehended a runaway slave, and sent him to his master! . . . it would be difficult to imagine sentiments and conduct more strikingly in contrast, than those of the Apostles and the abolitionists." Other examples of an attitude in the Bible favorable to slavery are mentioned, after which the author states: "I think, then, I may safely conclude, and I firmly believe, that American Slavery is not only not a sin, but especially commanded by God through Moses, and approved by Christ through his apostles. And here I might close its defence; for what God ordains, and Christ sanctifies, should surely command the respect and toleration of man." [30]

"Rabbi Morris J. Raphall stated the biblical argument in favor of slavery in its baldest form. There, in the Ten Commandments given on Mt. Sinai, he wrote, 'There where His finger scorched, the tablet shone.' The fourth commandment brought rest to all including 'Thy male slave and thy female slave' and the Lord forbade a man to covet his neighbor's house or 'his male slave, or his female slave, or his ox, or his ass.' And Abraham and Isaac, who themselves talked with God, were slave-holders. Why then invent a new sin not known to the Bible, and thus exasperate thousands of God-fearing, law-abiding citizens of the South." [31]

A similar defense warded off the humanitarian argument against slavery. The system at times might be cruel; but so were the industrial conditions of the laborer in England and in the North. In fact, so the reasoning ran, the slaves were better off than the workers in other parts of the world.[32] Indeed, slavery was a boon to all mankind, for it supplied the cotton clothing of the poor of all lands.

By enabling the poor to obtain cheap and becoming clothing, it inspired a taste for comfort, the first stimulus to civilization. Does not *self-defence*, then, demand of us steadily to resist the abrogation of that which is productive of so much good? It is more than self-defence. It is to defend millions of human beings, who are far removed from us, from the intensest suffering, if not from being struck out of existence. It is the defence of human civilization.[33]

Since slavery was a great advantage to the Negro, why not extend it to the white laborer?[34] "If some superior power should impose on the laborious poor of some other country—this as their unalterable condition—you shall be saved from the torturing anxiety concerning your own future support and that of your children."[35]

That slavery had evil effects upon the morals of young men, southern writers could not deny.[36] Here the defence mechanism took two forms. First, there was the rationalization that slavery protected the "honor" of the white women of the South.[37] What was lost in the moral behavior of the white man was compensated for by the chastity of the southern woman.

The second form of defence closely resembles *projection*. The southern writer liked to point out the immoral conditions of the North, the "horrible sin of white prostitution."[38] Mention is made of "New York Free Love, and Oneida Incest; and Mormon Polygamy."[39] The North was the land of "free love, free lands, free women and free churches."[40] The South defended itself from the idea of its own moral conditions by hunting out those of the North.

It is characteristic of an individual who has constructed defence mechanisms to resist bitterly any attempt to break them down. The same resistance may be found in the social group. Even the principle of "freedom of speech" must give way for the protection of the defence material.[41] In times of war, the justice of the nation's position must not be questioned. The reader can without doubt recall instances that will serve as most satisfactory examples of this resistance during the recent war. It has been remarked that "When Republicans were 'black abolitionists' they would have

regarded any attempt to suppress *The Liberator,* as edited by
William Lloyd Garrison, as an assault upon the constitutional
liberties of the whole nation. But they are not now (1919) particularly interested in preserving the constitutional liberties of the
nation as represented in the right of circulation of the *Liberator,*
edited by Max Eastman." [42]

The South, in order to protect the defence mechanism built
around its "Peculiar Institution" from the penetrating criticisms of
the abolitionists and anti-slavery men of the North, found it necessary to deny the "fundamental doctrine of freedom of speech."
Hence, we have the "gag rule," the refusal to permit anti-slavery
propaganda to pass through the mails, and the prohibition of public
addresses and discussions on the question of slavery. The following
quotation from a southern writer is an excellent example, not only
of the rationalization of the prohibition of freedom of speech, but
also of the process of constructing defence mechanisms.

A comparison of opinions and institutions . . . will lead to kinder
and more pacific relations. Hitherto, such comparisons could not be
made, because the South believed herself wrong, weak, and defenceless; and that Abolition was but an attempt to apply the brand
to the explosive materials of her social edifice. She is now equally
confident of her justice and her strength, and believes her social
system more stable, as well as more benevolent, equitable and
natural, than that of the North. Whilst she will never tolerate radical agitation and demagogical propagandism, she is ready for
philosophical argument and discussion, and for historical and
statistical comparison.

A Southerner employs the term "discussion" as equivalent to
agitation; for the South does not proscribe the discussion of any
subject, by the proper persons, at the proper places, and on the
proper occasions. (Who are proper persons, and what are proper
times and places must be left to a healthy, just and enlightened
public opinion to determine.) But men shall not lecture our children, in the streets, on the beauties of infidelity; parsons shall
not preach politics from the pulpit; women shall not crop the
petticoat, mount the rostrum, and descant on the purity of Free
Love; incendiaries shall not make speeches against the right of
land-holders, nor teach our Negroes the sacred doctrines of liberty
and equality.[43] . . . We want to be friends with them (the North)
and with all the world.[44]

Here we have clearly placed before us the process that had taken place in the South between 1830 and the Civil War. At first the South believed herself "wrong, weak, and defenceless." At the end of the period she has become "equally confident of her justice and her strength, and believes her social system more stable as well as more benevolent, equitable and natural than that of the North." No reason is given to explain why the South set about to discover that slavery was a "positive good." No mention is made about the profit of cotton culture. A defence mechanism against criticism has been built around the doubts of the South as to the ethical basis of its "Peculiar Institution." As with all such mechanisms, the question is not open to discussion, except "by proper persons, at proper places, and on proper occasions." If the defence is broken down, the moral sense of the South will be shocked, the "Peculiar Institution" will be doomed, and the supposed profits of the system lost. The entire southern position depended on the moral righteousness of slavery.

The denial of the freedom of speech on the slavery question is rationalized on the basis that "men shall not lecture our children, in the streets, on the beauties of infidelity . . . nor (here the basic reason crops closer to the surface) teach our Negroes the sacred doctrines of liberty and equality."

Although the South tried hard to convince herself that slavery was a "positive good," when the critical point of actual secession came, she was forced to find a more satisfactory justification of her action. There had been developing in the South another rationalization, the Calhoun doctrine. When the crisis came, this, rather than the justice of slavery, became the battle cry.[45] Rhodes has well expressed this view in the following words:

The justification alleged by the South for her secession in 1861 was based on the principles enunciated by Calhoun; the cause was slavery. Had there been no slavery, the Calhoun theory of the Constitution would never have been propounded, or, had it been, it would have been crushed beyond resurrection by Webster's speeches of 1830 and 1833, and by the prompt action of President Jackson. The South could not in 1861 justify her right to revolution, for there was no oppression, no invalidation of rights. She could not, however, proclaim to the civilized world what was true, that she went to war to extend slavery. Her defence, therefore, is that she made the contest for her constitutional rights, and this attempted vindication is founded on the Calhoun theory.[46]

The North, on the other hand, was as anxious to extend the free labor system into the territories as was the South to extend slavery. Once the war was under way, Unionism and anti-slavery became broad enough standards to include a sufficient force of popular support.

While the conflict lasted, and for many years afterwards, the more basic reason, the supposed profit of slavery on the part of the South and the demand for free western lands by the North, dropped into the background so far as public propaganda and popular history were concerned. The war became apparently a struggle for political ideals and moral convictions. Many writers of that period (and we still have echoes from them) concerned themselves with erudite constitutional arguments and moralistic philosophy on the right and wrong of slavery, and missed entirely the significance of the Homestead Act of 1862.

It is not enough to recognize only the economic and political factors in the social process; there is another, a more important phase, the psychological. Some day the historian will make use of the valuable tools which have been prepared for him by theoretical, physiological, experimental, pathological, and social psychology. Antiquated conceptions of human nature will be replaced by scientific knowledge of human behavior. A true understanding of history cannot be had without the application of modern psychology. Nor is it sufficient, as McDougall has pointed out ". . . for the historian and the political philosopher to be willing to recognise the mental factors in the phenomena with which he deals. It is necessary to recognise that these factors are of overwhelming importance, and that they cannot be satisfactorily dealt with by aid of obscure and confused psychological concepts of popular thought and speech. We must recognise these political problems for what they truly are—namely, psychological through and through, and only to be attacked with some hope of success if we call to our aid all that psychological science can give us." [47]

Notes

1 For an excellent survey of the situation see Barnes, H. E.: Psychology and history, *Amer. J. Psychol.*, 1919, 30:337–376.

2 Münsterberg, *Psychology—General and Applied*, 356.

3 Garrisons', *William Lloyd Garrison*, I, 80.

4 Garrisons', *William Lloyd Garrison*, I, 140.

5 *The Liberator*, Boston, I January, 1831.

6 Garrisons', *William Lloyd Garrison*, I, 84.

7 Garrisons', *Garrison*, I, 74–76.

8 Garrisons', *Garrison*, I, 100.

9 Barnes, H. E., *Psychoanalytic Review*, 1921, 8:25.

10 From the *Liberator*, April 9, 1831. Some satirical verses by "G—n" under the caption "Apologies." The quotation above is "Apology No. 1."

"For unless we can kidnap and purchase at pleasure,
We must do our own labor, and sport—when we've lcisure:
Oh! shocking the thought, that these delicate hands
Must take hold of the plough, and cultivate lands."

11 Pillsbury has pointed out the importance of "hate as a social force." *Psychology of Nationality and Internationalism*, Chap. III. See, also, Martin, E. D., *The Behavior of Crowds:* Chap. V, "The Crowd as a Creature of Hate."

12 Pillsbury, W. B., *Psychology of Nationality and Internationalism*, 86.

13 Pamphlet in the Columbia University Library (quoted by F. T. Carlton in *Organized Labor in American History*, 147).

14 *Quarterly Anti-Slavery Magazine*, New York, April, 1836.

15 Carlton, *Organized Labor in American History*, 146.

16 Dodd, W. E., *Expansion and Conflict*, 161.

17 Commons, J. R., *Political Science Quarterly*, v. 24, 487.

18 Angell: *Chapters from Modern Psychology*, 217.

19 Fitzhugh, George, *Cannibals All! or Slaves without Masters*, Richmond, Va., 1857, p. 368.

20 *Ibid:* 287.

21 Reynolds, E. W., *The Barons of the South;* Boston, 1862, pp. 18–19.

22 Channing, *History of the United States*, V, 151.

23 Hart, A. B., *Slavery and Abolition*, 136. See also Channing, *History of the United States*, V, 154.

24 Hart, *Slavery and Abolition*, 159.

25 *Ibid:* 136.

26 Calhoun Works, II, 630.

27 "Debate on Emancipation in the Virginia Legislature, in 1832"—quoted by Channing, *History of the United States*, V, 143.

28 Channing, *History*, V, 140; also Hart, *Slavery and Abolition*, 162.

29 For the view of the group as limited to accepting or rejecting, see Pillsbury, *Nationality and Internationalism*, 198.

30 Hammond, *Pro-Slavery Argument* (1852), p. 108.

31 Channing, *History*, 162.

32 Hammond in *Pro-Slavery Argument*, 134–38.

33 Harper in *Pro-Slavery Argument*, 88.

34 See Hart, *Slavery and Abolition*, 144. For the reaction of the North to this type of argument, see ante pages 6–7.

35 Here we find this type of rationalization: "Providence has placed him (the slave) in our hands, for his good, and has paid us from his labor for our guardianship." *Pro-Slavery Argument*, 275.

36 *Pro-Slavery Argument*, 42–44, 61, 228–29.

37 *Ibid*: 43.

38 *Ibid*: 228.

39 Fitzhugh, *Cannibals All!* 376–79.

40 *Ibid*: 368.

41 For the "sanctions of common approval," see Pillsbury, *op. cit.* 208.

Barnes (*Amer. J. Psychol.*, 1919, 30:374) has suggested that southern chivalry may have been a collective compensation for sexual looseness, racial intermixture, and maltreatment of the Negro.

42 Martin, E. D., *The Behavior of Crowds*, 264.

43 We note that the doctrines of liberty and equality are sacred for the white man—not for the slave. No matter how inferior a "poor white" might be, he had the satisfaction of feeling that a great many blacks were far beneath him. This compensation for inferiority, and the *prestige* of the great planter, may account to a relatively great degree for the loyalty of the "poor white" to the cause of the slave-holder.

44 Fitzhugh, *Cannibals All!* 377–79. Richmond, Va., 1857.

45 For an interesting account of the struggle the South had during the Civil War to uphold these rationalizations, see Stephenson, N. W., *Atlantic Monthly*, v. 123, p. 750.

46 Rhodes, *United States*, I, 52–53.

47 McDougall, *The Group Mind*, 99.

2

JOHN BROWN

WHILE JOHN BROWN WAS YET ALIVE, HE HAD BECOME A LEGEND, perpetuated even today through such works as Stephen Vincent Benét's long poem, *John Brown's Body,* and Leonard Ehrlich's powerful novel, *God's Angry Man.* His badly conceived and executed attempt to capture the arsenal at Harper's Ferry and instigate an uprising of the slaves sparked the imagination of extremists of the North and repelled the die-hards of the South. The former saw Brown as a God-inspired prophet, the latter a murderer who would arm the slaves to commit more crimes. In 1859, the moderate position in both sections was difficult to maintain. But "Brown's execution accomplished what his audacious raid failed to do, and his canonization preceded, if it did not initiate, a bloody war that a few far-sighted Americans had anticipated a generation before." [1]

The first fifty-five years of John Brown's life were haunted by failure and poverty (see the later chapter on Ulysses S. Grant—"Forty Years of Failure"). He fathered twenty children and raised

---

1 Aaron, Daniel (Ed.). *America in Crisis.* New York: Alfred A. Knopf, 1952, p. 108.

them in want. In thirty-five years he experienced twenty different business reversals in six states. But in the last few years of his life, Brown was so able to convince well-placed men of the North of his integrity and single-mindedness of purpose that he was successful in securing funds to carry out, eventually, his attack on Harper's Ferry. While Professor Woodward suggests caution in dismissing Harper's Ferry as "merely the work of a madman," he does this on the basis of the "respectability" of the men who secretly supported and financed Brown. But then Adolf Hitler had his respectable backers too—Krupp and Dr. Hjalmar Schacht, as ready examples. So have—and have yet today—other super-patriotic leaders, who by their profound sincerity, undeviating purposefulness and glib articulateness (all symptomatic of the paranoid personality) managed to find financial backers with social status and prestige.

However, events leading up to and including the assault on Harper's Ferry give evidence of John Brown's instability. His senseless and merciless massacre of innocent settlers at Pottawatomie; his obsession with the God of Vengeance of the Old Testament which he used to rationalize and justify his behavior; his revolutionary government which was, in actuality, a military dictatorship; his "war of liberation" in order to found an abolitionist republic; the supreme monomaniacal, singleminded assuredness of the correctness of his activities; and finally, the violation of elementary military tactics (expressive of the need to be caught and martyred?) which resulted in the dismal failure of his abortive insurrection—all are symptomatic of Brown's probable paranoid, or at least, psychopathic, state.

Woodward, in the following essay, points up Brown's emotional lability and the recurrent instances of psychosis in his family, in both the agnate and cognate lines. At least twenty-four of them, at one time or another, were attested to as "insane," the term commonly used in the nineteenth century. Woodward's analysis of Brown and Harper's Ferry throws light on the American mind in the midst of crisis. He gives us many clues to the psychology of the fellow-traveller of today, to the murky mentality of the violent revolutionary, and to treason.

John Brown's Private War

C. VANN WOODWARD

IN SOME RESPECTS Harper's Ferry bears closer resemblance to the crisis of our own time than do the other American crises under consideration. For one thing, it has more of the characteristics of an international than of a domestic crisis. It was a clash between two Americas, each struggling for dominance. Each of the antagonistic systems had its own set of interests, institutions, and values, and in the long perspective of nearly a century the clash between them takes on aspects typical of other historic struggles for power. In the mid-nineteenth century, however, the differences were usually expressed in terms of moral or ideological conflict.

In the 1850's as in the 1950's the issue was dramatized as a conflict between labor systems—free labor versus slave labor. Confident of the superiority of its system of wage labor, the North attacked the South's system of slave labor as wasteful, immoral, and inhuman. The South replied with many of the arguments later used by Marxians against capitalism, one being that free labor was really wage slavery minus the security enjoyed by the slave. Since world opinion regarded slavery as incompatible with advanced civilization, the moral advantage naturally lay entirely with the North in the labor dispute. It was therefore to the North's interest to make the labor issue the symbol of the whole conflict and at the same time to play down the issues of tariff, money, banks, subsidies, and other economic privileges, in which the North enjoyed no special moral advantage.

In a crisis as great as that which led to the American Civil War the importance of the Harper's Ferry raid should not be overestimated. It was but one of a series of violent border incidents that occurred between 1856 and 1861—from "bleeding Kansas" to Fort Sumter. They constituted a continuation of a longer war of propaganda and served as the prelude of formal war following Fort Sumter.

For present purposes, the significant thing about Harper's Ferry is the light it throws upon the American mind in the midst of crisis. Among the aspects illuminated by the incidents are several that claim attention because of their relevance to our own time. It is well to remember in comparing two crises a century apart that analogies are never perfect and that there are important differences between the two eras. With this *caveat* in mind it is possible to speak of the revolutionary mentality of the 1850's and the psychology of the fellow traveler, the intellectual and his involvement in conspiracy, subversive groups and their relation to the Bill of Rights, loyalty and the problem of treason. Rarely have Americans been more sharply torn between conflicting values—between the "higher law" and the statutory law, between principles and the Constitution, between home and country. Rarely has the traditional code of American political ethics been challenged more openly by the doctrine that the end justifies the means. And perhaps there has never been in our history a clearer instance of an insecurity complex, with its attendant hysteria and bellicosity, than that offered by the South; nor a better example of how rival powers infect each other with aggression in a war crisis.

After ninety years the figure of John Brown is still wrapped in obscurity and myth. Of the fourteen biographies of Brown published since 1859 not one has been written by a professional historian. The myth and legend makers have done their part, but much of the difficulty is inherent in the nature of Brown's life and character. His fifty-nine years were divided sharply into two periods. The obscurity of his first fifty-five years was of the sort natural to a humble life unassociated with events of importance. The obscurity of his last four years, filled with conspiratorial activities, was in large part the deliberate work of Brown and his fellow conspirators and their admirers.

Poverty and failure haunted the first fifty-five years of John Brown's life. The father of twenty children, he was compelled to see his family drag along in want and at times something approaching destitution. In thirty-five years he was engaged in more than twenty different business ventures in six states. Most of them ended in failure, some in bankruptcy, and at least two in crime. Brown was involved for years as defendant in one litigation after another brought against him for failure to meet his financial obligations. "Several of the cases in question leave no doubt of flagrant dishonesty on his part in both business and family relations," concludes Professor James C. Malin. The historian suggests that "this record of unreliability proven in court" might serve as "an index to the reliability of John Brown as a witness after he became a public character." The remarkable thing about this record is that it seems to have interfered in no way with the second of his careers. After 1855 John Brown abandoned his unprofitable business career when he was almost penniless and for the rest of his life was without remunerative employment. He depended for support upon donations from people whom he convinced of his integrity and reliability. Here and elsewhere there is strong evidence that Brown was somehow able to inspire confidence and intense personal loyalty.

The Kansas phase of Brown's guerrilla warfare has given rise to the "Legend of Fifty-six," a fabric of myth that has been subjected to a more rigorous examination than any other phase of Brown's life has ever received. Malin establishes beyond question that "John Brown did not appear to have had much influence either in making or marring Kansas history," that his exploits "brought tragedy to innocent settlers," but that "in no place did he appear as a major factor." He also establishes a close correlation between the struggle over freedom and slavery and local clashes over conflicting land titles on the Kansas frontier, and points out that "the business of stealing horses under the cloak of fighting for freedom and running them off to the Nebraska-Iowa border for sale" is a neglected aspect of the struggle for "Bleeding Kansas." John Brown and his men engaged freely and profitably in this business and justified their plunder as the spoils of war. Two covenants that Brown drew up for his followers contained a clause specifically providing for the division of captured property among the members of his guerrilla band.

It would be a gross distortion, however, to dismiss John Brown as a frontier horse-thief. He was much too passionately and fanatically in earnest about his war on slavery to permit of any such oversimplification. His utter fearlessness, courage, and devotion to the cause were greatly admired by respectable antislavery men who saw in the old Puritan an ideal revolutionary leader.

One exploit of Brown in Kansas, however, would seem to have put him forever beyond the pale of association with intelligent opponents of slavery. This was the famous Pottawatomie massacre of May 24, 1856. John Brown, leading four of his sons, a son-in-law, and two other men, descended by night upon an unsuspecting settlement of four proslavery families. Proceeding from one home to another the raiders took five men out, murdered them, and left their bodies horribly mutilated. None of the victims was a slaveholder, and two of them were born in Germany and had no contact with the South. By way of explanation Brown said the murders had been "decreed by Almighty God, ordained from Eternity." He later denied responsibility for the act, and some of the Eastern capitalists and intellectuals who supported him refused to believe him guilty. In view of the report of the murders that was laid before the country on July 11, 1856, in the form of a committee report in the House of Representatives, it is somewhat difficult to excuse such ignorance among intelligent men.

It was shortly after this report was published, however, that Brown enjoyed his most striking success in soliciting contributions and making friends for his war on slavery among men of wealth and intellectual distinction in Boston and other Eastern cities. In the first four months of 1858 he succeeded in raising twenty-three thousand dollars in cash, supplies, and credit to support his guerrilla activities.

In the spring of 1858 plans for the raid on Virginia began to take definite shape. To a convention of fellow conspirators in Chatham, Canada, in May, John Brown presented his remarkable "Provisional Constitution and Ordinances for the People of the United States." It represented the form of government he proposed by force of arms to establish with a handful of conspirators and an armed insurrection of slaves. Complete with legislative, executive, and judicial branches, Brown's revolutionary government was in effect a military dictatorship, since all acts of his congress had to be approved by the commander-in-chief of the army in order to become valid. Needless to say, John Brown was elected commander-in-chief.

By July 1859, Commander-in-Chief Brown had established himself at a farm on the Maryland side of the Potomac River, four miles north of Harper's Ferry. There he assembled twenty-one followers and accumulated ammunition and other supplies, including two hundred revolvers, two hundred rifles, and nine hundred and fifty pikes specially manufactured for the slaves he expected to rise up in insurrection. On Sunday night, October 16, after posting a guard of three men at the farm, he set forth with eighteen followers, five of them Negroes, and all of them young men, to start his war of liberation and found his abolitionist republic. Brown's first objective, to capture the United States arsenal at Harper's Ferry, was easily accomplished since it was without military guard. In the federal armory and the rifle works, also captured, were sufficient arms to start the bloodiest slave insurrection in history.

The commander-in-chief appears to have launched his invasion without any definite plan of campaign and then proceeded to violate every military principle in the book. He cut himself off from his base of supplies, failed to keep open his only avenues of retreat, dispersed his small force, and bottled the bulk of them up in a trap where defeat was inevitable. "In fact, it was so absurd," remarked Abraham Lincoln, "that the slaves, with all their ignorance, saw plainly enough it could not succeed." Not one of them joined Brown voluntarily, and those he impressed quickly departed. The insurrectionists killed one United States Marine and four inhabitants of Harper's Ferry, including the mayor and a Negro freeman. Ten of their own number, including two of Brown's sons, were killed, five were taken prisoner by a small force of Marines commanded by Robert E. Lee, and seven escaped, though two of them were later arrested. John Brown's insurrection ended in a tragic and dismal failure.

When news of the invasion was first flashed across the country the commonest reaction was that this was obviously the act of a madman, that John Brown was insane. This explanation was particularly attractive to Republican politicians and editors, whose party suffered the keenest embarrassment from the incident. Fall elections were on, and the new Congress was about to convene. Democrats immediately charged that John Brown's raid was the inevitable consequence of the "irresistible-conflict" and "higher-law" abolitionism preached by Republican leaders Seward and

Chase. "Brown's invasion," wrote Senator Henry Wilson of Massachusetts, "has thrown us, who were in a splendid position, into a defensive position. . . . If we are defeated next year we shall owe it to that foolish and insane movement of Brown's." [1] The emphasis on insanity was taken up widely by Wilson's contemporaries and later adopted by historians.

It seems best to deal with the insanity question promptly, for it is likely to confuse the issue and miss the meaning of Harper's Ferry. In dealing with the problem it is important not to blink at the evidence, as many of Brown's biographers have done, of John Brown's close association with insanity in both his heredity and his environment. In the Brown Papers at the Library of Congress are nineteen affidavits signed by relatives and friends attesting the record of insanity in the Brown family. John Brown's maternal grandmother and his mother both died insane. His three aunts and two uncles, sisters and brothers of his mother, were intermittently insane, and so was his only sister, her daughter, and one of his brothers. Of six first cousins, all more or less mad, two were deranged from time to time, two had been repeatedly committed to the state insane asylum, and two were still confined at the time. Of John Brown's immediate family, his first wife and one of his sons died insane, and a second son was insane at intervals. On these matters the affidavits, whose signers include John Brown's uncle, a half-brother, a brother-in-law, and three first cousins, are in substantial agreement. On the sanity of John Brown himself, however, opinion varied. Several believed that he was a "monomaniac," one that he was insane on subjects of religion and slavery, and an uncle thought his nephew had been "subject to periods of insanity" for twenty years. [2]

John Brown himself, of course, stoutly maintained that he was perfectly sane, and he was certainly able to convince many intelligent people, both friend and foe, that he was sane. He firmly refused to plead insanity at his trial. Governor Henry A. Wise of Virginia went so far as to write out orders to the superintendent of the state insane asylum to examine Brown, but endorsed the orders, "countermanded upon reflection." On the other hand, John Brown pronounced Governor Wise mad. "Hard to tell who's mad," jested Wendell Phillips to a laughing congregation in Henry Ward Beecher's church. "The world says one man's mad. John

Brown said the same of the Governor. . . . I appeal from Philip
drunk to Philip sober." He meant future generations when, he said,
"the light of civilization has had more time to penetrate." Then it
would be plain that not Brown, but his enemies were mad.

We, the Philips sober of the future, with some misgivings about
how far "the light of civilization" has penetrated, do think we
know a little more about insanity than did our great-grandfathers.
We at least know that it is a loose expression for a variety of mental disorders, and that it is a relative term. What seems sane to
some people at some times seems insane to other people at other
times. In our own time we have witnessed what we consider
psychopathic personalities rise to power over millions of people
and plunge the world into war. Yet to the millions who followed
them these leaders appeared sublime in their wisdom.

"John Brown may be a lunatic," observed the Boston *Post,* but
if so, "then one-fourth of the people of Massachusetts are mad-
men," and perhaps three-fourths of the ministers of religion. Begging that Brown's life be spared, Amos A. Lawrence wrote
Governor Wise: "Brown is a Puritan whose mind has become disordered by hardship and illness. He has the qualities wh. endear
him to our people." [3] The association of ideas was doubtless unin-
tentional, but to the Virginian it must have seemed that Lawrence
was saying that in New England a disordered mind was an endearing quality. The Reverend J. M. Manning of Old South Church,
Boston, pronounced Harper's Ferry "an unlawful, a foolhardy, a
suicidal act," and declared: "I stand before it wondering and
admiring." Horace Greeley called it "the work of a madman," for
which he had not "one reproachful word," and for the "grandeur
and nobility" of which he was "reverently grateful." And the New
York *Independent* declared that while "Harper's Ferry was insane,
the controlling motive of this demonstration was sublime." It was
both foolhardy and godly, insane and sublime, treasonous and
admirable.

The prestige and character of the men who lent John Brown
active, if sometimes secret, support likewise suggest caution in
dismissing Harper's Ferry as merely the work of a madman. Among
Brown's fellow conspirators the most notable were the so-called
Secret Six. Far from being horse-thieves and petty traders, the
Secret Six came of the cream of Northern society. Capitalist, philan-

thropist, philosopher, surgeon, professor, minister, they were men of reputability and learning, four of them with Harvard degrees. With a Harvard Divinity School degree, a knowledge of twenty languages, and a library of sixteen thousand volumes, Theodore Parker was perhaps the most prodigiously learned American of his times. In constant correspondence with the leading Republican politicians, he has been called "the Conscience of a Party." What Gerrit Smith, the very wealthy philanthropist and one-time congressman of Peterboro, New York, lacked in mental endowments he made up in good works—earnest efforts to improve the habits of his fellowmen. These included not only crusades against alcohol and tobacco in all forms, but also coffee, tea, meat, and spices—"almost everything which gave pleasure," according to his biographer. Generous with donations to dietary reform, dress reform, woman's rights, educational, and "non-resistance" movements, Smith took no interest whatever in factory and labor reform, but was passionately absorbed in the antislavery movement and a liberal contributor to John Brown. Dr. Samuel G. Howe, of Boston, husband of the famous Julia Ward Howe, was renowned for his humanitarian work for the blind and mentally defective. In his youth he had gone on a Byronic crusade in Greece against the Turk. These experiences contributed greatly to his moral prestige, if little to his political sophistication. The most generous man of wealth among the conspirators was George L. Stearns of Boston, a prosperous manufacturer of lead pipe. In the opinion of this revolutionary capitalist John Brown was "the representative man of this century, as Washington was of the last." Finally there were two younger men, fledgling conspirators. The son of a prosperous Boston merchant who was bursar of Harvard, Thomas Wentworth Higginson became pastor of a church in Worcester after taking his divinity degree at Harvard. Young Franklin B. Sanborn was an apostle of Parker and a protégé of Emerson, who persuaded Sanborn to take charge of a school in Concord.

The most tangible service the Secret Six rendered the conspiracy lay in secretly diverting to John Brown, for use at Harper's Ferry, money and arms that had been contributed to the Massachusetts Kansas Aid Committee for use in "Bleeding Kansas." This dubious transaction was accomplished by George L. Stearns, chairman of the committee, exercising as a private individual an option

he held of foreclosing upon the property of the committee, then
promptly transferring the arms to Brown and notifying only the
conspirators. By this means the Kansas Committee was converted
into a respectable front for subversive purposes, and thousands
of innocent contributors to what appeared to be a patriotic organization discovered later that they had furnished rifles for a treasonous attack on a federal arsenal. Even Sanborn admitted in 1885
that "it is still a little difficult to explain this transaction concerning
the arms without leaving the suspicion that there was somewhere
a breach of trust." It still is.

The Secret Six appear to have been fascinated by the drama of
conspiratorial activity. There were assumed names, coded messages, furtive committee meetings, dissembling of motives, and
secret caches of arms. And over all the romance and glamor of
a noble cause—the liberation of man. Although they knew perfectly well the general purpose of Brown, the Secret Six were
careful to request him not to tell them the precise time and place
of the invasion. The wily old revolutionist could have told them
much that they did not know about the psychology of fellow travelers. Brown had earlier laid down this strategy for conspirators
who were hard pressed: "go into the houses of your most prominent and influential white friends with your wives; and that will
effectually fasten upon them the suspicion of being connected with
you, and will compel them to make a common cause with you,
whether they would otherwise live up to their professions or not."
The same strategy is suggested in Brown's leaving behind in the
Maryland farmhouse where they would inevitably be captured all
his private papers, hundreds of letters of himself and followers,
implicating nobody knew how many respectable fellow-travelers.

When the news of the captured documents arrived there occurred a most unheroic panic among the Secret Six, who saw stark
ruin and an indictment for treason facing them. Stearns, Sanborn,
and Howe fled to Canada. Parker was already abroad. Gerrit
Smith's secretary did not stop until he reached England. Smith
himself issued pitiable and panicky denials of his guilt, then found
refuge in insanity and was confined to an asylum. Howe published
a denial unworthy of respect. Higginson alone stood his ground.
Stearns and Howe denied any knowledge of the attack before a
congressional committee, and both of them told Sanborn "they

found the question of the Senate Committee so unskillfully framed that they could, without literal falsehood, answer as they did."

The assistance that the Secret Six conspirators were able to give John Brown and his legend was as nothing compared with that rendered by other Northern intellectuals. Among them were the cultural and moral aristocracy of America in the period that has been called a "Renaissance." Some of these men, Emerson and even Thoreau among them, had met and admired Brown and even made small contributions to his cause. But they were safely beyond reproach of the law, and were never taken into his confidence in the way that the Secret Six were. Their service was rendered after the event in justifying and glorifying Brown and his invasion.

In this work the intellectuals were ably assisted by a genius, a genius at self-justification—John Brown himself. From his prison cell he poured out a stream of letters, serene and restrained, filled with Biblical language, and fired with overpowering conviction that his will and God's were one and the same. These letters and his famous speech at the trial constructed for the hero a new set of motives and plans and a new role. For Brown had changed roles. In October he invaded Virginia as a conqueror armed for conquest, carrying with him guns and pikes for the army he expected to rally to his standard, and a new constitution to replace the one he overthrew. In that role he was a miserable failure. Then in November he declared at his trial: "I never did intend murder, or treason, or the destruction of property, or to excite or incite slaves to rebellion, or to make an insurrection." He only intended to liberate slaves without bloodshed, as he falsely declared he had done in Missouri the year before. How these statements can be reconciled with the hundreds of pikes, revolvers, and rifles, the capture of an armory, the taking of hostages, the killing of un-armed civilians, the destruction of government property, and the arming of slaves is difficult to see. Nor is it possible to believe that Brown thought he could seize a federal arsenal, shoot down United States Marines, and overthrow a government without com-mitting treason. "It was all so thin," as Robert Penn Warren has observed of the trial speech, "that it should not have deceived a child, but it deceived a generation." At Lincoln's funeral Emer-son compared it with the Gettysburg Address.

Emerson seemed hesitant in his first private reactions to Harper's Ferry. Thoreau, on the other hand, never hesitated a moment. On the day after Brown's capture he compared the hero's inevitable execution with the crucifixion of Christ. Harper's Ferry was "the best news that America ever had"; Brown "the bravest and humanest man in all the country," "a Transcendentalist above all," and he declared, "I rejoice that I live in this age, that I was his contemporary." Emerson quickly fell into line with Thoreau, and in his November 8 lecture on "Courage" described Brown as "The saint, whose fate yet hangs in suspense, but whose martyrdom, if it shall be perfected, will make the gallows as glorious as the cross." [4] Within a few weeks Emerson gave three important lectures, in all of which he glorified John Brown.

With the Sage of Concord and his major prophet in accord on the martyr, the majority of the transcendental hierarchy sooner or later joined in—Channing, Bronson and Louisa May Alcott, Longfellow, Bryant, and Lowell, and of course Wendell Phillips and Theodore Parker. Parker pronounced Brown "not only a martyr . . . but also a SAINT." Thoreau and Henry Ward Beecher frankly admitted they hoped Brown would hang. To spare a life would be to spoil a martyr. They were interested in him not as a man but as a symbol, a moral ideal, and a saint for a crusade. In the rituals of canonization the gallows replaced the cross as a fetish. Louisa May Alcott called the gallows "a stepping-stone to heaven," Parker "the road to heaven," Theodore Tilton "a throne greater than a king's," and Phillips concluded that "henceforth it is sacred forever." [5]

Among Western antislavery men there were fewer intellectuals of fame or notoriety, but abolitionist preachers, teachers, and orators joined in apotheosizing Brown. Citizens of Oberlin erected a monument to three Negroes who gave their lives in Brown's raid. And Theodore D. Weld, once the genius of Western abolitionism, though now in retirement, permitted the burial of two of the Harper's Ferry raiders at his school in New Jersey. Not all of the Northern intellectuals became members of the Brown cult. Hawthorne and Whitman were two notable dissenters. Devotees of the cult showed little tolerance for dissent. Emerson declared that "all people, in proportion to their sensibility and self-respect, sympathize with him [Brown]," and Thoreau carried intolerance to the point of moral snobbery. "When a noble deed is done, who is likely to appreciate it? They who are noble themselves," answered Thoreau. "I was not surprised that certain of my neighbors spoke of John Brown as an ordinary felon, for who are they? They have either much flesh, or much office, or much coarseness of some kind. They are not ethereal natures in any sense. The dark qualities predominate in them. . . . For the children of the light to contend with them is as if there should be a contest between eagles and owls."

The task to which the intellectuals of the cult dedicated themselves was the idealizing of John Brown as a symbol of the moral order and the social purpose of the Northern cause. Wendell Phillips expressed this best when he declared in the Boston Music Hall: " 'Law' and 'order' are only means for the halting ignorance of the last generation. John Brown is the impersonation of God's order and God's law, moulding a better future, and setting for it an example." In substituting the new revolutionary law and order for traditional law and order, the intellectuals encountered some tough problems in morals and values. It was essential for them to justify a code of political methods and morals that was at odds with the Anglo-American tradition.

John Brown's own solution to this problem was quite simple. It is set forth in the preamble of his Provisional Constitution of the United States, which declares that in reality slavery is an "unjustifiable War of one portion of its citizens upon another." War, in which all is fair, amounted to a suspension of ethical restraints. This type of reasoning is identical with that of the revolutionaries who hold that the class struggle is in reality a class war. The assumption naturally facilitates the justification of deeds otherwise unjustifiable. These might include the dissembling of motives, systematic deception, theft, murder, or the liquidation of an enemy class.

It is clear that certain enthusiasts found in Brown's reasoning a satisfactory solution to their moral problem, but it was equally clear that the mass of people were not yet ready to accept this solution and that some other rationalization was required. The doctrine of the "Higher Law" and the doctrine of "Civil Disobedience" had already done much to prepare the way for acceptance of the revolutionary ethics. They had justified conduct in defiance of the Constitution and the government by appeal to higher moral ends. Transcendental doctrine was now used to extend the defiance of tradition even further. Thoreau's reply to attacks upon John Brown's methods was: "The method is nothing; the spirit is all." This was the Transcendentalist way of saying that means are justified by the ends. The old theologians would have spotted this instantly as the antinomian heresy. According to this doctrine, if the end is sufficiently noble—as noble as the emancipation of the slave—any means used to attain the end is justified.

The crisis of Harper's Ferry was a crisis of means, not of ends. John Brown did not raise the question of whether slavery should be abolished or tolerated. That question had been raised in scores of ways and debated for a generation. Millions held strong convictions on the subject. Upon abolition, as an *end*, there was no difference between John Brown and the American and Foreign Anti-Slavery Society. But upon the *means* to attain abolition there was as much difference between them, so far as the record goes, as there is between the modern British Labour Party and the government of Soviet Russia on the means of abolishing capitalism. The Anti-Slavery Society was solemnly committed to the position of nonviolent means. In the very petition that Lewis Tappan, secretary of the society, addressed to Governor Wise in behalf of Brown he repeated the rubric about "the use of all carnal weapons for deliverance from bondage."[6] But in their rapture over Brown as martyr and saint the abolitionists lost sight of their differences with him over the point of means and ended by totally compromising their creed of nonviolence.

But what of those who clung to the democratic principle that differences should be settled by ballots and that the will of the majority should prevail? Phillips pointed out that: "In God's world there are no majorities, no minorities; one, on God's side, is a majority." And Thoreau asked: "When were the good and the brave ever in a majority?" So much for majority rule. What of the issue of treason? The Reverend Fales H. Newhall of Roxbury declared that the word "treason" had been "made holy in the American language"; and the Reverend Edwin M. Wheelock of Boston blessed "the sacred, the radiant 'treason' of John Brown."

No aversion to bloodshed seemed to impede the spread of the Brown cult. Garrison thought that "every slaveholder has forfeited his right to live" if he impeded emancipation. The Reverend

Theodore Parker predicted a slave insurrection in which "The Fire of Vengeance" would run "from man to man, from town to town" through the South. "What shall put it out?" he asked. "The White Man's blood." The Reverend Edwin M. Wheelock thought that Brown's "mission was to inaugurate slave insurrection as the divine weapon of the antislavery cause." He asked: "Do we shrink from the bloodshed that would follow?" and answered: "No such wrong [as slavery] was ever cleansed by rose-water." Rather than see slavery continued the Reverend George B. Cheever of New York declared: "It were infinitely better that three hundred thousand slaveholders were abolished, struck out of existence." In these pronouncements the doctrine that the end justifies the means had arrived pretty close to justifying the liquidation of an enemy class.

The reactions of the extremists have been stressed in part because it was the extremist view that eventually prevailed in the apotheosis of John Brown, and in part because by this stage of the crisis each section tended to judge the other by the excesses of a few. "Republicans were all John Browns to the Southerners," as Professor Dwight L. Dumond has observed, "and slaveholders were all Simon Legrees to the Northerners." As a matter of fact Northern conservatives and unionists staged huge anti-Brown demonstrations that equaled or outdid those staged by the Brown partisans. Nathan Appleton wrote a Virginian: "I have never in my long life seen a fuller or more enthusiastic demonstration" than the anti-Brown meeting in Faneuil Hall in Boston. The Republican press described a similar meeting in New York as "the largest and most enthusiastic" ever held in that city. Northern politicians of high rank, including Lincoln, Douglas, Seward, Everett, and Wilson, spoke out against John Brown and his methods. The Republican party registered its official position by a plank in the 1860 platform denouncing the Harper's Ferry raid. Lincoln approved of Brown's execution, "even though he agreed with us in thinking slavery wrong." Agreement on ends did not mean agreement on means. "That cannot excuse violence, bloodshed, and treason," said Lincoln.

Republican papers of the Western states as well as of the East took pains to dissociate themselves from Harper's Ferry, and several denounced the raid roundly. At first conservative Southern papers, for example the *Arkansas State Gazette*, rejoiced that "the leading papers, and men, among the Black Republicans, are open . . . in their condemnation of the course of Brown." As the canonization of Brown advanced, however, the Republican papers gradually began to draw a distinction between their condemnation of Brown's raid and their high regard for the man himself—his courage, his integrity, and his noble motives. They also tended to find in the wrongs Brown and his men had suffered at the hands of slaveholders in Kansas much justification for his attack upon Virginia. From that it was an easy step to pronounce the raid a just retribution for the South's violence in Kansas. There was enough ambiguity about Republican disavowal of Brown to leave doubts in many minds. If Lincoln deplored Brown, there was his partner Billy Herndon, who worshipped Brown. If there was one editor who condemned the raid, there were a half dozen who admired its leader. To Southerners the distinction was elusive or entirely unimportant.

Northern businessmen were foremost in deprecating Harper's Ferry and reassuring the South. Some of them linked their denunciation of Brown with a defense of slavery, however, so that in the logic that usually prevails in time of crisis all critics of Brown risked being smeared with the charge of defending slavery. Radicals called them mossbacks, doughfaces, appeasers, and sought to jeer them out of countenance. "If they cannot be converted, [they] may yet be scared," was Parker's doctrine.

Among the Brown partisans not one has been found but who believed that Harper's Ferry had resulted in great gain for the extremist cause. So profoundly were they convinced of this that they worried little over the conservative dissent. "How vast the change in men's hearts!" exclaimed Phillips. "Insurrection was a harsh, horrid word to millions a month ago." Now it was "the lesson of the hour." Garrison rejoiced that thousands who could not listen to his gentlest rebuke ten years before "now easily swallow John Brown whole, and his rifle in the bargain." "They all called him crazy then," wrote Thoreau; "who calls him crazy now?" To the poet it seemed that "The North is suddenly all Transcendentalist." On the day John Brown was hanged church bells were tolled in commemoration in New England towns, out along the Mohawk Valley, in Cleveland and the Western Reserve, in Chicago and northern Illinois. In Albany one hundred rounds were fired from a cannon. Writing to his daughter the following day, Joshua Giddings of Ohio said: "I find the hatred of slavery greatly intensified by the fate of Brown and men are ready to march to Virginia and dispose of her despotism at once."[7] It was not long before they *were* marching to Virginia, and marching to the tune of "John Brown's Body."

The Harper's Ferry crisis on the other side of the Potomac was a faithful reflection of the crisis in the North, and can therefore be quickly sketched. It was the reflection, with the image reversed in the mirror, that antagonistic powers present to each other in a war crisis. To the South John Brown also appeared as a true symbol of Northern purpose, but instead of the "angel of light" Thoreau pictured, the South saw an angel of destruction. The South did not seriously question Brown's sanity either, for he seemed only the rational embodiment of purposes that Southern extremists had long taught were universal in the North. The crisis helped propagandists falsely identify the whole North with John Brownism. For Harper's Ferry strengthened the hand of extremists and revolutionists in the South as it did in the North, and it likewise discredited and weakened moderates and their influence.

The risk one runs in describing the reaction to Harper's Ferry is the risk of attributing to that event tendencies long manifest. The South had been living in a crisis atmosphere for a long time. It was a society in the grip of an insecurity complex, a tension resulting from both rational and irrational fears. One cause of it was the steady, invincible expansion of the free-state system in size and power, after the Southern system had reached the limits of its own expansion. The South therefore felt itself to be menaced through encirclement by a power containing elements unfriendly to its interests, elements that were growing strong enough to capture the government. The South's insecurity was heightened by having to defend against constant attack an institution it knew to be discredited throughout the civilized world and of which Southerners had once been among the severest critics. Its reaction was to withdraw increasingly from contact with the offending world, to retreat into an isolationism of spirit, and to attempt by curtailing freedom of speech to avoid criticism.

One of the South's tensions sprang from a lack of internal security—the fear of servile insurrection. By the nature of things a slave uprising had to be secret, sudden, and extremely bloody, sparing neither men, women, nor children. The few occurrences of this kind had left a deep trauma in the mind of the people. The pathological character of this tension was manifested in periodic waves of panic based largely on rumor. It is significant that two of the most severe panics of this sort occurred in the election years 1856 and 1860, and were accompanied by charges that abolitionists from the North were fomenting uprisings. Harper's Ferry was therefore a blow at the most sensitive area of Southern consciousness.

The first reaction to the raid, outside Virginia, was surprisingly mild. The newspapers, particularly in the Lower South, pointed out that after all the slaves had remained loyal, that Brown's invasion was a complete failure, and that it was quickly suppressed. This mood did not last long, however. The hundreds of captured documents belonging to Brown and his men persuaded Virginia authorities that the conspiracy was widespread and that the Harper's Ferry strike, had it been successful, was intended to be merely the signal for uprisings throughout the South. Among the documents were maps of seven Southern states with certain widely scattered areas and localities marked with symbols. The symbols may have indicated nothing at all, of course, but they were enough to grip the localities concerned with fear.

Another document that inspired terror was a long letter from one of Brown's emissaries reporting, two weeks before the raid, on a tour of the South. Written from Memphis, the letter suggests the presence of an extensive "fifth column" established in the South by Brown's organization. In Tennessee and Arkansas there were reported to be "an immense number of slaves ripe and ready at the very first intimation to strike a decided blow," and the writer was amazed to find "so large a number of whites ready to aid us" in Memphis. A "thorough scouring" of Arkansas convinced him that the readiness of the slaves was such that "a bold stroke of one day will overthrow the whole state." In Brownsville, Tennessee, a subversive white schoolteacher urged that "we must send out more well qualified men to the south as school teachers, and work them in everywhere," that there was "no avocation in which a man can do so much good for our cause" since the people had "so much confidence in a school teacher." The writer of the letter assured John Brown that "Southern people are easy gulled." His report reveals the man as a wishful thinker and a naïve enthusiast, but after Harper's Ferry the Southern mind was in no state to distinguish between responsible and irresponsible sources of evidence.[8]

Letters from all parts of the South deluged Governor Wise's mail with reports that Brown conspirators had been seized or punished. These, and the Southern newspapers of the time, portray a society in the throes of panic. Convinced that the South was honeycombed with subversives, Southerners tended to see an abolitionist behind every bush and a slave insurrection brewing in the arrival of any stranger. Victims of vigilante and mob action ranged from aged eccentrics and itinerant piano-tuners to substantial citizens of long residence. The mob spirit was no respecter of person or class. A sixty-year-old minister in Texas, who was a believer in the Biblical sanction of slavery and a Democrat of Kentucky birth, made the mistake of criticizing the treatment of slaves in a sermon and was given seventy lashes on his back. A schoolteacher who had lived in Louisiana and Arkansas for ten years was given thirty-six hours to leave the latter state. The newly arrived president of an Alabama college, who came from New York, was forced to give up his job and flee for his life. In December 1859, twelve families, including thirty-nine people associated with antislavery schools and churches of Berea, Kentucky, were forcibly expelled from the state for abolitionism.

Southern fire-eaters swore that no Northerner could be trusted and that all should be expelled. Even the humblest workmen from the North were in danger of insult, violence, or lynching. An Irish stonecutter in Columbia, South Carolina, was beaten, tarred and feathered, and expelled from the state by a mob. Three members of the crew of a brig from Maine were brutally flogged in Georgia, and a New England mechanic was driven out of a village in the same state because he was found to have a clean shirt wrapped in a New York paper containing one of Beecher's sermons. Two Connecticut book-peddlers were roughly handled in Charleston when lists of slaves were found in their bags, and two printers were ridden out of Kingstree, South Carolina, on rails. Four men "suspected of being abolition emissaries" were arrested in two days in Columbus, Georgia, and ten peddlers were driven out of the village of Abbeville, Mississippi. Four months after Harper's Ferry a man was lynched in South Carolina as "one of Brown's associates." Not only Northerners but associates of Northerners were subject to persecution, for guilt by association was an accepted principle in the crisis.

Then there was the Southern enemy within the gates to be dealt with. Hinton R. Helper of North Carolina had written an antislavery book, quantities of which were burned in public ceremonies at High Point in his own state, at Greenville, South Carolina, and Mayesville, Kentucky. Other public book-burning ceremonies took place at Enterprise, Mississippi, and at Montgomery, Alabama, while at Palestine, Texas, the citizens appointed a committee "to collect all said dangerous books for destruction by public burning." Thought control extended to the suppression and seizure of newspapers, a method long practiced, and in Alabama a resolution was introduced in the legislature prohibiting the licensing of teachers with less than ten years' residence, "to protect the state against abolition teachers." Not content with cutting off intellectual commerce with the North, extremists organized to end economic intercourse as well. They published blacklists of Northern firms suspected of abolitionist tendencies, organized boycotts, and promoted nonintercourse agreements. The Richmond *Enquirer* advocated a law "that will keep out of our borders every article of Northern manufacture or importation." On December 8, 1859, thirty-two business agents of New York and Boston arrived in Washington from the South reporting "indignation so great against Northerners that they were compelled to return and abandon their business."

Southern zealots of secession had no better ally than John Brown. Rhett, Ruffin, and Yancey all rejoiced over the effect of Harper's Ferry. Non-slaveholders saw dramatized before them the menace of a slave uprising and readily concluded that their wives and children, as much as the home of the planter, were threatened with the horror of insurrection. They frequently became more fanatical secessionists than the planters. In face of the Northern apotheosis of Brown there was little that Southern moderates could say in answer to such pronouncements as that of the New Orleans *Picayune* of December 2: "Crime becomes godliness, and criminals, red from slaughter of the innocent, are exalted to eminence beside the divine gospel of Peace." The Charleston *Mercury* of November 29 rejoiced that Harper's Ferry, "like a slap in the face," had roused Virginia from her hesitant neutrality and started her on the road to secession. "I have never before seen the public mind of Va. so deeply moved," wrote a Virginian sadly. "The people are far in advance of the politicians, and would most cheerfully follow the extremist counsels. Volunteer companies, horse & foot, are springing up everywhere." [9]

The crisis psychology of 1859 persisted and deepened in the fateful year of 1860 into a pathological condition of mind in which delusions of persecution and impending disaster flourished. Out of Texas came wild rumors of incendiary fires, abolitionists plotting with slaves, and impending insurrection on a vast scale. Rumors of large stocks of strychnine in the possession of slaves and of plans for well-poisoning were widely believed, though unproved. One scholar has aptly compared the tension of the South in 1860 with the "Great Fear" that seized the rural provinces of France in the summer of 1789 when panic spread the word that "the brigands are coming." In that atmosphere the South made the momentous decision that split the Democratic Party at Charleston in April, and before the mood was gone it was debating secession.

In the course of the crisis each of the antagonists, according to the immemorial pattern, had become convinced of the depravity and diabolism of the other. Each believed itself persecuted, menaced. "Let the 'higher law' of abolitionism be met by the 'higher law' of self-preservation," demanded the Richmond *Enquirer*. Lynch law was the only answer to pikes. "What additional insults and outrages *will* arouse it [the North] to assert its rights?" demanded Garrison. And Garrison's opposite number in Mississippi, Albert Gallatin Brown, cried: "Oh, God! To what depths of infamy are we sinking in the South if we allow these things to pass." Paranoia continued to induce counterparanoia, each antagonist infecting the other reciprocally, until the vicious spiral ended in war.

"John Brown's **Body**" was one of the most popular war songs America ever sang. In singing it millions of people hitherto untouched by the Brown cult became involved in the rites of apotheosis. In joining the worship of the hero, as Professor Malin has said, the victors "partook vicariously in his martyrdom" and furthered the rationalization of their conquest as a holy cause. "It is easy to see what a favorite he will be with history," declared Emerson of John Brown. And Thoreau wrote: "I foresee the time when the painter will paint the scene, the poet will sing it, the historian record it." Never did Transcendentalists utter more inspired prophecy. The poets, the painters, and the historians have been prolific. One scholar, who apologizes for an incomplete task, has studied two hundred and fifty-five poems on John Brown, together with fourteen biographies of the hero and thirty-one plays, eleven short stories, and fifty-eight novels in which he figures. This does not embrace the harvest of the last decade.[10]

Recantations were rare among the original Brown cult. A half century after Harper's Ferry, however, William Dean Howells, who said he was one of those who had given the martyr "unqualified reverence and affection," confessed to some misgivings. He reflected that in 1910 there was "a large and largely increasing number of conscientious Americans who regard the prevalent system of capitalism with the abhorrence that Brown felt for the system of Southern slavery." He speculated on what might happen if a "latter-day John Brown" would get into "a mood to go, say, to Pittsburgh, as John Brown of fifty years ago went to Harper's Ferry," arm the proletariat, seize the steel mills, and kidnap or liquidate the millionaires. Recalling what had happened to the anarchists of Haymarket Square, he had his doubts about the experiment.

But Howells did not shake the hero's pedestal. The conservative classes of the North have been remarkably steadfast in their devotion in spite of certain implications of the legend. The Marxian revolutionaries and their fellow travelers, on the other hand, have not overlooked the potentialities of the John Brown heritage. That heritage, as a matter of fact, could be appealed to as readily by conservatives to justify some new antinomian heresy of preventive war or diabolical weapon in a world crusade for capitalism as it could by revolutionaries to justify treason in a crusade for Communism. And the tradition still remains intact, "at once a sacred, a solemn and an inspiring American heritage," according to Oswald Garrison Villard. It is likely to remain unshaken a long time, for it is buttressed by words of some of the most admired of American poets and philosophers.

Notes

1 Henry Wilson to S. E. Sewell, December 10, 1859. Norcross Papers (Massachusetts Historical Society, Boston).

2 The nineteen affidavits were submitted by Samuel Chilton, counsel for John Brown, to Governor Wise, "with the object of praying you to grant a postponement of the execution of the prisoner." Chilton to Wise, November 21, 1859, John Brown Papers (Division of Manuscripts, Library of Congress).

3 Lawrence had supported Brown earlier but had grown skeptical of his methods by this time. Lawrence to Wise, October 26, 1859, John Brown Papers (Virginia State Library, Richmond).

4 There are at least three different versions of this famous passage in print. Emerson struck it out of the lecture in his published work. I have accepted the version of the passages used by Ralph L. Rusk: *The Life of Ralph Waldo Emerson* (New York: 1949), p. 402.

5 A convenient collection of the public tributes to the martyr, more than 500 pages of them, is James Redpath: *Echoes of Harper's Ferry* (Boston: 1860).

6 Lewis Tappan to Wise, November 6, 1859, John Brown Papers (Virginia State Library).

7 Joshua Giddings to Molly Giddings, December 3, 1859, Giddings-Julian Papers (Library of Congress).

8 Lawrence Thatcher to John Brown, October 3, 1859, John Brown Papers (Virginia State Library). "Thatcher" was evidently an assumed name for one of the conspirators close to Brown. A rather extensive search of Brown manuscripts, with Professor Malin's generous assistance, has so far not identified the handwriting.

9 John C. Rutherford to W. C. Rives, Jr., December 18, 1859, W. C. Rives Papers (Division of Manuscripts, Library of Congress).

10 Joy K. Talbert: "John Brown in American Literature," 2 vols., Ph.D. dissertation, University of Kansas (1941).

3

ABRAHAM LINCOLN

THE AMERICAN PUBLIC HAS LONG BEEN INTERESTED IN, AND VITALLY affected by, the health of its Presidents. In the past three generations, we have been concerned with Franklin Roosevelt's paralysis and cerebral vascular spasm, Dwight Eisenhower's coronary thrombosis and regional ileitis, and John Kennedy's lower back derangement and glandular illness.

The following four articles will give the reader the opportunity to learn about the physical health of Abraham Lincoln as well as to compare various psychoanalytical theories about him. Dr. Kempf's case history attempts a reconstruction of the medical history of Lincoln, both organic and functional. Dr. Clark's article, dealing with Lincoln's unconscious motives, classifies the President as a depressive type of psychoneurotic with only a tendency toward emotional disturbance, a tendency carefully kept in check by a sense of humor, physical activity, self-discipline and ordinary common sense. At no time did Lincoln pass beyond the limits of so-called normality. (It should be kept in mind that Clark's statement about the common causative factor of depression as hereditary is no longer fully acceptable in psychological circles.) Dr. Wilson writes about a prophetic dream reported by Lincoln, and

65

it is instructive to read what Clark has to say about the same dream. The final article, by Dr. Feldman, uses the Freudian approach in its attempt at an understanding of the psychology of the cult of Lincoln and explodes, as well, some of the myths surrounding the Civil War President.

Though medical explanations of Lincoln's health vary almost as widely as political attitudes toward him once did, there seems to be general agreement that in modern times he would be classed as a psychoneurotic. Some believe that Lincoln's ungainly appearance and awkwardness may have precipitated feelings of anxiety and insecurity, and made him an easy prey for depression following even minor setbacks. Another view is that both gawkiness and moodiness may have come from an endocrinal imbalance, possibly thyroid dysfunction coupled with hypogonadism. Still others feel that the injury Lincoln received as a youth from a horse's kick over his left eye may have been responsible for the eye-strain from which he long suffered, with recurrent headaches, fatigue, irritability and depression. The Freudian interpretation traces Lincoln's depressive traits to an unsuccessfully resolved Oedipal conflict, noting the lack of sympathy between Lincoln and his father and the intense devotion to both his mother and stepmother. Thus, despite the difficulties in determining the etiology of Lincoln's melancholy, the diagnoses and evidence all point to it conclusively.

Abraham Lincoln's Organic and Emotional Neurosis

EDWARD J. KEMPF, M.D.

THE PHYSICAL CONSTITUTION of Abraham Lincoln has perplexed his biographers and portrait sculptors and painters, as it did his personal friends, because of certain enigmatical qualities in his face and personality. More books, articles, and speeches are said to be presented yearly on Lincoln than on any man in history, and his philosophy of democratic government of the people, by the people, and for the people has become the philosophy of the democratic political organization of the United Nations, as well as the United States. It is therefore important that any new evidence on his physical constitution and neuroses that would be helpful in understanding his personality should be published.

The following discussion presents a new consideration of the evidence on his genetic and endocrine constitution, followed by new, recently discovered evidence of an accidental fracture of his skull in childhood from the kick of a horse. This fracture left certain permanent injuries and functional impairments of his brain that greatly influenced the schizoid, melancholic-euphoric development of his personality and thereby his marital life and legal and political career.

HEREDITARY DETERMINATION

Lincoln's face gave evidence of unusual hereditary genetic predispositions in its embryonic development, and hence in the development of his brain and personality. The creases in the skin of the human face are produced principally by the activities of the muscles of the face with attachments to the skin. In most faces, the crease that runs on either side from the nose continues below the cheek and around the upper lip and corner of the mouth, and then passes more or less distinctly around and under the lower lip. In Lincoln's face, as shown by his life mask and photographs, these creases, one on each side, pass from the nose part way only around the upper lip and then turn sharply backward, well above the corners of the mouth. Here they join unusually deep creases that run downward from in front of the cheekbones, between the buccinator muscle of the cheek and the masseter muscle of the jaw, and then curve forward, well back of the mouth, to pass under the chin, where they meet. The expressive effect of this unusual, though not rare, type of facial creasing was enhanced by the length and narrowness of his face. This type of facial creasing is characteristic of the great apes, and when it exists in man it indicates a primitive type of hereditary nervous differentiation.[1]

Three genetic moles, one on the right side and two on the left side of the face, gave, in relation to these creases, a distinguishing quality to Lincoln's face, which, once seen, was not likely to be forgotten and was, therefore, socially and politically invaluable. The largest and most prominent mole was located on the right side of his face, just above the crease as it turned backward from the upper lip to join the crease lying between the muscles of mastication and the mouth. The mole actually divided the crease, producing a perpetually dimpled, smiling effect on that side of the face. On the left side of the face, one of the other two moles lay on the cheek above the crease where it turned backward from the upper lip, and the other lay lower down on the side of the face, back of the crease, after it joined the masticator-buccinator crease. The positions of these moles in relation to the mole on the right cheek indicate that early in embryonic development, when the head was very small and the face was beginning to form, the right and left moles appeared in symmetrically opposite positions. If this is true, the mole on the left cheek later became divided, and the two parts separated progressively as the muscles and bones of the face enlarged.

Although the psychological effect of these unusual facial characteristics is now unknowable, they gave his face a ready-to-smile set and an unusually comical quality that surely must have reinforced the development of his great sense of humor and propensity to laughter. They probably also combined with other unusual inherited and acquired facial and bodily qualities in reinforcing the formation in his boyhood of the conviction that he was an unusual person, predestined to perform some great mission to be revealed to him, a conviction which developed later into his unique, fixed, lifelong humanitarian inspiration and compulsion.

As an adult, his hair was coarse and black, and his eyes were small, gray, and deeply set. His ears were large, and thick-lobed and extended almost at right angles to his head. His usually long and generally disheveled hair hid this grotesque, comical, inferior feature. His nose was not actually oversized, but it looked large because of his long, thin face. The nostrils did not extend as far into the tip of the nose as in most people, so that the end looked heavy. Lincoln was thought, when young, to be somewhat sensitive about his nose, but not about his ears. He was sometimes ridiculed for being "horse-faced."

HYPOKINETIC CONSTITUTION

Lincoln's body growth and energic constitution show gross evidence of pituitary hyperactivity and gonadal hypoactivity. He was a long, thin baby at birth, with unusually long, thin arms and legs. His body was morphologically like that of his tall thin mother. She was said by her cousins John Hanks and Dennis Hanks (Hertz[2]) to have been "5 feet 8 inches [173 cm.] high" and to have weighed about 130 lb. (59 kg.), whereas his father was 5 ft. 10 in. (178 cm.) tall and weighed about 190 lb. (86.2 kg.). Lincoln grew to 6 ft. 4 in. (193 cm.) in height and generally weighed less than 180 lb. (81.6 kg.). His legs and arms were disproportionately long for his body, which, when seated, was about the length of an average six-footer.

The skin of his face was weather-beaten, coarse, deeply grained, dark, and generally sallow or muddy. Many years of close exposure in youth before an open wood fire where he read, possibly left a permanent trophic effect. Deep creases over the forehead, at the outside corners of the eyes and around the mouth indicate an unusual amount of facial work in using the eyes and in laughing.

The neuromuscular tonus of his body was more relaxed than that of the average man. This was shown in the slow, drawling, staccato monotone of his speech; the deliberate, contemplative, meditative manner and slow mental reaction time, and the flat feet. He seems also to have had a lower blood pressure than normal, which probably, when too low, contributed to the production of nervous depression. Self-conscious of his height, he tended to slouch, with stooping of the shoulders and slight bending at the knees; but he generally held his chin up, his posture indicating an ego attitude of humility counterbalanced with well-determined self-reliance and self-respect.

Wold[3] has also reviewed the evidence on Lincoln's physical constitution in relation to his health. He has concluded that any endocrinopathy was limited to indications of thyroid dysfunction, and possibly a slight postpubertal overactivity of the pituitary, which might account for his disproportionately long legs and arms for the rest of the body. Attempts to explain Lincoln's melancholic disposition on an endocrinologic basis would be, Wold says rightly, "merely a venture in the realm of fancy."

However, even though his endocrine constitution is not fully known, it would be more erroneous to disregard the indications of some degree of pituitary, thyroid, and gonadal endocrinopathy than not to consider these factors as having possibly contributed to his hypokinetic constitution.

Many years of hard farm work and wood chopping from childhood to adulthood, out of dire necessity for living, gave him an unusually large and powerful muscular development of the hands and arms, back, and shoulders. His neck, though strong, was long and scrawny in relation to his head and sloping shoulders. His lower jaw was long and heavy and inclined to the acromegalic form.

His constitutional morphologic type was predominantly Kretschmerian asthenic[4] or Sheldonian ectomorphic and cerebrotonic,[5] and his energic constitution was Kempfian hypokinetic.[6] These qualities indicate that Lincoln was probably somewhat hyperpituitary and hypogonadal in endocrine ratio. His constitution disposed to some reduction of autonomic pressure of energy in sexual directions and tended to produce shyness with women and a preference for the company of men, factors of endlessly contributory and determinative influence on the social conditioning and development of his personality.

His slow, drawling speech, slow reaction time, mental deliberateness, and pedestrian rhythm in style of speaking and writing were so consistent with his energic constitution and morphologic type that the latter, obviously, largely determined the former. In Lincoln, the physiopsychological cyclical sequence dominated the psycho-physiological cyclical sequence of reactions. In other words, he must be, and generally was, guided by his feelings in what he said and did, for if they did not support him in the work of fulfilling certain self-commitments he would become miserable, if not melancholic.

LINCOLN'S FACE

If we examine the full-face photographs of Lincoln and the Volk (1860) life mask of his shaven face, we see that the forehead is narrow and high and bulges slightly in the midline. There is an unusual depression in the forehead of the mask, with a palpable edge, near the midline above the left eye. This deformation indicates the place of fracture of his skull. His head was said by some of his schoolmates, over 50 years later, to have looked small to them (probably relative to his height). Measurement of the Volk life mask between the bases of the tragi of the ears shows a breadth of 15.3 cm., which is somewhat greater than the breadth of the average head. Hence biographical statements that his head was small are erroneous.

In his photographs and masks, the left eye is set higher than the right. His left eyebrow is usually elevated more than the right, to help in keeping the upper lid retracted and the pupil of the left eye exposed. The tendency of the left eye to turn upward left uncovered more of the white surface of the sclera below the iris, giving a slightly staring effect on that side, in strange disharmony with the appearance of the right eye. In the best frontal photograph the left eye is definitely out of focus and turned reflexly slightly upward, and possibly outward. This deviation is due to weakening of certain extraocular muscles—possibly the inferior rectus, which is innervated by the third cranial nerve, and/or the superior oblique, which is innervated by the fourth cranial nerve. Lincoln's right eye was used dominantly for general vision and no doubt entirely for reading.

Further examination of the face shows that the left half of the upper lip is somewhat thicker than the right half and less expressive, that is, less unvolitionally and volitionally active. Also, the right half of the lower lip protrudes more markedly than the left and is pulled toward the right by the muscles of the cheek. This action characteristically holds the lower lip and facial muscles slightly toward the right. The right side of the chin is also slightly larger than the left, indicating stronger muscle tonus and development from more active use. The right nasofacial crease, previously described, runs somewhat farther from the midline than the left, and the tip of the nose crooks significantly toward the right. These muscles are supplied by the seventh, or facial, nerve. Although his larynx was large, he had a rasping, high-pitched voice, which grew shrill and squeaky upon emotional excitement, indicating some increase in muscle tonus of the vocal cords or the pharyngeal muscles, under control of the 10th cranial (vagus) nucleus.

Further examination of the life mask, especially measurement for corresponding right and left points from the midline, shows marked differences in the growth of the bones. Although such differences may be genetic or developmental in relation to loss of teeth or defective use from other causes, and cannot be taken as definitely indicative of the effects of an injury of the brain in youth, like the differences in tonic contraction of the ocular and facial muscles, they should be considered and functionally correlated. His cheek bones were unusually high and prominent. The right was larger than the left, and the right orbital ridge and lower jaw were more heavily developed than the left, giving the whole face a decided morphological curve toward the right.

This deformation becomes distinctly visible when the full-face photograph is turned upside down. When the Volk mask is turned upside down, the larger size of the face, the greater prominence of its lip, chin, and lower jaw, and the greater depression of the face under the cheek bone on the right side are striking.

FRACTURE OF SKULL AND INJURY OF BRAIN IN BOYHOOD

All these differences in the development of the facial muscles and bones, and the weakened functioning of the ocular and facial muscles on the left side in particular, indicate that Lincoln suffered a serious injury to his brain before adulthood. The sharp depression in the forehead above the left eye with a definitely palpable edge in the life mask, previously described, shows where his skull had been fractured, and the permanent differences in the nervous tone of the muscles of the two sides indicate that his brain was then permanently injured.

With this conclusion in mind, I searched the history of Lincoln's childhood for evidence of such an accident and found that it occurred in his 10th year. He was driving an unshod horse hitched in a circular mill for grinding corn or sugar cane; and, growing impatient of her slow pace, he shouted, "Get up, you hussy," and gave her a whack with a stick. She kicked back, hitting him in the forehead. He was knocked unconscious for many hours and was thought for a time to be dead. He seems to have recovered without apparent serious after-effects, since he received no special medical attention for the head injury, the doctor living many miles away.[7]

Fracture of the skull and cerebral after-effects were never suspected, or at least never reported, by any of his physicians, although after the age of 30 he consulted several for treatment of melancholia and other nervous symptoms.[8] This omission is not surprising, for it was not until after 1890, upon application of x-ray photography, that neurophysiology learned how to explain some of the cerebral effects and nervous consequences of fractures of the skull (Mock[9]).

Ample recording methods now show that an appalling amount of damage to the brain follows blows on the head, at the point of impact and from hydrostatic repercussion (contrecoup), through the production of petechial internal hemorrhages, as well as larger subdural blood clots, without external evidence of fracture. Blows on the forehead in boxing have been found to bruise by concussion the frontal lobes of the brain, sometimes with permanent, stupefying, "punch-drunk" effects, without visible injury on the outside of the head.

TENTATIVE DIAGNOSIS OF NATURE OF CEREBRAL INJURY

Although modern neurology requires for diagnosis a far more complete examination of the living subject for positive or negative evidence of nervous impairment, a tentative consideration of several types of injury to the brain that might have produced the unusual complex of symptoms in Lincoln's case, as far as is known, is desirable.

The blow on the forehead over the left eye evidently fractured the skull at the point of impact. The size and depth of the depression are evidence of its severity. It is most likely that a subdural hematoma of considerable size and petechial hemorrhages developed. The left frontal lobe was certainly damaged, which, in a right-handed, right-eyed person, would possibly have some modifying after-effects on the personality. These will be considered later.

The evident, permanent weakness of conjugate movements of the left eye, with the tendency of the eye to turn slightly upward and outward, and the weakness in tonus of the left facial muscles constitute a symptom complex that cannot be satisfactorily explained by a single area of permanent injury to the brain. The lifelong hypertension of the muscles of the pharynx and/or larynx is also indicative of involvement of autonomic nervous action, as are also his daily repetitive moodiness and emotional instability.

Hydrostatic repercussion within the skull on the opposite side (*contrecoup*) might have damaged, by shock or limited subdural hemorrhage, the right cerebral cortex in the lower frontoparietal area, where the weakened muscles have motor representation close together in a small area. But since the facial muscles have bilateral cortical representation, the effects of such an injury in a boy would have been completely compensated for within a few weeks; hence permanent damage must have occurred in some other area.

Several small hemorrhages in the midbrain or brain stem might have produced the particular ocular and facial effects. If the nucleus of the left third cranial nerve supplying the inferior rectus muscle were partly damaged, so as to weaken this muscle, the left eye would then tend continuously to turn more or less upward and slightly outward, as shown in Lincoln's photograph, while some degree of volitional coordination would be left. If another spot of hemorrhage damaged the nucleus of the left seventh cranial nerve, the facial muscles on that side would have been permanently weakened. If a third spot touched a certain portion of the midbrain, disturbance of sympathetic nervous action with permanent vocal tension might have followed.

Such weakening of the left facial muscles would probably have only minor secondary effects on the personality.

The production of a high-pitched, rasping voice was more important, but Lincoln largely overcame this professional deficiency by speaking thoughtfully, slowly, and clearly, always with the common-sense intention of expressing himself directly in the simplest words and thoughts that fitted the subject.

Decoordination of the left eye was more serious in that it tended to produce diplopia and severe eyestrain, which was increased upon fatigue or emotional excitement, with the sequelae of headache, nausea, indigestion, and depression. The deformation of facial expression and stress of diplopia required the development of the mental counterdefenses and compensations which characterized his personality.

Lincoln had other symptoms of permanent nervous lesions. With his rasping, high-pitched, nervous voice, he spoke in a slow, staccato monotone, indicating deficiency in sense of inflection in a public speaker, who naturally would have greatly desired this ability.

But most significant of all the symptoms was the repetitive tendency to lapse automatically into a lower conscious state, of mental detachment or abstraction, with characteristic facial expression, described by some of his friends as "ugly and stupid-looking," and by others as "dull," or "sad and abstract," or "detached," or "withdrawn." He told his friends, when a man in the 40's, that he was never without "melancholy." Upon being stimulated by his environment in a way that aroused autonomic-affective reactions of interest, as by some incident or some person's talk, or by reading, his facial expression was observed to change quickly from dull indifference to animated interest, with the tendency to smile and laugh. Herndon, his law partner, said he would sometimes burst out laughing to himself without apparent cause.[2]

Several men and women friends (Mary Owens, W. H. Herndon, L. Swett, and Mrs. Lincoln) saw in him an unusual lack of appreciation of beauty, nicety, and refinement and an inordinate fondness for laughing over vulgar, witty stories with clever, practical, or moral application. In contrast to this kind of aesthetic lapse, he was extremely fond of certain beautiful qualities of prose and poetry and memorized many passages from the Bible, Shakespeare, Burns, Gray, Goldsmith, and other poets. Most of all, he was highly conscientious about being truthful, reliable, honest, kind, fair, just, and loyal. His sense of fitness in the clarity and logic of his statements, his discrimination of innocence and guilt, truth and deception and justice in the courtroom, and his sense of definition and appropriateness in his speeches, were masterly. These aesthetic contrasts, of deficiency in some respects and of supremacy in others, might have been the effects of cultural preference more than of cerebral capacity.

The continuous tendency to lapse into melancholy or gloomy "blues" was, however, probably consistent with a permanent, cerebrally initiated, schizoid tendency to lapse automatically into a mentally dull, detached, drowsy state, and then to react, upon interpersonal stimulation, with excessive euphoric compensations.

This inhibitory-reaction tendency was also relatively overcome by the culture of certain forms of self-excitation, such as reading aloud to himself or other people, telling humorous stories, and becoming particularly adept in engaging in legal fights for justice. He liked to read aloud, he said to Herndon,[10] for thereby he gained the benefit of hearing, as well as seeing, what he read and remembered it more easily.

Two different loci of cerebral injury might have produced the complex volitional mental instabilities with the unstable sympathetic nervous reactions under stress or fatigue. One such locus would be a subcortical disruption (thalamic-sensory or hypothalamic-motor) at the head of the autonomic nervous system that depressed sympathetic nervous action and tended to produce dulness or drowsiness upon lack of excitatory stimulation. The other would be an impairment of the frontal cortex on the left side (of a right-eyed and right-handed person), involving the corticothalamic cycle of nerve impulses, that reduced the volitional production of the conscious stream of visual imagery of self-in-its-environment, so that such a person would require more external stimulation than would a normal one in order to remain mentally attentive. A person with this type of cerebral lesion, in order to keep mentally alert, would have to be involved, or keep himself involved, in emotionally stimulating situations by cultivating special stimulating interests and objectives, such as a passion for legal justice for all people. Lincoln did just this, as a humorist seeking happiness and as a humanist seeking justice, in an endless fight to overcome the tendency to lapse into a rut of sad, gloomy, suicidal preoccupations.

DIPLOPIA AND ASTIGMATISM

The earliest evidence of Lincoln's visual decoordination has been recorded by Shastid,[11] as told to him by his father, Dr. Shastid, an oculist who practiced in Pittsfield, Ill. The elder Dr. Shastid, when a boy, lived in New Salem and knew Abe Lincoln, then in his mid-twenties, as the storekeeper and postmaster of the town. He described him as a melancholy but kindly spoken person, who liked to amuse children, as well as grown-ups. Abe would sit on a box in front of the store when not waiting on a customer, generally with a dejected and abstracted expression. He would sometimes lie on the ground near the store, with his bare feet elevated against the trunk of a tree, and read. Shastid noticed that Lincoln's left eye looked queer at times and would suddenly get crossed and turn upward.

Some 20 years later, when a physician and oculist, Shastid saw Lincoln in several debates with Douglas and in several trials in court as a lawyer. He then recognized the ocular condition as hyperphoria from a certain weakness of the muscles of the left eye, which continuously caused the eyeball to turn upward. Upon excitement this condition would suddenly increase and produce a severe cross-eyed effect. Dr. Shastid suggested that the hyperphoria caused intense eyestrain and uneasiness and was at least partly the cause of Lincoln's moodiness or "chronic inexpressible blues." He thought that Lincoln possibly was also color-blind, for Lincoln once said to his (Shastid's) mother, when she showed him her flower garden, that flowers and sunsets had no beauty for him, as they did for other people.

Lincoln's right eye was dominant and was always used for vision, while the tendency of the left eye to turn upward and outward produced more or less overlapping of visual images. Like most such persons whose diplopia begins in youth, he soon adapted to this condition by reacting attentively to the imagery that he saw more clearly, that is, the image of the right eye, while ignoring what the left eye saw. This required more or less volitional brain work, which was carried on easily enough until manhood, when at times mental visual fatigue or emotional strain became too severe.

Through the adult years Lincoln had many nervous attacks, characterized by eyestrain, headache with nausea, and indigestion, so severe that he often became unable to work and had to lie down with a cold compress over his eyes. He had couches in his law office, at home, and in the White House for this purpose.

Probably in youth and maturity Lincoln was unable to focus both eyes for any length of time without volitional effort. Herein existed an unconscious, self-protective influence on conscious learning. He must not only use right-eyed instead of left-eyed vision, but he must consciously and conscientiously see mentally the right side and better side of things in order to reduce the emotional strain of being wrong. His highly persistent work in developing a clear thinking, logically visualizing, auditizing, and verbalizing mind counteracted the mentally befuddling effects of diplopia and protected him against the tendency toward gloomy mental visualizing.

In 1857, at the age of 48, while shopping in a jewelry store, he bought, upon the recommendation of a friend, his first pair of "spectacles" for reading. He tried on several pairs and paid 37½ cents for the glasses that he read best with. Until a few years before he had probably normal vision and effective accommodation of the right eye, although the accommodation was always attended by more or less strain from decoordination of the left eye.

The following reports on Lincoln's eyes and glasses are taken from several later authoritative sources. The glasses were reported by Almer Coe, of Chicago, to have in each lens the strength of +6.75 D. This indicated that Lincoln probably had 4 or 4½ D. of hypermetropia, or farsightedness, at the age of 48. This severe disability had no doubt been developing for a number of years and required constant effort to produce sufficient accommodation for reading.

Dr. W. H. Crisp,[12] an ophthalmologist, recorded the following observations: Full-faced photographs show an upward deviation of the left eye, great enough to produce a lack of fusion of its images with those of the right eye. The two eyes did not work together, possibly as a result of a vertical strabismus of the left eye.

Dr. S. Mitchell[13] found evidence of left hyperphoria and hypertropia and suggested that the corrugations of his brow and the crow's-feet at the corners of the eyes showed that Lincoln habitually used auxiliary facial muscles to support the external muscles of the eyes in the work of visual coordination.

Dr. K. C. Wold[3] suggested that the diplopia was caused by a decoordination of the external muscles of the left eye, which was inherently connected in some way with the other facial asymmetries.

No physician on record, so far as I know, has attempted to explain the origin and nature of the asymmetrical functioning of the facial and ocular muscles on the left side, although some have discussed the nervous effects of eyestrain.

All the known symptoms are grossly explainable, I think, as the result of a cerebral injury attending the fracture of his skull in boyhood, and producing permanent, specific forms of nervous decoordination (organic neurosis).

PRACTICAL ADAPTATION TO GLOOMY EYESTRAIN

The continuous tendency to visual decoordination was sufficient to increase nervous fatigue and depression of mood or "spirit" upon prolonged use of the eyes, particularly for reading. Such conditions tend in most youths to induce discouragement of reading, lethargy with laziness, and a preference for reading from a reclining position to ease the eyestrain. Despite his impairment, Lincoln was an eager student and liked to lie on the floor and read aloud by the light of the open wood fire. Later, as a man, he often read in a reclining position on a couch or on the floor and preferred to read aloud.

We have additional evidence of how Lincoln's neurovisual difficulties influenced him in everyday life. His work as a lawyer and politician required him to read excessively. He adapted to this by learning to scan pages rapidly for essentials and by developing a highly retentive memory. When it was unnecessary to use his eyes or mind, he would lapse into his characteristic semiwithdrawn mental state, previously described.

ENIGMATICAL EXPRESSION

The right side of Lincoln's face was animated and emotionally expressive, whereas the left side functioned more weakly, looked duller, and was out of harmony. The meaning of the duality and changes in his facial expression baffled everyone. Strangers, who estimated the man by his dull, perplexed face and sad, tired eyes, were always astonished at the quick change of his expression to alertness when he became interested in their conversation and wanted to make some contribution to it. Many strangers, including lawyers, generals, and members of his cabinet, upon first acquaintance, thought themselves superior to this ugly, dull, sad, weak-looking man, only to find themselves amazed and mastered by the ready wit, common sense, logical intelligence, and strength of character that became evident upon his being required to look out for himself.

As his law partner from 1843 to 1861, Herndon was no doubt the most frequent, intimate, and interested observer of Lincoln's personality and physical constitution day after day. He[10] has stated that Lincoln's most marked and persistent characteristic was a predisposition to become melancholy or sad and depressed. This attitude showed in his facial expression when he was sitting alone or when he was in a group and not taking an active interest in the conversation. Many other intimate friends of Lincoln were similarly impressed, as recorded in various biographies. Some of his friends thought, because of the muddy, leathery condition of his skin, that this facial lapse was due to indigestion and insufficient secretion of bile.

Herndon imagined that the morbidity was caused by some "occult" condition, which could not be explained by observation or reasoning. It was "ingrained," he said,[2] and "could not be reduced to rules or the cause assigned. . . . It was necessarily hereditary. . . . It was a part of his nature and could no more be shaken off than he could part with his brains. Simple in carriage or bearing, free from pomp or display, serious, unaffected, Lincoln was a sad looking man whose melancholy dripped from him as he walked." Herndon observed that "the look of sadness was more or less accentuated by a peculiarity of one eye (left), the pupil of which had a tendency to turn or roll slightly toward the upper lid, whereas the other one maintained its normal position equidistant between the upper and the lower lids." He also noticed that the tip of Lincoln's nose and his mouth turned toward the right. "Mr. Lincoln was a peculiar, mysterious man—had a double consciousness, a double life. The two states, never in the normal man, co-exist in equal and vigorous activities though they succeed each other quickly. One state predominates and, while it so rules, the other state is somewhat quiescent, shadowy, yet living, a real thing. This is the sole reason why Mr. Lincoln so quickly passed from one state of consciousness to another and different state" (letter from Herndon to J. Weik, Feb. 2, 1891, Hertz[2]).

Josiah Crawford (Herndon and Weik[10]) remembered that as Lincoln became occupied with reading, his lower lip stuck out. This, he thought, was only a lifelong "habit." Actually, as his mask (1860) and photographs show, the right half of the lower lip always protruded more than the left half and was pulled with the other muscles of the mouth slightly to the right side. When he was reading quietly or thinking actively, the degree of dominance in neuromuscular activity of the right side of his face tended generally to increase. When he was mentally inattentive, the lack of nervous stimulation tended to let the right side of his face decrease in activity faster than the relatively hypotonic left side, giving his expression a perplexed quality, which was misunderstood by those who would read his face.

SUPERSTITIOUS INTERPRETATION OF DIPLOPIA

Most persons with hyperphoria learn to disregard the dimmer, overlapping visual image without being conscious of such work. However, when eyestrain and fatigue or emotional excitement grow excessive, the visual decoordination increases until the two more or less distinct images tend to be seen with increasing mental confusion and uneasiness. Lincoln learned to cultivate a calm, humorous, kindly attitude, happy interpersonal relations, and a common-sense philosophy of life, which generally protected him from emotional provocation and increase of this distress. Yet he needed to have certain qualities of sympathetic excitation in order to maintain his best working pressure.

His description of a particular experience shows how he mystically interpreted his first experience with complete diplopia. Upon learning of his nomination for the presidency, in 1860, by the national convention of the young Republican party, Mr. Lincoln returned to his home, after a strenuous day, tired and nervous, and lay down on a couch in his wife's sitting room to rest. Directly across the room, facing him, was a large mirror on the bureau. In it he saw for the first time a double image of his face, and it perplexed him greatly. He described the experience as follows:

As I reclined, my eyes fell upon the glass, and I saw distinctly two images of myself, exactly alike, except that one was a little paler than the other. I arose and lay down with the same result. It made me feel quite uncomfortable for a few minutes, but, some friends coming in, the matter passed from my mind. The next day while walking the street, I was suddenly reminded of the circumstance, and the disagreeable sensation produced by it returned. I had never seen anything of the kind before, and did not know what to make of it. I determined to go home and place myself in the same position, and, if the same effect was produced, I would make up my mind that it was the natural result of some refraction or optics, which I did not understand, and dismiss it. I tried the experiment with the same result; and, as I had said to myself, accounted for it on some principle unknown to me, and it ceased to trouble me. But the God who works through the laws of Nature might surely give a sign to me, if one of his chosen servants, even through the operation of a principle in optics.

Lincoln had been a devoted reader of the Bible since boyhood and superstitiously believed, as it taught by numerous episodes in many chapters, that God revealed his wishes and commands to chosen people by natural and occult signs, such as visions, voices, and dreams, as well as by the feelings of the heart and conscience. He said that he felt himself "to be aided and enlightened by One who is stronger and wiser than all others."

Lincoln's comments on his first experience with complete diplopia, as a double visual image of his face in a mirror, shows that, while he regarded it with common sense, it also excited him superstitiously, mystically, religiously, and wishfully. He hoped somehow to receive an inspiring sign, as a chosen servant of the people and of God, to think of a way of solving the violent conflict between the free and the slave states that would be acceptable to both sides and eventuate in the peaceful preservation of the Union. By his form of thought, feeling, belief, and faith in having received a definite sign and divine inspiration, he was able to maintain high, consistent integrity of purpose against the subconscious tendency to schizoid indecision and confusion.

He did not really dismiss this double vision of his face as being caused by a law of optics that he did not understand. It continued to mystify him, and he often thought of it. When he was President, after a dream, a few days before his assassination, in which he saw himself dead in state in the White House, he confided to Ward Lamon how he finally interpreted its premonitional meaning for his destiny. He would have two terms as President, and in the second term he would be killed.[14]

PREFERENCE FOR PHOTOGRAPHS OF RIGHT SIDE OF FACE

The collected photographs of Lincoln published by Frederick Mill Meserve and Carl Sandburg,[15] and by Stefan Lorant,[16] show that in many of them he has a similar serious, solemn, dignified, unsmiling but kindly, reposeful, mentally inactive facial expression. In a few, the face is so moody, depressed, and unusually perplexed, and the eyestrain so pronounced, that many people doubt whether they are authentic reproductions. Not until one examines the lines of the eyes, mouth, and skin closely in such photographs is the identity fully established.

Lincoln's usual facial expression, when not being photographed, was that of patient humility, kindness and naturalness of attitude, honesty, simplicity, and serenity of thought, with the tendency to smile pleasantly or to burst into a good-humored laugh. His face also showed great self-reliance, courage, and firmness, with thoroughgoing dignity and repose, when he was not tending to lapse into dull conscious detachment. The left side of his face, being less mobile and not in completely harmonious affective tone with the right, and contributing less volitional kinesthesis to his brain, was less truly representative of his state of mind.

The differences in expression seem to have influenced Lincoln, or his photographers, to prefer photographs of the right side of his face, since most photographs were taken from the right quarter or the profile. Only a few were taken from the left side or from the front. Although a great laugher, he tended to keep his mouth closed firmly, with more protrusion of the right lower lip than of the left when being photographed. Even though Mrs. Lincoln chided him for persisting in looking too solemn, he could not be persuaded to smile freely before the camera. Herndon said that from the moment Lincoln faced the camera his face would grow serious and sad.[2]

Lincoln's face was completely shaven until, in his campaign for the Presidency in 1860, he was persuaded to grow a beard. The numerous changes in the style of cutting his beard and hair indicate that he and his barbers or Mrs. Lincoln indulged in no little experimentation for the best effect. His photographs show they tried a number of different trimmings, with one constant feature, namely, shaving the upper lip, lower lip, and upper half of the chin, while letting a beard grow on the lower half of the chin and throat and the sides of his face. The coarse, black hair on his head was generally cut so as to remain unusually long, probably for reducing the prominence of his ears. He liked to play with his hair and parted it on either the right or the left side, as he fancied. Its generally disheveled appearance indicates that he habitually, self-consciously mussed it with his fingers.

VICIOUS CIRCLE OF ORGANIC AND EMOTIONAL NEUROSES

The nausea and headaches from exacerbation of such continuous malfunctioning of the eyes are not uncommonly attended by a depressed, dark, gloomy outlook on life. Many ophthalmologists hold on physiopsychologic grounds that the mental state follows from the physical condition, constituting primarily an organic neurosis. Most psychiatrists hold that, although such organic causes of visual malfunction tend to increase headaches and depressions upon mental fatigue and emotional discouragement or excitement, the tendency to visual decoordination is psychopathologically increased by internal mental conflict and emotional depression or excitement, with the formation of a progressive vicious circle. Abundant evidence from the biographical study of Lincoln shows that the organic and emotional neuroses formed a vicious circle and worked pathologically, daily throughout his life, and that he cultivated a common-sense attitude to protect himself from himself and his personal relationships that was largely successful but not infrequently broke down.

It is impossible to understand the effects on the development of Lincoln's personality of the injury to his brain in childhood without considering their connections with the conditioning influences of the different members of his family and his social and professional relationships. Conversely, we cannot estimate soundly his personal adjustments to the great crises of his life without correlating them with the organic factors in his neurosis. The thousands of biographical studies and estimations of Lincoln in books, papers, editorials, and speeches published since his death have largely been based on a fundamental misunderstanding of the determining factors in the development of the man's personality and his great motives, although many have estimated ably the part he played in history.

The studies of Lincoln's facial expression made by physicians have related it to his ocular symptoms only as an auxiliary effort to control vision. The permanently destructive effects on his brain by the accident in boyhood, as the cause of his visual, facial, and vocal impairment and melancholic detachment, have been entirely overlooked. Of course, the definite history of the accident and the dent in his forehead discredit the theory of cerebral injury at birth or of hereditary factors as the cause. A biography will be published soon giving special attention to the interactions of his organic and emotional neuroses with the origin and development of his great inspirations, leading up to and including his Presidency. It will show for the first time how the cerebral injury and family environment in boyhood influenced the development of his personality and mental convictions as a man.

Because of limited space, it must suffice here to add the well-known fact that Lincoln (born and raised in a wilderness log cabin) had an unusually attractive, intelligent, heroic, although semiliterate mother, to whom he was greatly attached in childhood. She died tragically of an epidemic fever when he was 9 years old, and his father married again when he was 10. His stepmother, an unusually intelligent pioneer woman, was very kind and devoted to her stepson and encouraged him to learn to read and write and to educate himself. He always retained a persistent, gloomy mother fixation, with interest in melancholy and tragic songs and poetry about the dead and the past.

His betrothed, Ann Rutledge, died in 1837 of an epidemic fever, and he reacted with suicidal melancholia, which lasted for several months. The following year he courted Mary Owens and proposed marriage but was unable to complete this obligation because of conflicting emotional revulsions against it.

In 1840 he courted Mary Todd, and suffered such intense schizoid depression that he was unable to appear for the wedding ceremony. He again became melancholic, incoherent, and suicidal but recovered sufficiently in a few weeks to return to his office. He married Mary Todd in 1842; but, although she had four sons by him, he was never able to love her. He continued to have repeated attacks of emotional nervousness, with headaches and indigestion, for the rest of his life, particularly when forced to endure some grave political or military frustration.

Abraham Lincoln, throughout his maturity, until his death, was never free for a day from the tendency to melancholy from the combined interactions of an organic visual neurosis and a specifically conditioned, emotional neurosis that worked in a repetitive, vacillating, vicious circle, against the miserable effects of which he protected himself by cultivating a practical, common-sense philosophy of humanism and humor.

Notes

1 A third cousin, now living, Jonas Basham, whose grandmother, Mimi Hanks, was a first cousin of Lincoln's mother, Nancy Hanks, inherited facial creases remarkably similar to those of Abraham Lincoln, indicating maternal transmission of this unusual characteristic. A genetically oriented genealogical investigation of these, and the hereditary facial characteristics in Lincoln's maternal and paternal ancestry, discussed in this paper would contribute important evidence on his family tree.

2 Hertz, E.: The Hidden Lincoln, from the Letters and Papers of William H. Herndon, New York, The Viking Press, 1938.

3 Wold, K. C.: Mr. President—How Is Your Health? St. Paul, Bruce Publishing Company, 1948.

4 Kretschmer, E.: Physique and Character, New York, Harcourt, Brace & Company, 1925.

5 Sheldon, W. H.: The Varieties of Human Physique, New York, Harper & Brothers, 1940.

6 Kempf, E. J.: Biological Differentiation of Energic Constitutional Types, M. Rec. 154: 295 (Oct. 15) 1941.

7 H. E. Mock (Skull Fractures and Brain Injuries, Baltimore, Williams & Wilkins Company, 1950) reports that about 7% of untreated fractures of the skull in children end fatally. Before the automobile most such fractures were caused by being kicked in the head.

8 Lincoln was also struck on the head with a club in a fight with Negro marauders while taking a flatboat down the Mississippi, when he was either 19 or 22. This blow, he said, left a permanent scar (of unknown location). However, it probably did no further damage, for he routed the hoodlums, saved his cargo, and continued the journey.

Congenital injury of the nervous system has also been suggested to account for the ocular and facial symptoms, but this is discredited by the definite history of a blow on the forehead in childhood that knocked him unconscious for many hours.

9 Mock, H. E.: Skull Fractures and Brain Injuries, Baltimore, Williams & Wilkins Company, 1950.

10 Herndon, W. H., and Weik, J. W.: Herndon's Lincoln: The True Story of a Great Life, Chicago, Belford, Clarke, & Company, 1889.

11 Shastid, T. H.: My Father Knew Lincoln, Nation 2:227, 1929.

12 Crisp, W. H.: The Eyes of Abraham Lincoln, Am. J. Ophth. 15:775, 1932.

13 Mitchell, S.: Diagnosis of Heterophoria from a Portrait, Ophth. Rec. 23:224 (May) 1914; cited by Wold. (See n. 3.)

14 Lamon, W. H.: The Life of Abraham Lincoln, from His Birth to His Inauguration as President, Boston, Osgood & Co., 1872.

15 Meserve, F. H., and Sandburg, C.: Photographs of Abraham Lincoln, New York, Harcourt, Brace & Company, 1944.

16 Lorant, S.: Lincoln; His Life in Photographs, New York, Duell, Sloan & Pearce, Inc., 1941.

Unconscious Motives Underlying the Personalities of Great Statesmen and Their Relation to Epoch-Making Events

A Psychologic Study of Abraham Lincoln[1]

L. PIERCE CLARK, M.D.

WHILE NO ONE would have the temerity in the present status of the development of historical science to revive the rather discredited theory of Carlyle that history is but the collective biography of a few conspicuous public figures, it cannot be denied that there is often a residuary influence to be detected in the course of events which must be assigned to the part played by the dominating personalities of the time. The present article will be concerned with suggestions regarding a more intensive and scientific study of the latter.

Critical periods in national life are often imperfectly understood because current events only are considered in their interpretation. Intensive study of the personalities of great statesmen of any epoch has but recently become an object of psychological research. When the events in the political and social order are properly coordinated with the conscious and unconscious personal motives and desires of its contemporary leaders, we may then expect a sounder and broader view of historic interpretation. At the culmination of a crisis in national life we find there have often been comparatively few issues that have shaped a final national outcome, and that two or three powerful leaders have forged the ideas and sentiments of the people *en masse* and forced the crisis to a decision. We thus find it said that "the time was not yet ripe," or that "events waited upon a leader sufficiently powerful," etc. Too much reliance, therefore, would seem to have been placed upon current issues and events to explain epochal history, and not enough upon the innate attitudes of certain great contemporaries. These, largely because of their fundamental reactions to certain deeper unconscious personal motives which control human behavior, seize upon the more or less obvious issues of their time and devote themselves to a particular cause with an assiduity altogether out of proportion to any casual reason. Instances bearing out such a contention might be multiplied indefinitely.

True historical interpretation, therefore, of any great epochal moment is not possible until we make a careful psychological study of the people of that particular period, especially its great men and leaders. The position in the main is not a new one, but heretofore historians have made a study of the more obvious characterology of the great statesmen and either have not been able, or were unwilling, to study such historic personages in the more scientific manner now possible, although this has already been done in several instances by those trained in methods of intensive mental analysis. The historian, therefore, has not fully exhausted the possibilities of his subject, because of inadequate psychological training, while the psychologist for the most part has not coupled up his accurate personal analyses with the events to which his characterological study forms a necessary part. Those interested in the two methods of approach in historic study should coöperate more than has been done in the past. This viewpoint is worthy of a more extended investigation than this brief outline will permit. When we shall have made a broader, more intensive analysis of men and events we can possibly comprehend why the souls of certain great leaders seem literally to have caught fire, and they have exhibited an almost superhuman energy in their lifelong devotion to a particular cause.

One may properly inquire, what are some of these deeper motives in the individual which serve the purpose of advancing social consciousness in a practical manner? Modern psychology has unearthed a host of primitive and infantile motives which, though they seem to disappear from the individuals' lives as they grow up, are really found not to have been lost, but are transformed and become operative to the more adult purposes of existence. Simple illustrations are found in creative geniuses whose preoccupation in childhood early portended a fruition in later life. The boy Stephenson made toy engines, while Newton in his early youth was observant of natural phenomena. But such obvious data are still more deeply analyzable, and to these primary and more genetic instincts modern psychology has already devoted much time and fascinating research. To make such intimate studies immediately serviceable in historic, literary and artistic interpretation, a group of investigators have collected data and published their studies in a journal devoted exclusively to this domain. From a historic point of view it would seem desirable to select the prominent leaders of an epoch and proceed to analyze their characters as to salient personality traits and life reactions, and then examine the previous succession of events in their childhood which may have led up to the main traits of the adult character. In order to confine the issue at this time to a concrete instance, I have undertaken a tentative study of the depressive personality of Abraham Lincoln and the possible developmental causes that might account for such a personality, and have briefly sketched the influence which such character-traits may have had upon the events and issues of his time.

That Lincoln suffered lifelong from periodic depression—indeed, that he never seemed entirely free from some vestiges of the more intense episodes, is well known to all, but an attempt to elucidate the deeper, more genetic causes for such states has not heretofore been undertaken. The difficulties of such a study are in more than one direction; first, in mental medicine we have only too recently formulated a tentative explanation of how retarded or periodic depressions occur. This formulation is still under investigation, as sufficient data upon many points are still lacking. Naturally in our present thesis such studies have to be made upon historic data which, while recorded accurately, were collected for quite other purposes than an innate delineation of the mental traits which might be considered essential for the precise purpose of making a clinical diagnosis. Often, too, as in the case of Lincoln, there is a natural and sublime reserve which great personages draw about their more intimate life. As has been said, the great often lead solitary lives and defy analysis in more ways than one. There seems to be little doubt, however, that if we could have employed the more modern methods of analysis to the heroic life of Lincoln, we might have acquired sufficient facts to have completely substantiated our present thesis. We are obliged, however, to rest the main tenets of our conclusions upon reliable historic documents. We shall develop the study by first giving a simple statement of the nature and cause of periodic, or retarded, depressions as psychiatry has come to know them through long experience. Next, we shall state the psychologic mechanisms or unconscious motives seemingly underlying the lives of individuals thus afflicted, and finally we shall examine such portions of Lincoln's life as have a bearing upon this view of the cause of his depressions.

It is well known that many individuals otherwise normal are subject to more or less marked fluctuations in mood, and these swings of emotional feeling may occur irregularly or periodically. Heredity is the most common causative factor in the induction of the temperament and personality from which such disorders are recruited. At least some marked occurrence of such hereditary traits is found in the family stock of nearly three fourths of these patients (Kraepelin). Often the relatives have suffered from outspoken forms of the same mental disorder, or there is present a constitutional bias to some degree of retarded depression.

Individuals who suffer from periodic depressions possess evidence of a peculiar type of personality previous to the onset of the psychosis.[2] Some show an open, expansive temperament, while others, predisposed to more marked depression, are of a depressive makeup. In the majority frequent and causeless changes of mood are in evidence; they are excitable, excessively shy, or reserved. The disorder usually appears independent of external causes, either physical or mental. Even when such alleged causes are present, the provoking factors are usually inadequate to account fully for the depressed state. The condition is often recurrent, being based upon a deep-seated constitutional mental makeup. It is essentially a benign affliction, and recovery from individual attacks are the rule. The first attack usually occurs in the first or second decade of adult life. The real nature of the underlying morbid process in the brain, if any exists, is most obscure. Several hypotheses have been formulated to account for the psychosis, but none have proven adequate. There are no constant demonstrable or structural changes in the nervous system which may be counted as characteristic of this condition. In the absence of structural changes in the brain, psychiatrists have lately turned their attention more specifically to the psychologic factors playing a rôle in the evolution of the disorder. These will be considered later.

For the sake of those unacquainted with the condition we may now hastily sketch the usual picture of the mental state. The onset of depression is generally gradual unless it follows acute illness or definite mental shock. First there appears a mental sluggishness; thought becomes slow and difficult. Decisions are poorly made. The patient has difficulty in forming sentences and in finding words with which to express his thoughts. It is hard for him to follow ideas either in reading or in ordinary conversation. The process of association of ideas is remarkably retarded. The patient does not talk because he has nothing to say. There is a dearth of ideas and a poverty of thought. Familiar facts are no longer at their command. Remembrance of most commonplace events is difficult. In spite of the great slowness of apprehension and thought, consciousness and knowledge of surroundings are well retained. The patient appears dull and sluggish and may explain that he really feels tired out. His usual daily activities are performed slowly, as though under a feeling of inward restraint. If he is sent out to walk or to work he loiters until the initial impetus has passed. His usual duties loom before him as huge, impossible tasks because he lacks the will to overcome the inner resistance. Sometimes a patient may become bedridden. Before the mental retardation becomes extreme, the individual may dwell upon and often attempt suicide. The majority of patients say they are "no good" and desire to die, and as they pass into and come out of the deeper depression the possible fulfillment of suicidal desires is most to be feared. As already stated, the emotional attitude is that of a more or less uniform depression, and the patient sees only the dark side of life. The past and future alike are full of misfortune. All aims in life have lost their charm. The patient feels himself unsuited to his environment, he has lost his religious faith and lives on day by day in gloomy submission to his ordained fate. Often patients are ill humored, shy, and pettish or anxious, and are frequently irritable and sullen. Compulsive ideas are not uncommon, and they feel compelled against their inclination to ponder over unpleasant scenes. They often possess insight into the nature of their condition but fail to correct their faulty emotional tone or the morbid trend of judgment. Often they sit helpless, unable to begin work, and may even permit themselves to be fed; in some cases they may refuse to take food. Thus we find the chief symptoms of the disorder are mental and physical slowness and retardation, absence of spontaneous activity, a dearth of ideas, and a depressed emotional state.

As an explanatory preface to the discussion of the causes that may have played a rôle in the depressive episodes of Lincoln, we may briefly outline some of the more recent hypotheses of periodic or retarded depression. One of the more acceptable formulations is that recently put forward by Hoch, who has studied a long series in the light of the Freudian psychology covering the operations of the unconscious motives.

For some time antedating Freud's work it was known that in hypnotic states it was possible for one to experimentally create motives for actions and the latter could be carried out without the motive itself entering consciousness. For instance, a person duly hypnotized might be told while in that state that on the day following at a certain hour he would leave his office, return home and go to bed. The hypnotic seance would then be closed, and the following day the suggestion would be unconsciously obeyed. It, however, remained for Freud to reveal to us a new world of such unconscious motives of which we had previously been comparatively unaware. He insisted that the motives of infancy and childhood did not disappear from the mental life of the adult but underwent further development. From the very nature of their further development the original form of their existence ceased to exist as a reality to the normal adult consciousness. Freud found on analysis one of the great unconscious motives of the strivings of earliest life was a tendency for a strong attachment of the child to the parent, and particularly of a great love for the parent of the opposite sex. One recognizes at once the possible rôle such a love attachment might play in the development of the adult love-instinct. But adult love contains sensual elements which are not present in the child, and can, therefore, play no part in that tender feeling toward the parent. As puberty approaches, however, these sensual elements appear. It has been shown that the great task of puberty is to dissolve the bonds of the home tie and to transfer a part of the affections shown previously for the parent to new objects in the service of the instinct of propagation. This puberty-process, for some as yet unknown reason, is not possible to every individual, and the assumption is made that in such instances the trend of the sensual impulse then flows in the direction of the tender feeling formerly felt for the parent. But the conscious personality strongly opposes this process, hence this sexually intensified part of the attachment for the parent remains repressed and unconscious. One may say, therefore, that in the course of adult development certain normal steps remain undeveloped, or are arrested. Hence this defect of underdeveloped instinctive desires—which later are the very core of the personality—results in a defective adaptation especially in the sexual sphere, and, as has been carefully pointed out, when one states there is a sexual cause in every neurosis it does not necessarily imply a sexual cause in the adult sense, but in the sense that the cause lies in the imperfect development of the instinct. It has been shown that the unconscious has different depths, as it were, and that the infantile motives just mentioned are undoubtedly among the deepest repressed strivings. But in order to understand these infantile motives aright one needs to free himself from the ordinary adult logical way of thinking and meet the situation on the infantile level. Not a few persons, and even physicians, knowing that Freud has spoken of sexual causes and the child's longing for the parent, have simply combined or translated this into terms of adult sexuality. This is probably wrong, because adult sexuality has many qualities added at puberty which have no such formulation in the infantile life. Often the ideas of desire, expressed in the depressive psychosis in particular, are much more vague. They not infrequently express a mere desire of possession of some sort. This is well shown in the severest forms of melancholia wherein the longing is often expressed as a wish to die and be with the mother, or the wish for removal of the other parent as shown in the delusive statement that the father is dead. For instance, a man may become neurotic when he becomes engaged as Lincoln did. After marriage he may be unable to meet the marriage relations and then he may develop a psychosis of an intense type in which the ideas expressed are essentially that his marriage is annulled, his father is dead, and that he himself is following the mother into her grave and is united with her in her coffin. In other words, it may be inferred in such a case that the man was unable to adapt himself to his married life and therefore regressed or returned to a union with the mother. It can readily be seen that this psychotic setting is not sexual in the adult sense, though it is an evidence of imperfect adaptation of the sexual life.

There still remains another important point, namely, the thoroughly illogical nature of the above example. On logical grounds it is absurd to wish—and we regard the delusions as expressions of unconscious wishes—that the father should die, when all that is desired is to be united with the mother in death. But the psychotic does not think logically. The wish for the father's death or removal exists, because to the child he is the rival in the affections of the mother. We must not forget that the ideas expressed in psychoses are often, so far as known, direct emanations of unconscious desires which cannot be understood by the observer or the patient when standards of logical thinking are applied to them. And, when we try to cast them into logical or adult forms, we are doing something which is, strictly speaking, not possible, and the formulation is apt to become onesided and artificial. To recognize this is important. The vagueness of these trends is not due to our imperfect knowledge of them so much as to their very nature, and we are not improving matters if we attempt to make them clearer than they really are.

It has been said that the infantile motives, upon which Freud lays so much stress, have been revealed by a method which is questionable, owing to the great latitude given in it to interpretation. But in studying the psychoses we find exactly the same motives as those which Freud has inferred, and here very often no complicated interpretation is needed, since the unconscious desires are expressed directly in the ideas of the patient. This is what should make the central claims of psychoanalysis so convincing to the psychiatrist. Freudian psychology, however, can be understood only when the dynamic importance of the deepest infantile motives is fully grasped.

In the foregoing brief outline, we have the principal teachings of Freud, elaborated and applied by Hoch to the mechanisms of the depressive episodes of the benign psychoses. It must be held in mind that in the milder forms of retarded depressions, those without hallucinations, delusions or disorientation, the expressions of sadness and dejection rarely go so far as to completely illustrate the hallucinatory or delirious form of the hypothesis. Thus it was in the life of Lincoln, where but the vaguer outlines of these ideas were in evidence.

We shall now undertake to sketch hastily the main facts of Lincoln's life, and note what bearing the above hypothesis has in the interpretation of the depressive episodes of this great man.

So far as we have knowledge, Lincoln's early childhood was in no way dissimilar to that of any number of other children whose parents were pioneers in what was then a desolate wilderness. Little is known of his likes and dislikes or his manner of behavior and conduct aside from the fact that he was a well-intentioned, obedient and affectionate child.

In 1817, when the family made their way from Kentucky to Spencer County, Indiana, it was decided that they remain in this locality instead of pushing further westward. A shack was built, one side of which was left entirely open as there was no chimney, and the first was built half in the home and half outside. During this bleak winter Abe and his sister enjoyed the rough pioneer life, but to the ill-clad, delicate mother it meant nothing but great deprivation and hard work. She coughed a good deal and seemed overtired and sad, but no one seemed to realize that she was seriously ill. One day, while lying on her bed she motioned to her son to come near, and reaching out one hand to the eight-year-old boy she pointed to the little sister and whispered, "Be good to her, Abe." Then she closed her tired eyes, and several hours elapsed before the children knew she was dead.

Next day Lincoln's father made a rude coffin, and the mother was laid to rest at the top of a little hill. Abe protected the grave from the wild animals by piling rocks upon it, and the two children went down the hill clinging to each other in their grief. The boy grieved that his mother had been laid away without funeral rites, and several months later he took a wandering preacher to the little mound, already covered with the snows of winter, and had him deliver a funeral sermon over her grave.[3] It is said that he suffered the mother's loss more than any other member of the family, and that this was the dreariest winter of his life. But before another year had passed Mr. Lincoln brought from Kentucky a new wife, who was to change the lot of the little family decidedly for the better. One might think in the natural order of events the introduction of a foster mother into the home so soon after his own mother's death would have made the boy contract a dislike, or a certain amount of distrust toward her position in the household. Instead, however, a steadily increased companionship developed between the two. The warmth of this friendship was made the deeper in that the stepmother gave Abe her support in enabling him to carry out his desires for a more elaborate education than the backwoods ordinarily afforded. Indeed, she even urged this in spite of the fact that the father desired him to engage in the more immediate issues of the home and upbuilding of the family income. It was probably at her instigation that he was permitted the few books which he borrowed or bought from his meagre savings. In view of the fact that the father himself had a fairly good education and was apparently disinclined to further his son's ambition in this direction, one can easily comprehend that not a little dislike was engendered in Abe's mind toward his father for thus curtailing his chances of gaining the education to which he aspired. Even antedating this rationalization for an innate lack of harmony between the son and father, there was probably also operative a more basic concept, which is common to all children. In such pioneering communities, the immediate necessity of expending effort toward overcoming the material disadvantages gave little opportunity for an expression of conjugal affection as seen in a more conventionalized society. With the intensive attachment that sons often feel toward the mother, it is natural in many instances for them to possess a keen desire to give the mother in a childish way the affection that the father seemingly neglects. However this may be, one is gradually made aware that Abraham Lincoln grew up much attached to the memory of his mother, and was companionable and kindly disposed toward his stepmother, but that there was a very loose bond of sympathy and attachment toward the father. For years Lincoln supported his father, who died at the age of seventy-three. For the sake of contrast, let us see the optimistic manner in which Lincoln met the death of his father, which took place in 1851. On receiving news of his father's illness, Lincoln felt "unable" for various reasons to go to his sickbed, but in writing to his stepbrother said, "Say to him, that if we could meet now it is doubtful whether it would not be more painful than pleasant; but that if it be his lot to go now he will soon have a joyous meeting with loved ones gone before, and where the rest of us, through the help of God, hope ere long to join them."[4]

To return again to an earlier period: While Abe was quiet and reserved in manner and had in many instances evinced a crude shyness as ordinarily seen in rustic youths of his time, he was nevertheless very tender and devoted to his friends and associates. That he was naturally open and generous in all that concerned his relationships was well shown by innumerable instances, and in his protection of the weak against the strong. One also finds that Lincoln showed practically no dependence upon his father in the selection of an occupation in life; in fact he took a diametrically opposite course in his approach to the world than that which his father did. Instead of spending his time in studies of inventions and speculative applications of mechanical principles for improving the machinery of the farm, etc., he desired an open and freer contact with young men of his own age. The intensity of the attachment to the mother-imago or ideal was shown in greater part by the fact that he was very little concerned with the sentimentalities of courtship such as other young men were engaged in, and when in the company of young people he was largely the boon companion of the men and rather reserved and cold toward the opposite sex. Instead of having a series of girl friendships and being the squire gallant, there is but one instance of a really sentimental attachment up to the age of twenty-five years, when he made the acquaintance of Anne Rutledge, who was the daughter of one of the proprietors of the settlement at New Salem. It will be remembered this young lady was openly known to be engaged to a man who called himself "John McNeill," who had gone East apparently for the purpose of bringing his parents back with him to New Salem; this duty performed, he was then to marry Anne. In view of this knowledge it seemed to have been relatively easy for Lincoln to form an attachment for Anne under the guise of her being already promised to another,—easier than if she had been entirely free and to be considered in the marriageable class. After a year had elapsed and McNeill failed to return and carry out his part of the contract, Lincoln succeeded in persuading Anne to consider her engagement to the recalcitrant lover as broken, and in the spring of 1835 she consented to become Lincoln's wife. A happy spring and summer followed, but during this time Anne fell ill, and her condition gradually became hopeless. On August 25, 1835, Lincoln was summoned, and after an anguished parting, she died.[5]

This calamity shook the very foundations of Lincoln's deep and sensitive nature. He was profoundly depressed, could not eat or sleep, did little work, and appeared shaken to the depths. One evening not long after Anne's death he entered the little public house in the settlement during a severe storm. In the bitterness of his loneliness and grief he buried his face in his hands and with a cry of almost unbearable anguish and despair exclaimed, "The thought of the snow and rain on her grave fills me with indescribable grief." To the lonely little spot Lincoln frequently went to weep over her grave, and to his friends he seemed to be in the shadow of madness.

In the course of several months, however, Lincoln recovered in greater part from the depression which followed this period, but now there began, apparently without reason, regular periods of slight depressions which were unaccountable, and, as he himself termed them, "unreasonable." We know little of the specific settings of the depressions from which he suffered prior to his engagement to Mary Todd at the age of thirty-one. It would seem as though his attachment was rather casual and very much helped on to an engagement by Miss Todd herself. She was pert, bright and vivacious, and showed a desire to dominate her companions; in contrary moods she was petulant—a trait which has been known in many instances to turn to other less pleasing channels in later life. It is interesting to note that when an actual cementing of the engagement into a marriage bond was to be carried into effect Lincoln became anxious and apprehensive, and showed an unusual amount of perturbation and dejection of spirit. The time fixed for the wedding was the first day of January, 1841. Careful preparations were made at the Edwards mansion; the rooms were decorated, the supper prepared, and the guests invited.[6] The latter assembled on the evening in question, and the bride, bedecked in veil and silken gown, nervously toyed with the flowers in her hair and waited in an adjoining room. Nothing was lacking but the groom. An hour passed; the guests, as well as the bride, were becoming restless. Another hour passed, and it became apparent that the principal in this little drama had purposely failed to appear. The bride, in grief, disappeared to her room; the wedding supper was left untouched; the guests quietly and wonderingly withdrew. What the feelings of a lady as sensitive, passionate and proud as Miss Todd were, we can only imagine. By daybreak, after persistent search, Lincoln's friends found him. Restless, gloomy, miserable, he seemed an object of pity. His friends, Speed among the number, fearing a tragic termination, watched him closely day and night. Every instrument that could be used for self-destruction was removed from his reach. Mrs. Edwards did not hesitate to regard him as insane, and her sister, Miss Todd, shared in that view.

Here one is at once struck with the fact that the depression immediately succeeding this episode was one in which there was not only an incomplete adjustment to Miss Todd as a bride, but, as we shall see later, Lincoln seemed unable to adapt himself to the full requirements of marriage itself. Hence the profound depression which came on at this time. This despondency was as deep as that ordinarily seen in the depressive psychosis; there was retardation in thought and action, periods of extreme silence, listlessness, indifference, loss of appetite, insomnia, alternating with moods of anxious restlessness. He had gloomy forebodings and thoughts of suicide. This depressive period extended over nearly ten months following his failure to appear on the date first set for his marriage. During this time Lincoln was absent from his regular duties in the State assembly, which he had up to this time carefully and painstakingly attended; he was finally taken by his good friend Speed to Kentucky to regain his health. The question has often been asked whether Lincoln actually had a short period of detention in a sanitarium. We have information, however, that he was kept under the careful watch of different members of the family in Kentucky and was permitted to occupy himself as he pleased upon the ranch. As the months wore on he gradually assumed a more natural attitude, and began to take a more normal interest in his surroundings. After several months he returned to take up his regular duties. He had not, however, entirely recovered his mental health even after this sojourn, and he still had feelings of inadequacy and doubt with periods of depression. The incomplete recovery was shown in his letter to Speed, who had himself married in the meantime after undergoing somewhat similar difficulties in meeting the marriage situation. It will be remembered that after Speed's marriage, when he was settled and contented upon a well-stocked plantation, Lincoln wrote as follows under date of October 5, 1842: "I want to ask you a close question—Are you now, in *feeling* as well as judgment, glad you are married as you are? From anybody but me this would be an impudent question, not to be tolerated; but I know you will pardon it in me. Please answer it quickly, as I am impatient to know." We also gain some idea of the triumph and final compromise in Lincoln's closing words in another letter to Speed, which strikes the keynote of the main difficulty of all whose love ideals are too high for fulfillment, when the mother-love still stands in the way or is not replaced by the independent adult love of marriage: "It is the peculiar misfortune of both you and me to dream dreams of Elysium far exceeding all that anything earthly can realize."[7] From this and other data it is shown that Lincoln was striving manfully to meet life situations as they were, and he gradually acquired a feeling as though he were given new power to readjust and to meet the marriage relation, for soon after we learn of the renewal of the engagement, and its final consummation. From that time, however, there succeeded attacks of periodic depression. Added to this, while the family life seemed to have been of a happy character, there was some mitigation of the uxoriousness of the marriage tie with the advent of children. When the marriage relations are not simple, natural and satisfying, the mother may transfer a part of her unrequited affection to the children, especially to those of the opposite sex, and the father similarly to the daughters. It seems likely that some of the love not requited in the marriage state was expressed by Lincoln in the fine comradeship that sprung up between him and his third son, William. This affectionate relationship continued to grow daily in importance, so that it was obvious to all that William was Lincoln's great favorite. One also sees that when periods of depression were in evidence, the mere presence of this son was a great comfort and satisfaction to the father and helped him to bear many of his onerous burdens.

Now we must digress a little to note the obverse of the mother attachment. Some time previous to his marriage, Lincoln had written an extensive thesis against the Church, particularly its authority and dominating position in the world and affairs of men. We gain a lurking suspicion that the clear and incisive mind of Lincoln was intent upon lessening the power of *authority* and *domi-*

nance which the Church had through the ages exercised over its devotees. One also gains a strong conviction more than once founded upon fact, as we have seen, that the deepest motive in such a rejection of authority as the portent of this thesis seemed to have implied, was the denial of the heavenly as well as the earthly father's dominance. It is obvious all through Lincoln's early life, his speeches, his addresses and his ordinary conversation that he often quoted the Bible as many another great statesman has done. These citations are the accrements of thinking and belief common to all people; Lincoln apparently comprehended this throughout his whole career, and in dealing with the masses he acted upon this facile fact in his use of it as a universal language understood by all people. Further, it is obvious if one read his speeches and addresses with these facts in mind, that until very much later in life he used these Biblical citations in a purely rhetorical sense, to express emotions that were most aptly handled in such phraseology, rather than as a fundamental belief springing from his own soul. In point of fact Mrs. Lincoln once said that he had no religious faith in the usual acceptance of the word, but that religion to him was a sort of poetry in his nature.[8]

We shall soon see the application of the foregoing in our thesis. The next great emotional crisis in Lincoln's life that we have to consider is the unforeseen death in 1862 of his favorite son, William. At the boy's sickbed he walked the floor, saying sadly, "This is the hardest trial of my life."[9] One would have expected from the nature of Lincoln's personality that the essence of his love brought forward from his attachments to his mother and Anne Rutledge would have been so concentrated in his attachment for this son that a depression of considerable intensity would have occurred; this, indeed, did happen. Instead of a long period of depression, however, in which there was inability to work, insomnia, thoughts of suicide, etc., as had been present at the death of Anne and at his failure to make the marriage bond with Mary Todd, the depression was very short. The whole period of sorrow, embraced in an incipient phase of sadness, was entirely removed in the short period of three days. It is interesting to observe by what mechanism this condition seemed to have been curtailed. Lincoln shut himself in his room alone, and saw little of his wife or other son, and in the depths of his despair he turned to religion. That which he had known purely as a form of speech or argumentative rhetoric, and embracing more deeply much which we have seen in an expression of antagonism to the concept of authority as proceeding from God, etc., was now transformed. At this religious experience following his son's death he made a full reconciliation with God and accepted him as his personal God, and from that time on it was seen that a calm and peace entered into his attitude toward life that he had never before known.[10] Coupled with this was an abiding sense that he was protected and guided by the Heavenly Father in all things that portended his attitude in official as well as private affairs. In the depth of this religious conversion we see more than is ordinarily supposed to exist in such an episode. We probably have evidence here that he reconciled himself to the earthly as well as to the Heavenly Father, and that at last antagonism toward the earthly father had been removed and he was at peace with the conflict within his own soul. One must remember, however, that the infantile situation in such states passes in two directions—an intensive attachment to the mother, and a dislike for the father. The latter, as we have seen, was greatly if not entirely removed; but not so the former; we shall see how it is still symbolized during the remainder of his life. For instance, the calmness and peace that reigned in his mind are shown in the last days of his life, when he seemed to be roused to a new sense of the beauty of peace and rest, taking pleasure in quiet spots, and reading over and over lines of poetry which expressed repose. The tranquility of death seemed to especially appeal. Mrs. Lincoln once related to a friend that while driving one April day with her husband along the banks of the James they passed a country graveyard shaded by trees, and where the early spring flowers were opening on nearly every grave. It was so quiet and attractive that they stopped the carriage and walked through it. Mr. Lincoln seemed thoughtful and impressed. He said, "Mary, you are younger than I. You will survive me. When I am gone, lay my remains in some quiet place like this."

It would carry us too far afield to explain in detail that the symbolic meanings of these and other musings of Lincoln have much of the idealized longings for the mother-image.[11] The enormous task for many to separate themselves from the home, and the mother in particular, is beautifully and poetically portrayed by Jung:[12]

. . . at the sunrise of life man looses himself painfully from the mother, from the ties of home, to fight the way to his destiny, his direst enemy not before him, but within him, that deadly yearning backward to the abyss of self, to drown in his own wellspring, for engulfing within the mother. His life is an unending struggle with this death, a violent and fleeting escape from ever-imminent night. This death is no outer foe, but his own and inner longing for the silence and deep quiet of not-to-be, a dreamless sleep upon the waters of creation and passing away. Even in his highest strivings towards harmony and balance, for philosophic depth and artistic skill, he yet seeks death, for stillness, for satiety and peace. Should he, like Peirithoos, rest too long in this place of morning calm, stupor lays hold of him, and the poison of the serpent has crippled him forever. If he shall live, then he must fight, and give up his yearning for the past, that he may rise to his true height. And when he has reached his noonday, then he must again sacrifice the love of his own greatness, since for him there can be no tarrying. So does the sun spend his fullest strength, hastening onward to the fruits of autumn, which are the seeds of immortality; in children, in work, in renown, to a new order of things—whose suns in their courses once more shall rise and wane.

According to Lincoln's most intimate friends, he was totally unlike other people, and indeed was looked upon as a "mystery." They considered him a sad and gloomy man, who did not know what happiness was. "Terrible" was the word which his friends used to describe him in his darkest moods.[13] His musical tastes were simple, and he loved plaintive songs and ballads. He liked best of all "Twenty Years Ago," a song depicting a man who revisits the playground of his youth and the graveyard where his boyhood friends are buried.

All through 1863 and 1864 Lincoln's thin face had day by day grown more haggard; his eye, always sad when he was in deep thought, had a look of unutterable grief. Through all these months Lincoln was, in fact, consumed by sorrow. "I think I shall never be glad again," he said to a friend.[14] But as one by one the weights lifted, a change came over him. He was in fact transfigured, and that indescribable sadness which seemed to be a part of his very being, suddenly changed for an equally indescribable expression of serene joy, as if he were conscious that the great purpose of his life had been achieved.

So we find that Lincoln at last accepted a religious outlet, as a means for unconsciously solving or sublimating a large part of his regressive relations with life which had heretofore taken the form of intensive and prolonged depressions. There can be little doubt had Lincoln lived, in spite of the fact that the reconstruction period would have been an enormous tax on his great powers in carrying it through to its final and just conclusion, he would not have suffered from deep depressions—at least not to the extent that had been characteristic of him for the years prior to his final reconciliation to a personal religious life. That the intense longing for the mother-ideal was unchanged and was still the dominant note in Lincoln's soul is shown in the persistence of his life-long characteristic dream. Its beautiful and classic significance should be at once obvious in its death symbolism. In this dream, he said he seemed to be in a singular and indescribable vessel, always the same, moving with great rapidity towards a dark and indefinite shore. Lincoln had implicit faith that events would shape themselves favorably when he had this dream, which preceded nearly every important event of the War. Lincoln said that victory did not always follow his dream, but that the event and results were important. On the night previous to his assassination Lincoln said, "I had this strange dream again last night. It must relate to Sherman; my thoughts are in that direction, and I know of no other very important event which is likely just now to occur."[15]

To his wife Lincoln said, "We have had a hard time of it, but the war is over, and with God's blessing we may hope for four years of peace and happiness." Lincoln looked forward to going back to practicing law, and such were his thoughts on the last day of his life. His little son "Tad" was overcome with grief at his father's death, and asked if his father had gone to Heaven, "for," he added, "he was never happy after he came here; this was not a good place for him."

In the main, it seems that the benignant attitude Lincoln took toward the weak and downtrodden, shown, for instance, in his making the abolition of slavery the slogan for continuing the struggle of the Civil War, was prompted not a little by the more than filial devotion he must have felt for his mother. His willing, often eager desire to pardon infractors of military discipline, unwise, perhaps, for the rigorous exactions of military demands, was born to no little degree from his signal inability to meet some phases of his own personal conflicts (*e.g.*, his wedding day). At times so keen was his desire to pardon that he accepted almost any apparently sincere excuse. In point of fact when this was met with remonstrance, he later came to give little or no explanation for such leniency. He often said that no mother was to be made to suffer any more than the necessity of war required, and not at all through any personal act of his own if he could help it.

We note that States rights—the right of a State to secede from the Union—was the first concern of all statesmen of the period before the war and even in the first year of the conflict. Lincoln, even two years after the war had begun, answered Greeley: "My paramount object is to save the Union and not either to save or destroy slavery. If I could save the Union without freeing any slave I would do it. If I could save it by freeing some and leaving others alone I would also do that." [16] Even at a much earlier period he had held that "the institution of slavery is founded on both injustice and bad policy but that the promulgation of abolition doctrines tends rather to increase than abate its evils." Again, at a much earlier period when discussing the thirteenth amendment of the Constitution, Lincoln held that there was no equality of the Negro with the whites either in color or in many other respects but in the inalienable rights as human beings they were certainly entitled to everything the white race enjoyed. However, Lincoln gradually discarded the States rights issue for the abolition of slavery. Lincoln was extraordinarily quick to feel the importance of transferring the motive for a long-continued struggle from a more or less academic issue to a keen personal one—one which would fire the popular imagination with the glowing emotional warmth and zeal comparable to the slogan in the recent world war in which the dominant note was to "Make the world free for democracy." Although the grinding life of toil which the downtrodden slave endured must have keenly touched Lincoln's sensitive soul, yet he seems to have taken a less personal interest in the slaves than did many another abolitionist, such as Garrison and the slave runners of the North. No doubt Lincoln was much more concerned with the general principle of freeing all sorts of oppressed peoples, and the slave incidentally. There seems to have been but one instance of Lincoln's close personal contact with the degrading treatment of the Negro slaves and that was when he was in the early twenties, at New Orleans. After witnessing some of the debasing spectacles in the slave market, he said, "Boys, let's get away from this. If ever I get a chance to hit that thing (slavery), I'll hit it hard." In his later speeches and utterances he was singularly silent upon the personal brutalities practiced upon the slaves. While no doubt Lincoln sympathized with the sentimental propagandists of abolishing bodily suffering, he devoted himself to expounding the more general cause of human liberty and freedom, which, of course, included the former incidentally. His was a general plan to redress all human wrongs even to extending mercy to those who had been in violent antagonism to the abolition of slavery itself—a difficult and often misunderstood position and which the strict conservatives about Lincoln frequently misconstrued. To many men of that memorable period who had been engaged in "force without stint," it seemed that the change which Lincoln's character underwent near the end of the war, after his favorite son's death and subsequent religious conversion, portended weakness rather than strength. It is a matter of history that the war party looked with grave foreboding upon Lincoln's general attitude of a feasible reconstruction. It seemed to many that Lincoln was about to undo the great purpose of the national struggle in allowing the South to go free from final punishment. Even in the last cabinet meeting before his assassination Lincoln showed his intent to deal leniently and fairly with the erring South when he said, "I shall bear no hate or vindictiveness toward the South. The worst of them we must frighten out of the country, let down the bars and scare them off."

On the basis of the interesting results revealed in this application of the newer dynamic psychology to an analysis of the personality of Lincoln, one may say that intensive psychological studies should be made of great national characters to throw as much light as possible upon the part which they may have played as well as to determine what influence their personal conflicts and motives may have had upon shaping the national events which they directed. Only by this broad cooperation of psychology and history are we likely to arrive at a comprehensive historical interpretation of the dominating personalities of any period.[17]

Notes

1 Read before N. Y. Psychiatrical Society, March 5, 1919.

2 As has been pointed out by Hoch and others, the fundamental type of makeup of the manic depressive psychotic is frequently found to be one of either an open type of personality, or one of general moodiness. It is held, however, that there are so many contributing physical and mental factors in the induction of this mental disorder that one must not rely unduly upon the type of personality otherwise than to indicate the main trends of mental reactions which may follow in such personalities.

3 Tarbell, Life of Abraham Lincoln, 1900, Vol. I, p. 27.

4 Francis R. Browne, Everyday Life of Lincoln, p. 113.

5 Tarbell, Life of Abraham Lincoln, Vol. I, p. 120.

6 William H. Herndon and Jesse W. Weik, Abraham Lincoln, the True Story of a Great Life.

7 Nicolay and Hay, Abraham Lincoln, A History, Vol. I, p. 197.

8 Francis R. Browne, Everyday Life of Lincoln, p. 478.

9 Francis R. Browne, *Ibid.*, p. 351.

10 Tarbell, Life of Abraham Lincoln, Vol. II, p. 92.

11 Lincoln often said, "All that I ever have been, and all that I hope to be, I owe to my mother."

12 Wells' review of Jung's Symbolism in the Unconscious, Psychiatric Bulletin, 1916.

13 Francis R. Browne, Everyday Life of Lincoln, p. 113.

14 Francis R. Browne, *Ibid.*, p. 545.

15 Francis R. Browne, Everyday Life of Lincoln, p. 583.

16 Ward H. Lamon, Life of Abraham Lincoln, p. 504.

16 Tarbell, Life of Abraham Lincoln, Vol. II, p. 118.

17 I want to extend my thanks to Prof. J. Harvey Robinson and Prof. Harry E. Barnes for their critical suggestions in preparing the manuscript.

A Prophetic Dream Reported by
Abraham Lincoln

GEORGE W. WILSON, M.D.

IT IS NOT MY INTENTION at this time to attempt any complete dynamic analysis of Abraham Lincoln's character. Others before me have made some attempts along this line, but their efforts were not very successful, probably for the reason that the attempts at reconstruction were not well formulated and because readers, especially those who have a sufficient curiosity about the life and doings of Abraham Lincoln and other prominent personalities out of American history, prefer to maintain their own illusions regarding their heroes, and verbalized or printed material that may in any way tend to destroy those illusions produces an immediate loss of interest or even a critical and hostile rejection of any proof of what they interpret as signs of weakness of character.

Most of us prefer to think of George Washington as the Father of Our Country, a great soldier and general and a man of unquestionable honesty. We read and remember his farewell address to his soldiers as an example of sound judgment and remarkable foresight. If some one suggests that this masterpiece of constructive thinking was a product of the brain and pen of Alexander Hamilton, we may listen but continue to remain unconvinced. In a like manner, we prefer to think of Andrew Jackson as a strong masculine character, who was a pioneer in the settlement, construction, and expansion of our Democracy, and to forget the fact that he was a moody, "hot tempered" man who killed several men in duels. Most Americans remember Benjamin Franklin as a great publisher, inventor, and diplomat, forgetting or caring not to know that both his enemies and his friends often referred to him as the "old whore master."

At one time I had some ambitions toward making a careful study and an attempt at a reconstruction of Abraham Lincoln's character, but I very soon abandoned this fantasy because I felt that the task was too great and that probably there would be insufficient interest to warrant such an exhaustive study. Instead, I turned my attention to a study of the neurotic impulses which impelled John Wilkes Booth to murder the President, and left to one side any discussion of the motives which prompted Abraham Lincoln—*to get himself murdered.* So in this paper I am not attempting even a superficial reconstruction of Abraham Lincoln's character but instead, to present sufficient factual material in such a way that the inferences or interpretations which I might make will be so obvious that their verbalization would be superfluous.

To the people who lived, worked, or played with Lincoln during his two terms as President of the United States, his assassination was received as the fulfillment of an expectation rather than as a surprise. Lincoln had been warned, coaxed, and cajoled by his friends and political associates for the utterly careless manner in which he exposed himself to physical attack. Secretaries Stanton and Seward, his private secretary Hay, as well as Mrs. Lincoln had repeatedly pleaded with him to utilize more fully the personal protection to which he was entitled as the chief executive of the United States. Lincoln never disagreed with the arguments that were propounded in support of these warnings but, as was his custom, he ignored their advice and followed his own dictates. He usually followed this pattern in other things as well. His customary reaction to admonitions relative to his defiance of the rules and regulations as applied to the physical protection of the President of the United States was to chide or belittle the admonisher and then go about unprotected.

In this same connection probably no other President of the United States was so lacking in caution regarding personal interviews. Almost any one could obtain an appointment with him, and people who had grievances to present were given preference over friends and political associates.

On the very afternoon of Lincoln's assassination, Secretary Stanton took the President to task because of his carelessness, and threatened to detail a whole company of infantry to accompany Lincoln everywhere he went. Stanton called attention to the President's contemplated attendance at Ford's Theater and requested that he insure himself of adequate and ample protection. To this advice Lincoln replied in a characteristic manner, by requesting that Stanton detail his own aide de camp who was working that night on some important war material. Lincoln was aware of the fact that Stanton's aide was almost indispensable in the War Department on this particular evening and undoubtedly made this request for the purpose of irritating Stanton.

On the night of his assassination, Lincoln attended the theater accompanied by his wife, a Major Rathbone and his fiancée, with one ex-policeman of "shady" reputation who was supposed to remain on guard outside the door of the presidential box during the performance. Actually this guard was not at his station when the murder was committed. I am stressing Lincoln's behavior in these respects because it contrasts so vividly with his "presentiments" and his verbalized, pessimistic attitude regarding his own fate.

Several times Lincoln publicly expressed the belief that he would not live through his second term as President. He often reported his "presentiments," fantasies, and even his dreams, not only to his intimate friends but to strangers as well. As far as I have been able to determine, he was the only President of the United States who made a common practice of taking people into his confidence regarding his dream and fantasy life.

Lincoln's habit of reporting his "presentiments" and dreams appears to have begun soon after his election to the presidency. At that time he said that he had the feeling that he would never take office. He predicted with some justification that his election would not be certified and that he would never be sworn in as President. The reason which lends some justification to this belief was that the sentiment against certifying him for the presidency was very strong in the South and by no means lacking in the North.

A bona fide plot to assassinate Lincoln during his journey to the Capitol was uncovered at about the time he departed from Chicago for Washington. Lincoln was warned of this plot, but it was only after he and his party reached Baltimore that he was persuaded to change his previously published plan of travel and to go by private vehicle from Baltimore to Washington, while his private coach and the remainder of his party continued as designated.

Lincoln claimed by inference that he could foretell the future. By that I mean he stated that he either dreamed about or had "presentiments" that revealed to him the probable outcome of state problems and of impending battles. He attributed a prophetic quality to all his dreams. He claimed to have had certain recurrent dreams and said that following these dreams some important event of the war invariably occurred and that the event was usually one of a favorable nature. One of these recurrent dreams was the following:

Lincoln was in some singular, indescribable vessel and was moving with great rapidity toward an infinite shore.

The President claimed that he experienced this dream preceding the battles of Sumter, Bull Run, Antietam, Gettysburg, Stone River, Vicksburg and Wilmington.

When Lincoln reported and offered this proof of the prophetic quality of this dream in the presence of General Grant, he was reminded by the General that the battle of Stone River was not a victory, but a distinct defeat, for the Union army. Lincoln's reply was an admission of the truth of General Grant's statement but he said that, nevertheless, he *had* the dream preceding that fight.

The reporting of a dream that was repeated by Lincoln a short time before his assassination, one which was dramatically re-enacted very soon after its production, does not mean that I am attributing to Lincoln the same omnipotence which he claimed for himself. It is my desire instead to demonstrate how accurately this dream portrayed the unconscious wishes of Abraham Lincoln and how clearly the manifest content of the dream depicted his exhibitionistic and self destructive impulses as well as demonstrating the omniscience and denial of actual death by the dreamer.

The two men who most often warned Lincoln about his personal safety were Stanton and Lamon. Robert Lamon was an old and trusted friend of Abraham Lincoln and had been in close contact with him from the days of his early political strivings, up to and including his residency in the White House. Lamon had observed Lincoln's gradual rise to that of a world figure and a legend, and it was he who tried to understand Lincoln the dreamer. He saw Lincoln, "Believing, like the first Napoleon, that he was a man of destiny, and that he accepted certain phases of the supernatural."

To quote Carl Sandburg, "What Lamon thought or surmised in this field had at least the value of the observation of an intimate." Lamon wrote: "Assured as he (Lincoln) undoubtedly was about omens, which to his mind were conclusive—that he would rise to power and greatness, he was firmly convinced by the same tokens that he would be suddenly cut off at the height of his career and the fullness of his fame. He always believed that he would fall by the hand of an assassin: and yet, with that appalling doom clouding his life, his courage never for a moment foresook him." Often, wrote Lamon, he heard Lincoln repeat the following lines from "The Dream," a Byron poem:

> Sleep hath its own world,
> A boundary between the things misnamed
> Death and existence: Sleep hath its own world,
> And a wide realm of wild reality.
> And dreams in their development have breath,
> And tears, and tortures, and the touch of joy;
> They leave a weight upon our waking thoughts,
> They take a weight from off our waking toils,
> They do divide our being.

To Lamon, Lincoln spoke more than once of his failure to reproduce a double image of himself which he once observed in a looking glass while lying on a lounge in his own chamber in Springfield. In this image Lincoln had two faces; one face depicted "The glow of life and breath and the other shone ghostly pale white." Lincoln interpreted this illusion as meaning that he would have a safe passage through his first term as President but that death would overtake him before the close of his second term.

According to Lamon's study, Lincoln held the belief that "Every dream had a meaning if you could be wise enough to find it, your wisdom perhaps leading you at times into preposterous tricks and vagaries of human mind and frame." Lincoln held to the belief that the best dream interpreters were the common people, the children of nature, as he called them. He considered himself one of these. He contended that the very superstitions of the common people had roots of reality in natural occurrences.

The dream that I am reporting occurred in the second week of April, 1865, and therefore was produced just prior to Lincoln's death. I believe it is best told in the language of Robert Lamon, who wrote: "Lincoln kept this dream secret for a few days, until one evening at the White House, in the presence of the writer, Mrs. Lincoln and one or two others, he began asking about dreams and led himself into telling the late one that haunted him. Lincoln proceeded to tell of the dream by saying, 'It seems strange how much there is in the Bible about dreams. There are, I think, some sixteen chapters in the Old Testament and four or five in the New in which dreams are mentioned; and there are many other passages scattered throughout the book which refer to visions. Nowadays, dreams are regarded as very foolish and are seldom told, except by old women and by young men and maidens in love.' Mrs. Lincoln remarked: 'Why, you look dreadfully solemn: do *you* believe in dreams?' 'I can't say that I do,' Lincoln replied, 'but the other night I had a dream which has haunted me ever since. I am afraid that I have done wrong to mention the subject at all, but somehow the thing has got possession of me and, like Banquo's ghost, it will not down. About ten days ago, I retired very late; I was weary, fell into a slumber and soon began to dream.' The dream:

'There seemed to be a death-like silence about me; then I heard subdued sobs as if a number of people were weeping. I thought I left my bed and wandered downstairs. There the silence was broken by the same pitiful sobbing, but the mourners were invisible. I went from room to room; no living person was in sight, but the same mournful sounds of distress met me as I passed along. It was light in all the rooms: every object was familiar to me: but where were all the people who were grieving as if their hearts would break? I was puzzled and bewildered: what could be the meaning of all this? Determined to find the cause of a state of things so mysterious and so shocking, I kept on until I arrived at the East Room, which I entered. There I met a sickening surprise. Before me was a catafalque on which rested a corpse wrapped in funeral vestments. Around it were stationed soldiers who were acting as guards; and there was a throng of people, some gazing mournfully upon the corpse whose face was covered, others weeping pitifully. "Who is dead in the White House?" I demanded of one of the soldiers. "The President," was his answer, "He was killed by an assassin!" Then came a loud burst of grief from the crowd, which awoke me from my dream. I slept no more that night; and although it was only a dream, I have been strangely annoyed by it ever since.'

Afterwards referring to this dream, Lincoln quoted from "Hamlet," "To sleep; perchance to dream! ay, *there's the rub!*"

I think it is fitting to close this communication with a quotation written by the man who reported the above dream: "I had my ambitions—yes—as every American boy worth his salt has. And I dared to dream this vision of the White House,—I, the humblest of the humble, born in a lowly pioneer's cabin in the woods of Kentucky. My dream came true, and where is its glory? Ashes and blood. I . . . have lived with aching heart through it all and envied the dead their rest on the battle fields."

BIBLIOGRAPHY

Clark, L. Pierce—Lincoln, A Psychobiography, New York, Charles Scribner's Sons, 1933

Herndon, William H., and Weik, Jesse W.—Abraham Lincoln, The True Story of a Great Life, New York, 1908

——Herndon's Life of Lincoln (Paul Angle, Ed.), New York, 1930

Lamon, Dorothy (Ed.)—Recollections of Abraham Lincoln, 1847–1865, by Ward Hill Lamon, Chicago, 1895

Lamon, Ward H.—Life of Abraham Lincoln from His Birth to His Inauguration as President, Boston, 1872 (Written by Chauncey F. Black)

Nicolay, John G., and Hay, John—Complete Works of Abraham Lincoln, New York, 1905

Sandburg, Carl—Abraham Lincoln, The War Years, New York, Harcourt Brace and Company, 1939

Abe Lincoln: The Psychology of a Cult

A. BRONSON FELDMAN

IN THE MYTHOLOGY of the United States the legend of Abraham Lincoln stands unrivalled as raw material for the psychology of the unconscious, especially in the field of social illusion, of racial and national dreams. Every patriot and critic of American ideals knows the legend as a classic illustration of the national day-dream come true, of the "local" boy who makes "good." Lloyd Lewis, in his valuable study *Myths After Lincoln* (1929), attempted to delineate the posthumous tales of the martyred president in the light of Sir James Frazer's theory of myth, picturing Lincoln as a Yankee reincarnation of the primordial divinity of the soil. In the opinion of Lewis "the American god" served as an image of agriculture, looked up to by a people whose dearest passion went out for the fertility of their farms. "This new god," Lewis says, "had died to save Man's barns from Jefferson Davis's raiders:" that is why Lincoln was worshipped (p. 405; cf. 335). In the following pages I should like to correct this agrarian conception of the legend, in the light of Sigmund Freud's discoveries of the unconscious motives of myths.

A short examination of the Lincoln myth enables us to recognize an urban element in it, political in the old Greek sense of the word. Certainly the town as well as the country contributed to the adoration of Lincoln, who was never a farmer himself but earned fame first as a village storekeeper and afterward as a railroad corporation lawyer and spokesman of the party of merchants and manufacturers. But the myth appeals to sentiments and passions that run deeper than political economy. The "American god" is nonpartisan. And his cult has qualities of profound affect for people who never saw the United States, even barbaric nomads, as Tolstoy bears witness. These qualities transcending national limits and the frontiers of culture form the objects of the present research. With

116

the assistance of Freudian psychology we can trace the process of Lincoln's apotheosis, stage by stage.

Nothing exists in our minds, according to an old principle of science, which did not first exist in the life outside our minds. On the basis of vast experience with the mental struggle known as the Oedipus complex, Freud concluded that the human race must have undergone at the beginning of its existence an adventure or series of adventures in love and murder corresponding to the oedipal fantasies. He attempted in several books, notably in *Totem and Taboo* (1913) and *Moses and Monotheism* (1939), to reconstruct the original tragedy of incest and parricide, whose mental reflexions he found everywhere in humanity in the form of repressed infantile yearnings and dreams. The outcome of Freud's studies in anthropology was a theory that might well be called the archmyth; for its pattern can be clearly traced in the fundamental myths of all nations.

Freud depicts the primeval fathers and mothers of the race living in small hordes, much like the great apes nowadays. The old primate who dominated the horde habitually killed or chased away the young fellows who interfered with his sole possession of the females. One day, Freud imagined, these exiled youths came together resolved on a united battle with the old leader. They succeeded in killing him. The exhilaration and new security resulting from this combined effort encouraged the youths not to restore the old order of single supremacy in the horde. Instead they resolved to limit their incestuous demands on the females in such a way that male cooperation could be sustained.

Thus a union of brothers was established. This union commemorated its formation by an act or ritual inculcating the lessons of the first sin, the murder of the "old man," the ancestor. He became their god, a ghost full of evil wishes toward them, yet somehow lovable, because he had protected their mothers from jungle enemies and sometimes relieved them from starvation. According to Freud the ritual commemorating the father's murder culminated in a feast symbolizing, unconsciously perhaps, the cannibalistic meal the brothers made of their horde-father in order to incorporate his virile qualities.

From this ritual and its accompanying myth developed, according to Freud, all the religious cults of the world,

Let us now see how Freud's theory applies to the Lincoln cult. Before Lincoln's assassination his figure in the imagination of the American people stood far inferior in stature to the idol which it afterward became. There is no evidence that any considerable quantity of men regarded him as a god, and plenty of evidence that large numbers considered him much less. His final election found only 55% of the voters of the Union in his favor. His home state, which later inscribed over the door of the court-house in Springfield, "Illinois clasps to her bosom her slain and glorified son," gave most of its franchise to his political enemies. He did enjoy the affection and respect of thousands of citizens, but none of them rose to revere him until they were bereaved of the big, shrewd, kindly, humorous and rather ugly leader. As president, of course, he became the object of strong feelings which multitudes directed toward him as the great white father of the United States, the incarnation of Uncle Sam. These feelings, however, were not qualitatively different from the feelings previously excited by other men in his awe-inspiring presidential office, regular state surrogates for the people's unconscious notions of paternity.

The exact degree of psychic consanguinity between Lincoln and his country was not always seen as fatherhood, in any case. In 1862 Nathaniel Hawthorne drew his portrait in another relation, in an article printed some years after the author's death. To Hawthorne Lincoln was "Uncle Abe." With characteristic honesty the novelist, a Democrat of long loyalty to the party, pictured the President as not only "about the homeliest man I ever saw," but also "the essential representative of all Yankees, and the veritable specimen, physically, of what the world seems determined to regard as our characteristic qualities." (Quoted by James T. Fields, *Yesterdays with Authors*, 1872.) Hawthorne voiced delight in the process—plainly an unconscious one—by which the nation had chosen its chief: "It is the strangest and yet the fittest thing," he wrote, "in the jumble of human vicissitudes, that he, out of so many millions, unlooked for, unselected by any intelligible process that could be based upon his genuine qualities, unknown to those who chose him, and unsuspected of what endowments may adapt him for his tremendous responsibility, should have found the way open for him to fling his lank personality into the chair of state. . . ." Few Americans who met "Uncle Abe" could resist the feeling of consanguinity. Private Jenkin Jones spoke for masses when he declared that "All regarded the loss of him as of a near and dear relative" (quoted by Carl Sandburg, *Abraham Lincoln: The War Years*, 1939, iv, 342).

The objection may well be raised here that the Confederates and their sympathizers did not see a kinsman in Lincoln. One Southern clergyman, exiled in Canada, informed hotel guests after hearing the news of his murder that "Lincoln had only gone to hell a little before his time" (Lewis, 69). Sidney Lanier, the Georgia poet, once described a banquet in the President's honor as "The Great Apotheosis of the Great Hog." In the North, too, there were skeptics. After the assassination ex-president Fillmore did not drape his home in black; he explained lamely to a threatening crowd that his wife was ill and he had not heard the news. Ex-president Pierce had to listen to another crowd jeer at him for not displaying a flag in honor of the martyred chief. These two gentlemen had known the intoxication of service as paternal figures of government. They could conceive of Lincoln as an equal, and perhaps felt an impulse of secret pleasure in the thought of their colleague's fall.

There was plenty of anti-Lincoln sentiment in the North. The New York *Herald*, on April 16, 1865, denounced much of the Northern journalism which was mourning Lincoln as brass hypocrisy: "That press has, in the most devilish manner, urged men to the commission of this very deed. They who jeered at the first attempt to assassinate Mr. Lincoln, in 1861, and said that it was gotten up to bring odium upon the South; they who coolly advertised that for one hundred thousand dollars Mr. Lincoln and Mr. Seward could both be killed before the 4th of March; they who thought the attempt to burn this city a very good joke—excellent food for laughter—and they who specifically incited to this murder by their invocation to the dagger of Brutus—they are indeed the real authors of this horrible crime." The political opponents, the "Copperheads," thus denounced, must have felt compassion for Booth, and hatred for Lincoln. The President was not a father to them in the reverential sense; he was a fiend. But one does not have to be expert in etymology to recognize fatherhood in the Devil, and his fellow fallen angels. The Devil is the "Father of Liars," and if the sons and sympathizers of Dixie cursed Lincoln as a hellion, they nevertheless viewed him with filial awe. "Resistance to Lincoln is Obedience to God," announced a banner in Alabama in 1861 (Sandburg, i, 5). To the Confederate and Copperhead conscience Lincoln stood for the apotheosis of beastliness, the same tyranny in essence which the ego learns to fear in the father, whose sexual intercourse is thought of by children as an onslaught of sadism.

Not all champions of Dixie and its "peculiar institution," slavery, considered Lincoln as an embodiment of Satan. Some of them discovered in him before the martyrdom a stalwart though somewhat cunning protector. Judge Campbell of Richmond, for example, beheld him ready to hazard the anger of Congress by stretching his dictatorial powers to the point where he would risk official recognition of Virginia's return to the Union under a government of "rebels," elected by themselves. The benevolence of the President toward the Secessionists was well known. Lincoln abhorred the antislavery partisans who conjured up visions of gallows or guillotine for the Confederacy. He dreamt not of the abolition of black bondage but of the healing of his country's breach, the resurrection of the Federal flock under a single shepherd, with the black-sheep of the Confederacy treated as equals. "The Union," said Alexander Stephens, vice president of the Confederate government, "with him, in sentiment, rose to the sublimity of a religious mysticism" (Sandburg, 1, 213). Celestial or infernal, Lincoln towered as a patriarchal figure in the broken nation's mental shrines.

From the viewpoint of Freudian mythology, the Southrons represented an alliance of brothers in revolt against the father. By their rebellion they accomplished what all the sons of Columbia wished in their hearts, and many had the nerve to wish in the pulpit and the press. More than one of them had the conscious wish to strike the blow for the father's downfall. The man who actually did it, and so lifted Lincoln from political fatherhood up the ladder of deity, seems to have been selected by destiny for his role in the myth.

The last words of John Wilkes Booth were "Tell mother I died for my country." What precisely the assassin meant by his "country" is not easy to say. In the letter of 1864 often called his testament Booth speaks of the whole United States as his country. But when he saw the Secessionist troops marching as prisoners of the Union army, he cried out, "I have no longer a country!" as if Dixie alone deserved that name (Lewis, 215; Sandburg, iv, 321). One thing is sure: Booth loved to conceive of himself as a Brutus, freeing his mother-country from a cruel Caesar.

To be a Brutus was his obsession. His father's name was Brutus; and there can be little doubt that at the core of his madness was an unconscious craving to take his father's place in his mother's heart. The Oedipus complex of the younger Booth manifests itself in his letter of 1864, where he describes his country in fervently feminine terms: "Oh! how I have longed to see her break from the mist of blood and death that circles round her folds, spoiling her beauty and tarnishing her honor. But no, day by day has she been dragged deeper and deeper into cruelty and oppression." The thought of this cruelty hung in his mind on the same frame of reference as his ideas of paternity. "I have lived," he writes, among scenes of Southern slavery "most of my life, and have seen *less* harsh treatment from master to man than I have beheld in the North *from father to son.*" But he dared not utter openly his hate for the domineering Brutus whom his mother loved. Desperately his ego wrestled to subdue the upsurges of his id toward patricide, until finally it arranged a fantastic transference of the wish from the father of his family to the father of the state.

The shift of emotion from family to state can be accounted for without difficulty if we keep in mind the fact that Booth regarded his country as feminine and its government as masculine.

For the passion of politics we use the term patriotism, indicating that government is generally viewed as a projection of fatherhood. Beneath the sanctions and dictates of patriotism, however lies a far older feeling, a passion for the territory under the government. For this passion we might invent a new term—matriotism. Matriotism concerns the maternal zone, by which I mean the environment of the child's unconscious identified with the source of its earliest milk. It embraces more than the breast and body of the mother (or her precious bottle). It includes nonsomatic portions of her world which the baby is unable to differentiate from her. Thus the image of a room may become as integral a part of the child's thought of motherhood as it is in the German word for woman, *frauenzimmer.* By extension of this elemental mother sentiment homes and their heavens, the landscapes surrounding the very young, rise to consciousness with endearing charms and seem to pulse with the erotic warmth and nourishment associated with the primitive, infant security. The notion of Mother Nature develops in this way.

This love of the land in which one lives, matriotism, cannot be separated from the desire—and the dread—of incest. Consequently men are reluctant to allude to the mother-country save in abstract and sublime terms. In the times that try their souls, however, the sexual affect of thoughts about the native land emerges with startling clarity. On the Monday after Lincoln's murder, for example, Andrew Johnson shouted from the White House that treason is a crime akin to rape. Those who commit treason are frequently propelled by the feeling that their country has been raped. In the masculine heads of the state they discern the sadists who violated her. Where the unconscious conception of sex is sadistic, the boy anxious to gain his father's place and mastery will express the matriotic emotion with violence. So it was with Booth.

His crime might have been carried out as early as February 1861. On the 18th of that month Jefferson Davis was inaugurated president of the Confederate States, and Lincoln was resting at Albany, before traveling the last miles of his triumphal tour to the Capital. John Wilkes Booth was also in Albany, acting in a tragedy entitled *The Apostate*. A strange accident happened in the last act of the play, when Booth was showing off his extraordinary acrobatic skill, with extraordinary violence. His role called for a fall, which he performed with rare energy and ended by inadvertently stabbing himself. (Sandburg, i, 43; iv, 313.) It is conceivable that thoughts of using his dagger on the rival of Jefferson Davis, with whose cause the "Apostate" had already identified himself, were seething in Booth's brain at this time. The accident could therefore be explained as the outcome of conflicting emotions, sudden rage against paternal tyranny, provoked by Lincoln's presence in the city, and abrupt contrition and guilt for the lust to kill the rival of Booth's Oedipus love. The guilty ego may have turned the would-be assassin's knife upon himself.

In any case it was not until the cause of Jefferson Davis went down to bloody defeat that Booth's mind resolved consciously and definitely to kill Lincoln. He felt that the failure of the fraternal insurrection left no other course open for the rescue of the mother-country from the father's brutality. He entered Father Abraham's theatre box carrying not only a revolver but a knife.

The assassination was a trauma for America. From the shock of it the nation emerged with a new vision of the man Lincoln, a vision shaped in the unconscious, in the dark backward abyss of the mind where the primitive and infant impulses, desires, and furies survive. Naturally the savage conception of the new god was not permitted by civilized nerves to mount into consciousness. Thousands of brains operated on the divine image, transmuting it in accordance with older religious convictions, or the demands of modern reason, and in accordance with the practical necessities of politics too. Above all, however, worked the influence of Christianity, shaken and altered substantially in the war that split American Christendom. It was a Christianity which had undergone violent regression to its Judaic roots that gave birth to the Lincoln cult, discerning the signs of a new world redeemer in the bosom of the dead Abraham.

We all know in what a dramatic setting the trauma occurred. Americans at the time were infinitely fonder of tragedy in the theater than their descendants are today. The principle of sacrifice, which lies at the core of tragic drama, they cherished in a way that would strike Americans of our own generation as foreign, darkly European. The fact that Lincoln was murdered during the performance of an English comedy which made fun of the Yankee character only rendered the tragedy of his loss more poignant, for he had been ridiculed across the land in precisely the same manner that Tom Taylor caricatured "Our American Cousin." And the President was killed by a notorious tragedian, the son and brother of actors famous for their playing of godlike martyrs and heroes of self-sacrifice.

Even more potent in the minds of the people than the scene of Lincoln's murder was the time of the tragedy. The "Emancipator" died on the night of Good Friday, the anniversary of the crucifixion of the Savior Christ. This coincidence left few intellects in the country unimpressed, particularly since it was the subject of innumerable sermons. Several pastors deplored the willingness of Lincoln to appear this night at a playhouse, the "Devil's chapel." These critics missed the Christian meaning of the President's coming to Ford's Opera House. According to Grover, the owner of a rival theater, who had invited Lincoln to witness his production of *Aladdin or The Wonderful Lamp* on the fatal night, Ford's playhouse was "the accepted House of the Bourbons," the favorite of Washington friends of the Confederacy. In Grover's opinion, the President's decision to hear a play that burlesqued the American character rather than a play expressing the popular daydream of rising from rags to riches was promoted by a desire "in furtherance of his general purpose, to extend the hand of conciliation" (Sandburg, iv, 261). In short, it appears to have been a gesture of Christlike forgiveness for the sins of Dixie and its Northern sympathizers, the Bourbons and Copperheads.

Let us take a closer look at the last episode in the President's life. "Our American Cousin" had begun grinding on its historic way some minutes before Lincoln and his wife arrived in the chief executive's box with their guests. The orchestra greeted his coming with an outburst of "Hail to the Chief." Among the observers in the audience was a Julia Shephard, whose report of the event contains a vivid memorial of the state of many American minds that night. "The young and lovely daughter of Senator Harris," she wrote, "is the only one of his party we see, as the flags hide the rest. But we know Father Abraham is there like a Father watching what interests his children, for their pleasure rather than his own" (Sandburg, iv, 280). Mrs. Lincoln apparently did not know that the Father of his country was invisible to the audience. She leaned amorously on his shoulder and whispered a wish to know what people would think of her daring. There was a more than merely erotic current in the President's party that night. Senator Harris's lovely daughter sat beside her fiancee, Major Henry Rathbone, oblivious of any significance in the fact that her lover was also her stepbrother. Yet it seems strange that there should be a hint of incest on the very scene where a majestic Father was to be murdered by a passionate, morbidly mother-bound son.

Major Rathbone was wounded by Booth's dagger as he grappled with him to prevent his escape. Tragedy followed Rathbone after that until the hour of his own death. He went crazy and murdered his stepsister-wife and then himself (Lewis, 263). The motive of these horrors is beyond our present ken.

Eye and ear witnesses differ sharply about what happened in the theater after Booth sprang from the President's box. He did not escape unscathed. In leaping from Lincoln's site the murderer's foot tangled in a Federal flag, and he fell to the stage breaking a leg bone. Possibly his ego suffered a flash of contrition after he shot Lincoln in the head, and he fell, as in Albany in 1861, punished by his conscience, his superego. Some witnesses declared that he ran off without a word. Others said he faced the spectators, brandished his bloody knife, and shouted the motto of Virginia: "*Sic semper tyrannis.*" Julia Shephard thought she heard him shriek, "The South is avenged!" But listeners not far from her were equally confident that Booth's utterance was "The South shall be free!" And others thought he confined himself to a laconic "Freedom!" or "Revenge!" (Sandburg, iv, 282.) The confusion of testimony bears witness to the traumatic effect of the crime, and the contagion of the trauma.

Among the spectators in the gallery that night sat Peter Doyle, whom Walt Whitman loved more than any other man. Doyle described to the poet the pandemonium that ensued on Booth's shot, and Whitman depicted the scene in his own operatic style: "the broad stage fills to suffocation with a dense and motley crowd like some horrible carnival. . . ." Some gentlemen endeavored to clamber up to Lincoln's box to see the dying chief, while mobs jostled on the floor below for glimpses of his bloodstains, striving to keep their feet clear from the red marks left by the President's wounds as he was carried from the theater. (Lewis, 55.) Inspired by the tragedy, Whitman produced two famous poems, "When Lilacs Last in the Dooryard Bloom'd" and "O Captain! My Captain!" The public embraced the latter elegy, probably embarrassed by the superior lyric's allusions to epicene love for Lincoln's "large sweet soul," and its sensual litany to the "Dark mother," death. Whitman's celebration of the Captain of the state—"Captain! dear father!"—was greeted with joy, and learnt by heart. His picture of the fallen father attained a popularity far greater than Herman Melville's tribute to "The Martyr," which rings more vivid changes on the theme of Lincoln's paternity: "He lieth in his blood—The father in his face. . . ."

The shock of the assassination could be absorbed by the nation's nerves by assimilating it to memories of crucial events which had been more or less fortunately lived through. Or it could be absorbed by assimilating it to memories of events which the nation had never lived through except in dramatic or mythical thought. There was no event on American record to which the murder of the President could be compared. But national fantasy was rich in material by whose light the assassination took on the air and radiance of a religious victory. For instance, the people had ready at hand for solace the fact that the martyr's name carried with it a sacred promise of immortality and redemption from pain. He was their Father Abraham, and like the Hebrew patriarch shone in their minds as the co-author with God of a covenant which elected the people to a liberty and power all their own, the covenant called the Emancipation Proclamation. When Lincoln came to New York in 1861 the city greeted him with the words of Yahveh to the father of the Chosen People: "Fear Not, Abraham, I Am with Thee." Not long after, volunteers for the Union were chanting to the *pater patriae*, "We are coming, Father Abraham, three hundred thousand more!"

The Old Testament analogy carried an especially poignant meaning for those Americans who saw a real likeness between the patriarchal images of the Bible and the paternalism practiced in Dixie. When they thought of the South in terms of the Old Testament they imagined it as Egypt, the land of bondage. Names of Southern slave-markets like Cairo and Memphis deepened the vividness of the comparison. The nature of the bondage itself was enough to promote in the national unconscious the religious passion of this metaphor. It was inevitable that long before the outbreak of the Civil War preachers against slavery should warn the country that a Moses was bound to come who would lead the Negroes to liberty, through a "Red Sea." The Abolitionist Owen Lovejoy, whose brother Elijah had been lynched in Lincoln's home state for agitation against black bondage, prophesied to the House of Representatives that the slaves would surely walk to emancipation as the children of Israel had journeyed to the Promised Land (William, 3).

The Emancipation Proclamation fastened in the mind of the nation the idea of Lincoln as the Moses of the children of Ham. The fact that the Proclamation was practically forced on the President, and that he tried to maintain it simply as a military measure within the Confederate zones, did not lessen the glory of the Mosaic metaphor by a single ray. On the Sunday following Lincoln's death the Northern clergy favored it above all other similitudes. Moses was the name most commonly bestowed upon Lincoln in the pulpit on "Black Easter." (Lewis, 107.) In the dazzle of the new myth even Andrew Johnson, Lincoln's successor, assumed an alien splendor. "Johnson," thundered the Rev. C. B. Crane, "is the Joshua whom God has appointed to consummate the work which our dead Moses so nobly commenced." There were certain awkward limitations to the popularity of the comparison between Moses and the President. It had more cordial appeal to the Negro chattel than to the white wage-earner and the white proprietor.

For the Negro, however, the analogy becomes remarkably life-like when we study it in view of Freud's theory of the martyrdom of Moses, expounded in his last book. For the slaves of the American Egypt the Emancipator appeared veritably as an alien prince— just as Freud pictured the Lawgiver of the Jews, Moses, as a man from the oppressors' race, the Egyptians. Lincoln's leadership and his tragedy confirmed in the souls of the liberated their determination to overcome urges of regression to African religion. They remained loyal to the religion of their Liberator, the theological economy and imperial simplicity of the single God. It is interesting to note the resurgence of monotheistic faith in America on the occasion of the modern Moses' death. "The great irreligion of our times," proclaimed the Rev. J. B. Thompson of the Home Missionary Society, on Black Easter, "is the exclusion of a living, personal God from human affairs. The sharp crack of a pistol," he went on, almost in exultation, "lays low the head of a nation and from the unseen comes the voice, 'Be still and know that I am God.'" (Lewis 95.) America answered Amen, with a Hebraic devoutness unknown to it since the day of New England theocracy.

"Abraham Lincoln's death by murder," announced the Rev. Dr. John Chase Lord of Buffalo, "canonizes his life. His words, his messages, his proclamations are now the American Evangel. God has permitted him to die a martyr because He wished to consecrate the works, the policy and proclamations of our President as the political gospel of our country, sealed in blood." (Lewis, 111.)

The faithful did not need any explanation of the way in which murder could consecrate a doctrine. "There is no sure foundation set on blood," says one of the nobles in Shakespeare's *King John*, but Christendom has never taken stock in such teaching. The judgment of the United States clergy on the crime of John Wilkes Booth may be succinctly defined by the words of one of them, E. B.

Webb of Boston, as a cry for blood for blood. "Give us back," said Webb, "the stern, inflexible indignation of the old Puritan, and the *lex talionis* of the Hebrew lawgiver" (Lewis, 85). It was the desire for retaliation that prompted the ministers to allude to Moses more frequently than to Jesus on the Sundays following the fatal night.

But while the Mosaic metaphor sounded most frequently from the pulpit, in the hearts of the congregation a younger metaphor rang with stronger magnetism, the analogy of Lincoln with Jesus. Of all the mythic memories to which the assassination of Lincoln was spontaneously chained, none sprang to the American mind with firmer conviction than the concept of the murder of Christ. Thus the Rev. James Freeman Clarke, a popular pastor, voiced the profoundest belief of his people when he assimilated the image of the martyred executive to that of the Crucified. "Perhaps the crime committed last Friday night in Washington," Clarke said, "is the worst ever committed on any Good Friday since the crucifixion of Christ. It was not only assassination, it was parricide; for Abraham Lincoln was as a father to the whole nation" (Lewis, 112). "It was parricide. . . ." From this insight into the tragedy of Lincoln are derived only part of the grandeur and the misery of his myth. Another, equally vital part comes from the idea of filicide suggested by his death. It was not simply the Father of his Country who founded by his blood "the American Evangel"; it was also the Son of the People, the child of the backwoods, who paid with his life for the guilts of the "conscript fathers" of the republic.

Comparison of the backwoods boy and the Son of Man emphasized the lowliness of both, including the traditional idea of Jesus as a figure of ugliness. (Cf. the Apocryphal *Acts of John* which portrays the Savior as "a small man and uncomely.") The very words by which the Rev. Henry Ward Beecher had despised and rejected Lincoln in 1862 could be turned in honor of the dead demigod in 1865. "It would be difficult," Beecher had observed, "for a man to be born lower then he was. He is an unshapely man. He is a man that bears evidence of not having been educated in schools or in circles or refinement" (Sandburg, i, 555). Even Beecher's sneering reference to the Illinois statesman as a "border-state eunuch" might have been remembered with religious awe in the light of the analogy with the Galilean, who extolled eunuchs in the service of the Kingdom of Heaven. Just as many recalled with a holy thrill how Lincoln had been reviled in 1861 for stealing into the Capital "like a thief in the night," as the Messiah was supposed to come before Doomsday.

A Baptist minister of Minnesota, years later, took pains to point out the common elements in the tragedies of Lincoln and Christ. "Joseph was a carpenter. Thomas Lincoln was a rough carpenter. Both Christ and Lincoln were reformers, maligned and abused. Like Christ Lincoln had been calm and meek and patient. The sins of man rested on both. Like the Man of Nazareth, Lincoln realized that he was not come to send peace on earth but a sword. Both were killed as a sacrifice for man." The minister could have added details of similarly powerful affect for the Christian frame of reference of the Lincoln legend. He could have recalled the backwoods boy's insistence that all that he was or ever hoped to be he owed to his angel mother, an avowal conjuring up in pious minds the vision of the Madonna at the Manger. But few Americans at the time of Lincoln's martyrdom required an exposition of the parallels between him and the Son of Man. The air resounded with similitudes linking the current drama with sacred history.

The news of the surrender of the Confederate army under Lee had come out on Palm Sunday, five days before the assassination, and Yankee soldiers were enabled to sing with heartfelt ardor: "Mine eyes have seen the glory of the coming of the Lord. . . ." while the partisans of Dixie expected the crack of Doomsday. One of Lee's soldiers cried out in the hour of his surrender, "Blow, Gabriel, blow! My God, let him blow; I am ready to die!" (Sandburg, iv, 202.) We may interpret this outcry as the expression of a wish to end the world because it looked as if the soldier's own microcosm of the South was tottering on the verge of extinction. We have already remarked how the sight of Southrons marching as prisoners of the Union army afflicted John Wilkes Booth with this same anguish for the lost mother-zone. The Jews to whom Jesus brought his evangel were likewise afflicted, watching the armies of Rome trample on their holy soil. Jesus tried to hearten them with his vision of the Kingdom of Heaven, a patriarchal paradise: "In my Father's house are many mansions," said the Nazarene, promising space and content to all who would believe in Him and yield their desires for the profane possessions of this world, the evil mother-earth.

For President Lincoln the end of the Civil War marked a Judgment Day for the United States. He welcomed it as a time for communion with the Almighty, thanksgiving for peace, and remission of the sins of the South. To his fellow citizens grieving over the rapine and harrowing that America had endured he held out the promise of healing and new happiness in a restoration of the Union: "that this nation, under God, shall have a new birth of freedom," glistening with all the spirituality of the old republic, with its ideals of justice and equality for men who would yield their desires for material privilege. Lincoln was angry at the politicians for whom the victory of the North signified a new distribution of the American earth, and its carnal powers of industry. The battle of the brother-states had settled, in his judgment, no question more incisive than the question of the states' right to secede. The "many mansions" of the Union were dearer to him than the "forty acres and a mule" favored by radical Republican politicians. Lincoln's utterances prior to his own doomsday were almost exclusively concerned with his wish to get the revolted states back into "their proper practical relation with the Union . . . safely at home."

In order to exalt and pour splendor on his policy of compromise with the slave-holders, the President spontaneously took refuge in the shadow of the Nazarene. He quoted with rapture Christ's sayings of humility and forgiveness to foes. The Christlike posture was not adopted by Lincoln in artifice; it came to him naturally. He too was a man of sorrows, acquainted with grief, and tortured with doubts of his mission. When he wrote for his own eyes in September 1862 that "In the present civil war it is quite possible that God's purpose is something different from the purpose of either party," he suffered something like the agony of Jesus in the garden of Gethsemane. (Sandburg, i, 590.) He meant every word of his second inaugural oration, which stated that if God willed the war should continue "until all the wealth piled by the bondsman's two hundred and fifty years of unrequited toil shall be sunk, and until every drop of blood drawn with the lash shall be paid by another drawn with the sword, as was said three thousand years ago, so still it must be said, the judgments of the Lord are true and righteous altogether."

But Lincoln could not bear any human imitation of the divine judge. "Let us judge not," he exhorted his countrymen, particularly his wife, "that we be not judged." Over and over he repeated these words, to persons who like Mrs. Lincoln demanded the hanging of Jefferson Davis for high treason, or similar punishment for the chief sinners of the South. His wife provoked him to one of his rare gestures of indignation, a gesture worthy of Christ, once when they were approaching Washington and she exclaimed, "That city is full of our enemies." Lincoln lifted his arm and his voice: "Enemies!" he cried, "We must never speak of that!" He was prepared to turn his cheek to the hand of Confederates who would consent to return on his terms to the Union fold.

No wonder the Rev. George Dana Boardman, in his Easter sermon on the significance of Lincoln's death, thanked the Lord "that He hath so woven the web of nations as to permit the American people to set before the ages the grandest human illustration the world has ever witnessed of that sublime principle which seems to pervade the universe and which lies at the very cornerstone of Redemption—Vicarious Sacrifice" (Lewis, 109).

After the trauma of Lincoln's assassination, and the submergence in the unconscious of the painful thoughts it aroused, and the assimilation of images from these thoughts to ego-ideals of theology, came the myth-making phase of transformation of the solemn and sad feelings thus generated into ideas of joy. The tragedy of Lincoln became the basis of a new evangel, glad tidings to the broken and sorrowing country. Now we hear that Booth's deed was actually a Providential deed, a sacrifice to God. "It is no blasphemy against the Son of God and the Savior of men," C. B. Crane assured his flock, "that we declare the fitness of the slaying of the second Father of our Republic on the anniversary of the day on which He was slain. Jesus Christ died for the world, Abraham Lincoln died for his country." Dr. Henry Bellows was equally confident that the murder presented "a mighty sacrifice" for the sins of America (Lewis, 110, 111). And the Rev. George Duffield, a fiery Presbyterian of Detroit, exhausted his rhetorical powers to prove that in the death of Lincoln the Lord had "pursued the same plan of his gracious Providence" as the scheme that brought the North in triumph out of the war (Lewis, 96).

In these pious expressions we catch a glimpse of the original notions which Booth's act called up from the id of Lincoln's antagonists South and North, the savage death-wishes that only a few

Confederates ventured to give tongue in the open air. Men of fidelity to the Union, or the Republican Party, had to repress the id-glee over the kill; they translated the slaughter, in Shakespeare's phrase, into a "dish for the gods," a divine sacrifice. As a tragedy with a Providential happy ending, it could be enjoyed by their superegos, the internal deputies of their Puritan parents. To appease the national conscience, stricken with horror by the crimes and atrocities of the fratricidal war, the fallen politician had to be changed into a martyr, a hero, a god; the accidental bullet had to be metamorphosed into a bolt from Paradise. This change took place in strict accordance with the principles of Freud's archmyth; the ruin of the hero is followed by the love-feast of his folk, celebrating his defeat while they sing and dance with woe for it, and finding in his broken body the means for freshly cementing the tribal ties. The unconscious rejoicing of the people over the corpse of Lincoln showed itself perhaps nowhere so clearly as in the New York Pageant of his funeral car, in the banner of the National Hook and Ladder Company on which were blazoned the words: "The assassin's stroke but makes the fraternal bond the stronger" (Lewis, 139).

Inevitably the Christian model for the Lincoln myth induced additions to it, like the belief that the martyr's tomb at Springfield is in reality empty (Lewis, 299). People have also fancied that the body it bears has been converted to stone. This particular legend may arise from the medieval story of King Barbarossa, who waits statuesque in his mountain tomb for the summons of Germany on her night of fiercest necessity. The pragmatic acumen of America does not permit any visions of Lincoln's return in the future. The Messiah here must be born anew for every crisis, as the new cult of Franklin Roosevelt demonstrates. Nevertheless, the yearning of the nation is for a savior of the Lincoln kind, and when he is not forthcoming the myth-peddlers of the land, such as Vachel Lindsay, mourn and wish that they could "rouse the Lincoln in you all." To the grave of Lincoln have come more pilgrims than to any other tomb in the civilized world. For no other leader has so perfectly exemplified the ego-ideal of the common, the anonymous, the mass.

"How vain," sighed Senator Sumner of Massachusetts, deploring what he thought was Lincoln's failure to live up to the heavenly opportunities of his office, "how vain to have the power of a god and not to use it, godlike." (Williams, 41.) The President really did use his dictatorial powers like a god; only it was not a god known to scholars like Sumner, antiquarians and anthropologists. It was a new diety, created by the United States—the god named Uncle Sam. Nobody ever resembled that diety as vividly as Abe Lincoln, both in external traits and in shrewdness, empirical horizon, opportunism, humor, easy-going ethics, pristine superstition, infinite rapid anxieties, and so on. He was alleged to be the tallest man in America, and exaggerated his height by a striking stovepipe hat. For some reason unexplained he grew whiskers when he was elected President. And he delighted in asserting himself as the lowest common denominator of the genus American. "Without mock modesty," he never tired of telling his constitutents, he was "the humblest of all individuals that have ever been elevated to the presidency" (Sandburg, i, 54). At the same time he proclaimed that, of all the presidents, he had the most difficult task. Like a true-blue Yankee he would not publicly complain about his lot; he was able to grin and bear it, and proudly showed the world his grin. The obduracy, indeed the arrogance of the grin marked the boundaries of his humility, the armor of the American ego against the dangerous liberties that might be taken with the "divine average," as Whitman named it. The most comic of the chief executives, Lincoln was the worthiest representative of a nation that loved buffoons more than savants or saints. At the same time he "dripped melancholy," as his friend William Herndon said, and by his moments of tragedy completed the gratification of his countrymen with a leadership that mingled kaleidoscopically laughter and tears. In a truer sense than Lincoln realized he was what he fondly styled himself—"public property" (Sandburg, i, 54).

It was inevitable that he should not only be considered worthy of death as the redeemer of the people's guilt, the representative of the incest-haunted and father-hating brothers who had ravaged Columbia and drenched her with blood. He had to be spiritually consumed by the people, introjected in their souls, converted by holiday feast into a part of the superego along with the other father-idols, half-sublime, half-devilish. On February 12—Lincoln's anniversary—the nation rehearses the tragicomedy of his deification, the vicarious killing, the unconscious rejoicing over his death, the introjection of his image by a process that may properly be defined as intellectual cannibalism. The repetition of ritual and drama serves to confirm the onlooking and listening children in their faith in the national gospel, the dogmas of the Declaration of Independence and the Gettysburg Address.

The secret magnetism of the Lincoln cult, I believe, consists of the craving of the masses for a paternal, a Mosaic liberation from their dull and deadly servitude. They wish to obtain freedom without their own endeavors, by magic, so to speak. So long as the people fail to exert their strength for sovereignty, and rely on saviors, Abraham Lincoln remains an idol of democracy. When they go into adult action for self-government the melancholy humorous god subsides into the frustrated and vacillant statesman, who hated slavery and yet considered it a lesser evil than the sundering of his country, the disunity of the States. The "house divided" caused him more pain than the sight of the race enslaved. In other words, he remained, deep in his unconscious, a victim of devotion to the home-goddess, the mother whom he had early lost. He remained in soul a child, a guilt-ridden son. It is the helpless child in us who looks to the image of "Father Abraham" for succor and solace in our periods of depression or desperate labor. It is the infant in us who seeks vengeance for his degradation in the constant renewal of the national happiness on February 12, with its attendant renewal of woe for his death.

4

JOHN WILKES BOOTH

JOHN WILKES BOOTH, BORN IN 1838, DEAD TWENTY-SEVEN YEARS later, lived long enough to know he had realized his adolescent fantasy of achieving immortality by destroying something famous. Junius Wilkes Booth, John's father, was one of the best known actors of the American stage. According to Wilson[1], he was a moody, aggressive, unpredictable man, kind to his family but demanding absolute obedience, frequently away from home for long periods of time, and subject to alcoholic bouts. Booth's mother was devoted to the family, doted particularly on John, her favorite, and experienced a grim and dire dream about her son's destiny which she would relate in the boy's presence. John's older brothers, Junius Brutus and Edwin, were among the most successful actors of the second half of the nineteenth century. A younger sister, Asia, presented no threat to the rising actor's ambitions.

In childhood, John Wilkes possessed much nervous energy, was defiant, headstrong, a poor student who was frequently disciplined by the school authorities but who was also able to escape punishment because of the winning personality and ready smile he was always able to produce. During adolescence, his behavior was marked by significant destructive fantasies, which Weissman reports in the next chapter, by surreptitious vocational ambitions and by the fantasy of writing his father's biography. Throughout his youth, he was pampered and spoiled by his mother and sister. Since his father and two older brothers were away during most of his formative years, the opportunity for identification with them was minimal. But the opportunity for developing repressed murderous rages against them found rich soil and was to blossom later on when John Wilkes did not receive the acclaim accorded them when he was to trod the boards.

The Oedipal conflict could only be resolved when the substitute father, the leading American actor on the national stage, was done away with. Acting out his fantasies, his penultimate phrase, "Mother, I died for my country," is readily translated into, "Mother, I killed my father because of you." And his last words, as he looked at his hands, "Useless, utterly useless," demonstrate his complete failure to adjust his unconscious to reality. "He could not successfully manipulate reality to conform to his own unconscious strivings," writes Wilson, "but it is interesting to note how dramatically he did manipulate reality so as to completely justify and fulfill the dream which his mother had repeated to him when he was a little child."[2]

---

1 Wilson, George W., "John Wilkes Booth: father murderer," *Amer. Imago*, 1:55, 1940.
2 *Ibid.*, p. 59.

Why Booth Killed Lincoln
A Psychoanalytic Study of a Historical Tragedy

THE MOOD of a melodrama must have been upon the twenty-six-year-old John Wilkes Booth as he scheduled the shooting of Abraham Lincoln in the Ford Theatre. The assassin planned to use the customary dramatic cue to indicate the moment for murder. It was to be synchronized with a line in the second scene of the third act of Tom Taylor's *Our American Cousin*. A humorous soliloquy with a note of ridiculous violence, intended to provoke laughter, was to be the distracting signal to squeeze the trigger.

He rode up on his horse at 9:30 p.m., half an hour before the selected fateful scene began. He dismounted, entered the theatre, "removing gauntlet gloves, bowing and smiling to fellow actors and whispered to an actor in the wings. The actor shook his head and pointed to the tunnel. Booth could not cross backstage at this time." After surveying the audience from the other wing, he stepped out of the theatre with the knowledge that he had ample time before his act. At the adjoining tavern of Peter Taltayul's, where he ordered a bottle of whisky and some water, he got into a discussion with an unidentified, intoxicated man who needled him, "You'll never be the actor your father was."[1] In this moment of frightened excitement John's unconscious became vulnerable, yet he replied pleasantly and calmly, "When I leave the stage, I will be the most famous man in America." What multiple unconscious meanings are hinted at in this brief, ambiguous retort!

The assassin was the younger brother of the famous American Shakespearean actor, Edwin Booth, and both were the sons of an English-born but famous American actor, Junius Wilkes Booth. The history student will recall that a month or so before, Lincoln had been inaugurated as President of the United States for a second term following his re-election the previous November. Booth shot Lincoln on April 14, 1865, a few days after Lee had surrendered to Grant and the Civil War was over. Lewis Paine, an underling in Booth's conspiracy, attempted a synchronized, unsuccessful assassination of William Seward, the Secretary of State.

After Booth shot Lincoln, he leaped on the stage, landing off balance because the spur of his riding boot had caught in the bow tie flag decorating the Presidential box. He sustained a fractured left ankle but felt no immediate pain since he thought only of escaping through the wing of the theatre to his waiting horse on the street. Nevertheless, Booth found time to declaim from the stage the Latin phrase, "Sic semper tyrannis!"

Already on three previous occasions during the three preceding months, Booth had planned to kidnap, no, to capture—as he preferred to think of it—Lincoln, always during a performance at the same Ford Theatre. His melodramatic kidnaping plots involved the cumbersome procedure of dropping Lincoln from his box on to the stage, from there carrying him off through the wings, and following the same escape route which he actually used on April 14.

To those who are driven by their own imagination to ruminate, a number of questions, doubts, inquiries and better ways of having done this may occur. Why did the actor's plan for either kidnaping or killing have to be carried out exclusively on the stage? Why did he have to use a plan which necessitated carrying the President on and off the stage? John Wilkes wanted to be seen, identified and eventually caught and killed. This was not the escape of the usual criminal. He was a well known figure in the theatre. Furthermore, he had written an undelivered letter to the newspaper *The National Intelligencer* (see Stern, 1939, p. 72), and a sealed letter to his sister Asia, to make sure that no other hand would be mistaken for this act.

The verdict of the period in which this tragedy occurred was that John Wilkes Booth was deranged. His loyalty to the South originated from a psychotic delusion in which he feared that Lincoln would become a "king" and reign over a dynasty, following his re-election. Credit our grandfathers with the evaluation that the "mad" Booth wanted primarily to become famous. They knew nothing of a possible unconscious hatred of a father, let alone the possibility that will be developed here, namely that John Wilkes' delusion in which he perceived and hated Lincoln as a reigning king was derived from the denial of rage against his brother Edwin.

In the final terrible days in hiding after John had shot the President and learned that he was dead, John scrawled a frantic and soul-searching note in his diary. Its contents reveal a direct expression of the unconscious aim of his murderous act. "I do not repent the blow I struck . . . I think I have done well. Though I am abandoned, with the *curse of Cain* upon me, when if the world knew my heart, that one blow would have made me great, though I did desire no greatness" (Ruggles, 1953, p. 192). In this desperate, defiant utterance, John labels his own act as the act of Cain, in which the good brother Abel was slain. This was not, as so many had thought, the act of a Brutus who killed a ruler, but the act of a brother who kills a brother unconsciously.

Psychoanalysis has shown that in paranoid delusions the deepest feeling involves an inordinate hatred of a loved person which is too frightening to be recognized.[2] John Wilkes was a man who hated so deeply and rivaled so intensely his family's elders that he was too frightened to know or show the slightest emanations of his feelings toward those involved. He had to remove these feelings to a vastly remote representative.

THE CONCURRENCE OF LINCOLN'S RE-ELECTION, EDWIN'S REIGN AND JOHN WILKES' PLOT FOR FAME

At the time of Lincoln's re-election, Edwin Booth came into the full bloom of his "reigning" career and within a few months—before April 14, 1865—established himself as the head of the tribe of Booth actors. At this particular moment, Edwin was heralded as the "Prince of Players," the greatest Hamlet who ever lived. In these few crucial months—from the time of Lincoln's re-election to his inauguration, events in Edwin's career cast him as the unrivaled actor who was destined to rule over the American theatre until his death.

Edwin had rented the Winter Garden for the current season of 1864-1865, and for several seasons to come. This was the beginning of a new adventure in Edwin's expanding career. Until then, like his father, he had been limited to the necessity of making arrangements with managers. Now he could select his own vehicles, cast, repertoire, and in New York! He had come of age as no Booth ever had.

On November 25, 1864, shortly after Lincoln's re-election, a benefit performance of *Julius Caesar* was given at the Winter Garden, under Edwin Booth's leadership. The proceeds were for the purpose of erecting a statue of Shakespeare in Central Park. For this occasion, Edwin gathered his talented brothers, Junius Jr. and John Wilkes, to contribute their efforts. Edwin played Brutus, Junius Jr. played Cassius and John Wilkes played Mark Anthony.

The following morning the entire family was gathered at Edwin's house for breakfast. The theatre reviews in the newspapers extolled the virtuosity of both John Wilkes and Junius Jr., which prompted Edwin to remark, "I must brush up or lose my laurels." Then they discussed the recent election. Edwin commented that he had voted for the first time in his life, and had voted for Lincoln. This infuriated John Wilkes who derogated the President with the term "Old Abe," and cursed him viciously. In spite of John's feelings for the South, this outburst was provocative since he was familiar with Edwin's pro-Lincoln sympathies.

Was this then a provident opportunity for John Wilkes to displace his inadmissible and unrecognized hatred of the reigning Edwin onto the issue of Lincoln's imaginary rule?[3] A year before, Lincoln had paid a surprise and unguarded visit to the Ford Theatre where he witnessed Edwin's Shylock and then commented, "A good performance, but I'd a thousand times read it at home if it was not for Booth's playing." That same night Edwin was entertained at dinner by Secretary of State, William Seward. These were the first signs of Edwin's rise to national fame. To dine with the Secretary of State and lure the President to an unplanned visit to his performance would be any actor's dream. What feelings would this stir in a rival actor brother from a family of notable thespians? John Wilkes had a pathological need for fame and had openly stated, "I want fame, fame, fame!"

Historians have been puzzled why Seward was John Wilkes' co-victim. Had this been exclusively a political plot, Secretary of War Stanton would have been a much more suitable target. His capture or death would have achieved a more complete disruption of the executive and military functions of the North. The choice of Seward as victim exposes the emotional origin of the crime. He was hated because, like Lincoln, he admired Edwin.

However, John Wilkes did not formulate his first plot to capture Lincoln until a year later, when Lincoln was re-elected. He developed his grandiose plans for November 1864 to April 14, 1865. This period coincided with the time during which his brother Edwin achieved outstanding theatrical success.

On the evening after the benefit performance of Julius Caesar, Edwin Booth began his career as his own producer, *sans frères*, playing Hamlet. His acclaim grew with each performance. "Booth never lost the name he made that season." "The fashion and the passion, especially among women," was how the New York critic who signed himself "Nyn Crinkle" described Booth's Hamlet. The New York *Times* pronounced it "a part in which he had no living equal." "What Garrick was in Richard III, or Edward Kean in Shylock, we are sure Edwin Booth is in Hamlet," suggested the editor of *The Easy Chair* of Harpers for April 1865. "Booth is altogether princely. . . . His playing throughout has an exquisite tone like an old picture. . . . The cumulative sadness of the play was never so palpable as in his acting." "Edwin Booth," writes William Winter, "was the simple absolute realization of Shakespeare's haunted prince, and raised no question and left no room for inquiry whether the Danes in the Middle Ages wore velvet robes or had long flaxen hair. It was dark, mysterious, afflicted, melancholy" (see Ruggles, 1953, pp. 169-170).

His success was accompanied by absolute recognition by his brothers. The transformation in Junius Brutus Jr. is the first to be noted. He had commented earlier. "Ted has the public. Yet, let him act a thousand years and he will never be able to approach father." However, after a few months of Edwin's Hamlet we find Junius saying, "that while father could make the cold shivers crawl down my back, he couldn't possibly have played Hamlet as Edwin has done for one hundred performances and done it as well."

Finally, the silent, younger rival, John Wilkes, with a tinge of psychotic unreality and extraordinary keenness, says, "No, no, no! There's but one Hamlet to my mind; that's my brother Edwin. You see, between ourselves, he is Hamlet—melancholy and all." We must remember that Lincoln too had a "melancholy" quality.

The "crowning" of Edwin's success was his recognition by the City of New York. A municipal Committee along with the Governor of New York State planned to present Edwin with a gold medal on the night of his hundredth performance of Hamlet, March 22, 1865.

On March 20, 1865, John Wilkes plotted for the third time to achieve his own unforgettable "fame." Had he succeeded, it would have shattered Edwin's day of honor into a day of disaster.

SIGNIFICANT EVENTS IN JOHN WILKES' LIFE

John Wilkes' intense unconscious hatred was mostly directed at his brother Edwin who was an alternate for both his real and fantasy-life father. Edwin was five and a half years older than John Wilkes. From the time of his birth until he was eight or nine, Edwin was consistently the oldest male at home, and must have appeared to John as a father as well as a brother. Therefore, Edwin occupied the double dais of a rival heir and substitute father. When Edwin was fourteen years of age, he replaced Junius Jr. as his father's touring companion—a role in which he was to guard his father against excessive drinking and the ensuing difficulties. This also served as a period of apprenticeship in acting. During the next four years, from the age of nine to thirteen, John Wilkes, with no older male about, was like a fatherless boy, always playing wild games.

In the spring of 1852, John Wilkes, age fourteen, was completing a year at a large boarding school, kept by the Quakers in Cockeysville. The elder Booth intended to buy a farm nearby and thus provide a home and future occupation for his two younger sons, John Wilkes and Joseph. He had in mind that no other sons of his would become actors. Consciously he wanted none of his sons on the stage, but all his actions indicated that he was shaping the theatrical careers of his two older sons.

That same year, Junius Jr., who was now a theatre manager on the West coast, induced his father to accompany him back to California to seek new theatrical horizons. Edwin, age nineteen, now an established professional actor in his own name, was persuaded to join them. Such an adventure, going from the East coast to the West coast, had in those days the implication of a permanent change. The family was now split. The father, in a theatrical unit with the older brothers, headed for San Francisco, and the other, domestic unit, with John Wilkes as the eldest male, his mother, two sisters and younger brother, remained on the Maryland farm (Kimmel, 1940, p. 151). John felt that he had been badly treated and neglected and that he was not accepted as a man and an actor by his father. He complained bitterly to his sister Asia, "How shall I ever have a chance on the stage. Buried here, torturing the grain out of the ground for daily bread, what chance have I of ever studying elocution and declamation." He began to plan defiantly for himself, for his acting and subsequent fame. From now on, in every way and at every moment, his acting developed a stealthy, surreptitious, aggressive quality that remained until the final day of the drama at the Ford Theatre.

At the end of the school year, the parents were invited to a picnic at the school. Asia escorted her mother in place of the migrant father. The entertainment for the occasion consisted of planned recitations by the students. One of the pupils recited Othello's declamation. Then, to the surprise of his relatives, John mounted the stage as Shylock and, as Asia put it in her Memoirs, "A master, who stood screened by the boys nearest the platform, read out Salarino's, the servant's and Tubal's lines, and Shylock had the stage to himself" (Clarke, 1938, p. 56). This unannounced but carefully plotted first stage performance was to be repeated with even greater melodramatic flavor throughout his subsequent, if short, theatrical career.

This surreptitious quality tainted all his future undertakings of acting. He confessed his first professional activity in Baltimore, when he was seventeen, to his sister Asia, as if he were a criminal, for he had originally pretended that he had to leave the farm for a few days on business. Outwardly the escapade had the style of a pleasant surprise, but it was inwardly structured as a stealthy, forbidden act. Asia reports this incident as follows: " 'Well, Mother Bunch, guess what I've done!' Then answering my silence he said, 'I've made my first appearance on any stage for this night only and in big capitals.' . . . . Mother was displeased as we to hear of this adventure. She thought it premature and that he had been influenced by others who wished to gain notoriety and money by the use of his name." Wilkes' mother was overprotective in this evaluation of her son's enterprise. As his adoring mother, she would find it hard to face the truth, for actually John Wilkes was taking advantage of the famous name of his father and brother and was seeking notoriety and money when it was "premature" for him to be starred at his "first appearance on any stage" considering his lack of training. He rebelled and competed as an actor with his father and Edwin.

As his stage career developed, he was described on one occasion as an "outrageous scene thief." He planned to confine his acting to the South because he "would never hope to be as great as father, he never wanted to rival Edwin but wanted to be loved by the Southern people above all things. He would make himself essentially a Southern actor." However, his actions proved otherwise. As soon as Edwin Booth had gone to England in the summer of 1861, John Wilkes invaded his brother's theatrical territory. Eleanor Ruggles (1953) writes in *The Prince of Players*, "When Edwin sailed for England, John saw his chance. He starred in St. Louis, in Chicago, then in Baltimore; and here in the city most associated with all the Booths, his posters proclaimed defiantly: 'I AM MY-SELF ALONE!'"

JOHN WILKES' ADOLESCENT FANTASIES—FEARS AND WISHES

The Unlocked Book, written by Asia Booth Clarke, who died in 1888, was not released for publication until 1938. Asia had concealed the manuscript during her lifetime. Prior to her death she passed it on to a trusted friend whose daughter finally published it. Asia had hoped that posterity would evaluate these memoirs of her brother John in the coolness of distance. She preserved for us the events, aspirations and fears of his boyhood. She also preserved her mother's aspirations and dreams for him. All of these helped shape Lincoln's assassin.

Along with her own manuscript, Asia left "A Book of Cuttings," stamped "J.W.B.," containing a variety of newspaper clippings. The six articles she selected to save for the future from the multitude written about John Wilkes during her lifetime showed extraordinary intuition and perception. The most significant of this group is entitled, "His Schooldays, by a Classmate." It is merely signed "A Marylander" and is dated December 3, 1878, New York—thirteen years after the notorious crime. This article was actually a letter written in response to a newspaper article by John T. Ford who had made a remarkable case for the theory referred to as John Wilkes' "Admiration for Brutus." [4] Ford felt that "the fact that the public had made assassination respectable by applauding the chief actor in the play of Julius Caesar, was the mainspring of his action."

The classmate from Maryland suggests that John Wilkes was *not* playing Brutus. He concludes, "I believe instead of following the Brutus idea, his thoughts were rather after Washington, Bolivar and Leonidas—but his great boyish aim would be accomplished. 'His name known in history, to live forever.' "

I think that the classmate has given us a meaningful hint in his phrase "but his great boyish aim would be accomplished." Credit the Marylander for recording in this article the boyhood fantasies which John Wilkes told him. They are crucial to our ultimate understanding. Their first meeting was in 1852, at school. I quote further from the Marylander:

Morris Oram always looked forward to the law as his profession, and in stating his views for the future his ambition was to be a greater orator than Daniel Webster, and a more profound lawyer than Reverdy Johnson, while Booth thought only of being a man admired by all the people. He asserted that he would do something that would hand his name down to posterity never to be forgotten, even after he had been dead a thousand years. Booth and Oram had red clay pipes, with reed stems about a yard long, and when they with their pipes lay on the ground, these daily conversations were always in order. Our opinions of the future were freely discussed. I recollect when we asked Booth how he expected to acquire such greatness and notoriety as he was constantly talking of. One of his answers was: "Well, boys, I'll tell you what I mean. You have read about the Seven Wonders of the World? Well, we'll take the Statue of Rhodes for example. Suppose that statue was now standing, and I should by some means overthrow it? My name would descend to posterity and never be forgotten, for it would be in all the histories of the times, and be read thousands of years after we are dead, and no matter how smart and good men we may be, we would never get our names in so many histories."—On another occasion when the same subject was discussed, I recollect he said, "I wish there was an arch or statue at the mouth of the

Mediterranean Sea across the Straits of Gibraltar, with one side resting on the rock of Gibraltar and the other on an equally prominent rock on the coast of Africa. I would leave everything and never rest until I had devised some means to throw it over into the sea. Then look out for history, English, French Spanish, and all Europe, Asia and Africa would resound with the name of John Booth. I tell you it would be the greatest feat ever executed by one man."

RECKLESS OF CONSEQUENCES

While speaking, his whole soul appeared to contemplate with satisfaction the future he had drawn.

Oram said, "Billy, suppose the falling statue took you down with it, what good would all your glory then do you?"

His answer was: "I should die with the satisfaction of knowing I had done something no other man would probably ever do."

The fantasies of this fourteen-year-old boy amaze us when we realize how thoroughly they were enacted a dozen years later, when they had been long forgotten by their weaver.

The destructive fantasies of smashing both the Statue of Rhodes and the Arch spanning the Straits of Gibraltar belong to the current events in John's life. He related these fantasies to his young friends some time after his father and two older brothers had left for the Northwest Coast. (As we noted before, John felt that he had come of age as his brothers before him had and that he was permanently bypassed by his father in his rightful turn to accompany him and become an actor.) The migration of the theatrical elders was undertaken by steamer. In those days there was no Panama Canal. The "Illinois" left New York, steamed past Mexico and landed at Colon. There they "poled up the Chagres River to Gorgona." Here they "mulebacked" through the jungle across the Isthmus, finally landing in Panama City on the Pacific. They boarded ship, sailed North, and arrived in San Francisco on July 28, 1852.

The route of their voyage is pertinent to John Wilkes' fantasies. The Straits of Gibraltar lie between the continents of Europe and Africa, between the Atlantic and Mediterranean, as the Isthmus lies between North and South America and separates the Atlantic from the Pacific. In his fantasy, John created an imaginary land arch spanning the Straits of Gibralter, similar to the Isthmus of Panama. The dangerous jungles of the Isthmus, where his father and brothers could easily have perished, were transformed into the fantasied arch for which he would devise "some means to throw it over into the sea."

What is hidden behind these fantasies are the murderous wishes against his father and Edwin. Junius Brutus Jr., also a father figure to John Wilkes, entered little into John's unconscious hostility since Junius was so much older and had been away from home completely during John's formative childhood years. Furthermore, he never became the theatrical rival to John that Edwin was. In his daydreams John willed the destruction of his male elders as he felt they had abandoned him and destroyed his dreams to become an actor like them and with them.

The Statue of Rhodes, the sixth wonder of the world, existed about 300 years B.C. on the Island of Rhodes. It stood 105 feet high, 50 feet short of the Statue of Liberty, and was, like our statue, a harbor statue. It is said to have stood at the entrance to the island's harbor, and the figure of Helios, the worshiped sun-god, stood with his legs straddled over the harbor's entrance. Again we note that John Wilkes' fantasy dealt with structures which were gateways to water voyages. The dangers of both the sea voyage and the jungle of the Isthmus which threatened his father and brothers were displaced onto distant waters. The statue of Helios, the sun-god, represents an unequivocal, universal symbol in man's unconscious for the father. Thus, again, John Wilkes' fantasied destruction intended the destruction of his father and his father-like brother Edwin.

The part of the fantasy in which the statue falls upon him as he destroys it contains a preview of his capture and death subsequent to his assassination of the President.

In the twelve intervening years between the boyhood fantasy and the act of murder, the life of John Wilkes Booth was a series of enactments dictated by the long repressed but lively fantasy. With Lincoln destroyed like his "statue," John died as he had promised, "with the satisfaction of knowing I had done something never before accomplished by any other man and something no other man would probably ever do."

THE NATURE AND ORIGIN OF JOHN WILKES' FANTASIES

John's fantasies were provoked by but did not originate from his father's adventures to California. Some explanations for both the basic origins of John's fantasies and the fuel for their enactment are found in Asia's Memoirs. She tells us that "his mother, when he was a babe of six months old had 'a vision' in answer to a fervent prayer in which she imagined that the fore-shadowing of his fate had been revealed to her, and as this incident was more painfully impressed upon her mind by a 'dream' when he had attained manhood, both vision and dream were familiarized to me by frequent repetition. . . . The oft-told reminiscence was put into this form and presented to the mother on her *birthday;* the lines claim no other *merit* than affording an explanation of her vision:"

THE MOTHER'S VISION

Written 1854, June 2nd, by A. B. (Asia Booth) Harford Co., Md.

'Tween the passing night and the coming day
When all the house in slumber lay,
A patient mother sat low near the fire,
With that strength even nature cannot tire,
Nursing her fretful babe to sleep—
Only the angels these records keep
　　Of mysterious Love!

One little confiding hand lay spread
Like a white-oped lily, on that soft bed,
The mother's bosom, drawing strength and contentment warm—
The fleecy head rests on her circling arm.
In her eager worship, her fearful care,
Riseth to heaven a wild, mute prayer
　　Of foreboding Love!

Tiny, innocent white baby-hand,
What force, what power is at your command,
For evil, or good? Be slow or be sure,
Firm to resist, to pursue, to endure—
My God, let me see what this hand shall do
In the silent years we are tending to;
　　In my hungering Love,

I implore to know on this ghostly night
Whether 'twill labour for wrong, or right,
For—or against Thee?
                 The flame up-leapt
Like a wave of blood, an avenging arm crept
Into shape; and COUNTRY shone out in the flame,
Which fading resolved to her boy's own name!
God had answered Love—
   Impatient Love!

This is the terrible vision of John's destiny, written as a poem for the mother's birthday by sister Asia when she was eighteen and John sixteen. The vision implies an early death, an act of brave but bloody violence, in the name of the Country. However, its morality is in doubt—"for wrong or right," "For—or against Thee?" Asia further tells us, "Mother and I often talked of her 'vision in the fire' and of her 'awful dream' . . ." John Wilkes was not spared from hearing this "talk" and became intensely preoccupied with its content.

We have recounted how John Wilkes, at thirteen, had unexpectedly recited Shylock at school. Immediately after that performance, he could hardly wait to show his sister Asia his written version of "what he called 'his fortune' which a Gipsey . . . had told him a few days since. 'See here,' he said, 'I've written it—but there was no need to do that, for it is so bad that I shall not soon forget it.'" The fortune read:

"Ah, you've a bad hand; the lines all cris-cras. It's full enough of sorrow—full of trouble—trouble in plenty everywhere I look. . . . You'll die young, and leave many to mourn you, many to love you too, but you'll be rich, generous and free with your money. You're born under an unlucky star. You've got in your hand a thundering crowd of enemies—not one friend—you'll make a bad end, and have plenty to love you afterwards. You'll have a fast life—short, but a grand one. Now, young sir, I've never seen a worse hand, and I wish I hadn't seen it, but every word I've told is true by the signs. You'd best turn a missionary or a priest and try to escape it."

. . . The fortune had not ceased to trouble him, and at intervals, through the course of the few years that summed his life, frequent recurrence was sadly made to the rambling words of that old Gipsey in the wood of Cockeysville.

Asia had no understanding that the constant talk between her mother and herself in his presence affected him. She naïvely accounts for his gullibility of the gipsy's story with "this seed of an inherent superstition [was] kept alive by early associations with Negroes, whose fund of ghost stories, legends and ill omens never knew exhaustion." She could not see that his mystical and fatalistic attitudes stemmed from her own and her mother's visionary attitudes. This interplay between John and the two women became organized in his psychic structure. He consciously shared in their anxiety for him as if the vision were his own, and indeed it became part of himself.

THE NATURE AND ORIGIN OF HIS MOTHER'S DELUSION

Her "vision" was actually a visual hallucination and her preoccupation with its contents throughout the years represented its transformation into a fixed delusion. The symptom was masked in the guise of a mother's conventional dreams, hopes and anxieties for her child's future. The content of a mother's intense anxiety about a child, even when not openly expressed, rarely fails to become the child's own anxiety. In the earliest phase of ego development, the infant feels himself and the outside world as one. In the normal development of the infant's ego, his self-representation becomes completely separated from that of his parents and the world about him within the first year of life. Recent psychoanalytic investigations show that in mental illness the representation of the parent remains fused with the self-representation, as it had been originally. Consequently, in psychotic behavior, the individual often enacts incorporated psychotic aspects of a given parent, but feels the actions as exclusively his own (Jacobson, 1954).

Such an organization of John Wilkes' delusion can be recognized from his last words, quoted by Ruggles (1953): "He . . . opened his eyes and moved his lips to shape the words, 'Tell . . . Mother.' Then he fainted again. When he came to he finished his sentence. 'Tell . . . Mother . . . I . . . died . . . for . . . my . . . country.'" His dying utterances expose the structure of his delusion to have been a part of his mother's delusion embedded within him. This is not to imply that Mary Ann shared her son's terminal political delusion in which he hatefully saw Lincoln as a reigning king.

As a matter of fact, she was prone to share Edwin's views and was somewhat pro-North and pro-Lincoln. Actually, the Booth family homestead was in northern Maryland where it was quite common to have pro-Northern feelings. Whenever John talked bitterly against Lincoln, his mother felt helpless, uncomfortable and concerned.

Why did his mother develop this symptom at this particular time, when John Wilkes was six months old?

Mary Ann and Junius Brutus Booth had shortly before suffered the loss of three children: four-year-old Frederick, their fifth child; Elizabeth, the sixth child, and their fourth child, Mary Ann. These deaths occurred within the span of a few weeks. The father developed an agitated depression and was cared for by his wife, whose troubles as a bereaved mother were compounded by the burden of her husband's temporary derangement. The next year, in 1836, the whole family went to Europe, where the father had a theatrical tour. Here their third child, eleven-year-old Henry, died of smallpox. But Mary Ann had more burdens in store. She became concerned that the world might learn that she was not the legal wife of Junius Brutus Booth.

During this trip, the elder Booth was blackmailed by his brother-in-law, Jimmy Mitchell, who had been a kitchen boy in the home of the elder Booth's father before he married the actor's sister. Mitchell, a drunk, the father of eight children, was always desperate for funds. He threatened exposure of Booth's first marriage and thus attempted to extort money from the well-to-do actor. From these unpleasant experiences the Booths gladly returned to America.

"Home again in Maryland, Booth sent his sister the wherewithal to leave her husband and join him at the farm with her eight children. But all ten Mitchells, including Jimmy came, and the unsavory tribe of Mitchell children . . . scuffled and snapped like scabby puppies over Booth's chosen refuge. Their father bullied their mother, wouldn't work, was constantly in liquor . . ." Thus, in 1837, Mary Ann had to live in a household in which her illegal union with the elder Booth was constantly in danger of being exposed to her children and the world.

That year Mary Ann became pregnant with John Wilkes. No previous pregnancy had been associated with any misfortunes, such as the deaths of four children and the threatened exposure of her illicit life. These trying conditions and qualms of conscience disturbed Mary Ann throughout her pregnancy, birth and early months of mothering John Wilkes. In the midst of this suffering she experienced her intense hallucinatory "vision."

A few years ago (1954) I described "a woman, who would occasionally visualize, whenever there was a severe exacerbation of her obsessional symptoms, the image of the muscular arm of her father threatening her with physical punishment." It was then shown that the avenging arm represented an early internalized image of a disapproving father. We will recall that in the vision of Booth's mother

> The flame up-leapt
> Like a wave of blood, an avenging arm crept
> Into shape . . .

Mary Ann Booth's evoked image of the avenging arm speaks directly of her pangs of conscience. These unfortunate circumstances led to the development of her significant vision and subsequent delusion which had such tragic repercussions on the life of her son and our nation.

THE ENACTMENT OF THE DELUSION

Granted that John Wilkes had a paranoid delusion derived from his mother's delusion which developed when he was an infant; granted that his delusion contained a deep unconscious hatred for his fatherly brother Edwin—Prince of Players—which found its transfigured representation in Abraham Lincoln; granted that this transformation into a psychotic hatred of Lincoln became possible via the coincidence of the President's re-election; granted that the assassination was an outgrowth of his geographic adolescent fantasies of Rhodes and Gibraltar with well-hidden death wishes against his traveling father and brothers, with everlasting fame as the reward for his "heroic" deeds. What distinguished him from the multitude of people in the history of the world who have had similar delusions about ruling men displaced from "father and brother," with similar unconscious death wishes against them and desires for undying fame and notoriety? Why did they rarely commit an Act of Cain, but rather lived out their lives, in spite of their murderous thoughts, in mundane mediocrity, undistinguishable from other citizens? What made John Wilkes enact his fantasies with such brazen indifference for his life?

His bravado and unconcern were rooted in his wild childhood play as he "stormed through the woods on horseback, screaming his throat dry at invisible enemies and whirling a Mexican sabre over his head . . . and his adoring mother saw in his escapades the germ of heroic deeds"—and we see the germ of his final murderous act.

His mother gave approbation to the enactment of their mutual visionary fantasies—though his wild play went beyond the normal boy's warlike games. The mother's sanction and timorous admiration of his wild nature and behavior nurtured the expansion of his future wild delusion, culminating in the act of murder. This special state of sanction and admiration from his mother, who shared in her "vision" his patriotic delusion "for my Country," distinguished him from the run-of-the-mill paranoid psychotic who believes his dreams but does not enact them; and so, Booth shot Lincoln.

<h3 style="text-align:center">THE AFTERMATH</h3>

Fourteen years later, on the eventful anniversary date of April 14, 1879, Edwin Booth began a four-week engagement in Chicago. On the night of April 23, while playing Richard III, he was shot at three times, but was missed. It is said that Edwin "rose at the third shot, walked to the footlights and pointed out to the audience the would-be assassin as the pistol was again levelled at his head. At the trial which followed, the man was proved to be insane, and he has ever since been confined at the asylum at Elgin, Illinois." What terrible memories and perhaps uneasy stirrings must have been mobilized in the unconsciously intended victim of Lincoln's murderer!

Edwin Booth died on June 7, 1893. "Booth's funeral was held two days later at the Little Church Around the Corner . . . As Booth's coffin was being carried out of the church after the Episcopal service to the sonorous 'Dead March' from Saul—in the same moment by an eerie coincidence, three stories of Ford's Theatre in Washington where Lincoln has been shot by John Wilkes Booth and which since had been made into government offices, collapsed with a splintering roar, killing over twenty persons" (Ruggles, 1953).

The life story of John Wilkes Booth ends as it was lived, with a mystical and unfathomable event. It was as if the dying Ford Theatre in the end confessed that it was intended to house and symbolize the murder of Edwin Booth and in its place was staged a historical tragedy—the assassination of Lincoln—with the leading role in both dramas played by the notorious and visionary actor, John Wilkes Booth.

Notes

1 Quotations are from Bishop (1955, pp. 202–204).

2 Nunberg (1938) noted the gratification of aggression as well as libido in the case of a paranoid patient. See Knight (1940) for full discussion and formulations, also Stärcke (1920) and van Ophuijsen (1920).

3 Lehrman (1939) notes that in homicide "by means of unconscious elaboration, the victim . . . becomes a composite personage—a fusion of rival sibling, parent and self."

4 Wilson (1940) contends that John Wilkes was identified with Brutus. Unfortunately, I did not encounter this paper until just prior to my own publication. In his paper, Wilson formulates that the act of the paranoid John Wilkes Booth "constituted unconscious father murder but represented unconscious suicide as well."

BIBLIOGRAPHY

Bishop, J. (1955), *The Day Lincoln Was Shot*. New York: Harper & Bros.

Clarke, A. B. (1938), *The Unlocked Book*, edited by Eleanor Farjeon. New York: C. P. Putnam Sons.

Jacobson, E. (1954), Contribution to the Metapsychology of Psychotic Identifications. *J. Am. Psa. Assn.*, 2:239–262.

Kimmel, S. (1940), *The Mad Booths of Maryland*. Indianapolis: Bobbs-Merrill Co.

Knight, R. P. (1940), The Relation of Latent Homosexuality to the Mechanisms of Paranoid Delusions. *Bull. Menninger Clin.*, 5:149–160.

Lehrman, P. (1939), Some Unconscious Determinants in Homicide, *Psychiat. Quart.*, 134:605–622.

Nunberg, H. (1938), Homosexuality, Magic and Aggression. *Int. J. Psa.,* *19*:1–16.

Ruggles, E. (1953), *Prince of Players—Edwin Booth.* New York: W. W. Norton.

Stärcke, A. (1920), The Reversal of the Libido Sign in Delusions of Persecution. *Int. J. Psa., 1*:231–235.

Van der Stern, P. (1939), *Man Who Killed Lincoln.* New York: The Literary Guild of America.

Van Ophuijsen, J. H. W. (1920), On the Origins of the Feeling of Persecution. *Int. J. Psa., 1*:235–240.

Weissman, P. (1954), Ego and Superego in Obsessional Character and Neurosis. *Psa. Quart., 23*:529–543.

Wilson, G. W. (1940), John Wilkes Booth, Father Murderer. *Am. Imago, 1*(3):49–60.

5

CHARLES SUMNER

HATED BY HIS OPPONENTS, ADORED BY HIS FRIENDS, FANATICAL, EGO-
tistical, puritanical, and yet somehow sympathetic—such was
Charles Sumner, the dedicated senator from Massachusetts who
was one of the most powerful and enduring forces in the government in a time when senators were often more influential than
Presidents.

Sumner's life, wrote David Donald in the preface to his Pulitzer
Prize winning biography of 1960, touched upon virtually every
significant movement in his time. He was an advocate of international peace; a leader of educational and prison reform movements; organizer of the antislavery Whigs; a founder of the
Republican Party; the principal antislavery spokesman in the
Senate during the 1850's; a chief of the Radical Republicans during
the Civil War; and an architect of the congressional program for
reconstructing the conquered South. He was a man inflexibly
committed to a set of basic ideas as moral principles. He was
further distinctive in that he alone of his contemporaries moved
with equal assurance in the antithetical worlds of New England
letters and of Washington politics. And he was almost the only
nineteenth-century American politician who was nearly as widely
known in Europe as in his own country.

The senator's boyhood was spent in Boston, where he was born on January 6, 1811. His father, a not too successful lawyer, was an unaffectionate parent, unsmiling, formal and rigid in his interpersonal relations, and punctilious in etiquette. His mother was equally lackluster and distant toward people and undemonstrative toward Charles and his eight siblings. A spinster until twenty-five, she apparently never learned to show her feelings. The cheerless, somber home also felt the pinch of a necessary frugality because of the struggling lawyer's income, inadequate to maintain a family of eleven.

Charles, a premature twin, was breast-fed by his mother, but his sister was given to a nurse's care. The separation, Sumner's biographer Donald says, had lasting consequences: "There never grew up between Charles and Matilda that closeness of feeling that so often characterizes twins." Furthermore, while Charles developed real affection for his younger sisters, he regarded his four brothers as rivals and competitors. As the oldest son, more was demanded of him; he felt he had to earn affection while the others reaped it without having to work for it. "It was no wonder that Charles came early to find *King Lear* the most satisfying of Shakespeare's plays," Donald writes, "for he could identify himself with Cordelia. Throughout his life his most frequently used quotation was the reproach of the mad King, which should have been directed against the faithless and undeserving Goneril and Regan, but instead fell upon the head of the inarticulate Cordelia: 'Nothing will come of nothing.' "[1]

The unprepossessing, shy and awkward boy tried to win his father's regard through scholarly learning, as his father before him had had a classical education and was wont to intersperse his elegant conversation with Latin phrases. At ten, he was enrolled in the Boston Public Latin School, and for the next five years, Charles "rejoiced in this wonderful opportunity to become a learned man like his father."[2] Although the boy mastered the most difficult of the Latin texts, and further emulated his father by becoming an ardent history student, his attempts at identification were pathetic but not

---

[1] Donald, David. *Charles Sumner and the Coming of the Civil War.* New York: Alfred A. Knopf, 1960, p. 8.

[2] *Ibid.*, p. 9.

wholly futile. With an unexpected favorable change in the family's income, Charles was sent to Harvard to follow in the footsteps of his father and grandfather.

He was an average student there, but his college years were to be the most enjoyable of his life. For the first time he was able to assert some independence and even indulge in some minor rebellions. He was able to make friends, too, for the first time, and "he learned from them that all social intercourse was not necessarily conducted with the gloomy formality that prevailed in the house on Hancock Street. Secure in the relaxed, affectionate company of these classmates, where there was no moody father or rival brother to pounce upon every careless word or to capitalize upon every failing, Sumner found that he had a hitherto undiscovered talent, conversation."[3] He was soon nicknamed "The Chatterbox," became a first-rate declaimer, orator and public speaker. It was almost inevitable that he should enroll in Harvard Law School and eventually enter politics.

As the leading Republican in the Senate and its most vociferous anti-slavery proponent, Sumner was subjected to virulent attacks from many quarters. In the following selection, David Donald writes about Sumner's illness and his protracted three year absence from the Senate Chamber. Apparently suffering from septicemia, the precise nature of Sumner's ailment was mysterious. Donald delves into the psychological origins of his ailment, stemming from a bodily attack on Sumner on the Senate floor by Preston Brooks in 1856. The attack was prompted by a harsh, vindictive polemic by Sumner against the South in general and against the state of South Carolina in particular, including a personal vilification against its senator, Andrew P. Butler. The latter's young cousin, Congressman Preston Brooks, also of South Carolina, felt Sumner's remarks to be personally slanderous. With a gold-tipped, gutta-percha cane, Brooks beat Sumner about the head and shoulders until the bloodied senator lost consciousness. The case history follows here.

---

3 *Ibid.*, p. 17.

The Vacant Chair

DAVID DONALD

IF SUMNER'S HEALTH was of great concern to his friends, both personal and political, it was of equal interest to his opponents, who from the beginning found something suspicious about his invalidism. As it was part of the standard Southern interpretation of the assault that Brooks had only "chastised" Sumner with a "light walking cane," proslavery congressmen never accepted as a fact that Sumner had been seriously injured. Their suspicions were confirmed when Dr. Boyle testified to the House investigating committee on May 27 that Sumner's injuries were "nothing but flesh wounds." When Senator Butler spoke in defense of Brooks on June 12, he argued: "For anything that appears in that testimony, if [Sumner] had been an officer of the Army, and had not appeared on the next day [after the attack] on the battle-field, he would have deserved to be cashiered."[1]

After Republicans made "Bleeding Sumner" one of the principal issues in the 1856 presidential campaign, supporters of both Buchanan, the Democratic nominee, and Fillmore, the American candidate, openly charged that the senator was shamming. His wounds, they noted, offered a most convenient political martyrdom. As Sumner was not too ill in June to prepare a carefully revised edition of "The Crime Against Kansas," the Boston *Courier* decided that he was "playing the political possum." In July the Washington *Union*, the official organ of the Pierce administration, charged that Sumner's wounds were entirely healed, but that he stayed away from the Senate because of "his wounded pride and his irrepressible anger and indignation." The Boston *Post* suggested that Sumner's doctors were conspiring to picture the senator as an invalid until just prior to election, when he could reappear before the public and capitalize "very much upon the

160

interest his protracted absence from public duty [would] excite to see and hear him, for party effect." By fall the Washington *Union* had uncovered an even worse plot: physicians were "nursing the disease, lest it should die a natural death," because Sumner was "resolved not to recover until after the next Senatorial election in Massachusetts." Noting that Sumner miraculously recuperated just in time to address the citizens of Boston on the day before the elections, the Philadelphia *News* concluded: "The Senatorial sophomore has no doubt done more by playing possum than if he had stumped the entire North with re-hashes and plagiarisms from Demosthenes."[2]

Sumner was furious over these accusations. "While thus suffering for more than four months," he exclaimed in September, "I have been charged with the ignoble deed of *shamming illness!* It seems to me, if any thing could add to the character of the original act it is this supplementary assault on my character." Republican politicians were also seriously troubled over these slanders, which seemed to attract much credence in the Northwest, and they urged Sumner to collect affidavits from his other physicians to counteract the influence of Dr. Boyle's damaging testimony. Wilson helped Sumner gather statements from Dr. Lindsly, Dr. Wister, Dr. Perry, and Dr. Jackson, all declaring that Sumner's brain had "received a shock from which it might not recover for months" and all emphatically affirming that Sumner was unable to resume his Senate duties. This combined medical statement, Sumner himself declared in private, "was specially intended for Indiana, where the calumny had been employed; and . . . it was necessary that it should be circulated before the Election. . . ."[3]

The publication did not down the suspicion of fraud. Throughout the next three years, while Sumner was generally absent from the Senate, hostile newspapers carried occasional stories that he was "malingering" with a "sham sickness." Sumner, declared the New York *Atlas* in 1858, "is rapidly acquiring the reputation of a charlatan, who, preceded by his servant in motley, with a trumpet and drum, cries his injuries and sufferings in the cause of freedom as saleable wares, for the purpose of putting money in his purse." "This most ridiculous of humbugs," announced another editor, "fairly stinks in the nostrils of the American people."[4]

This accusation, which has found some defenders among later

historians of pronounced antiabolitionist sympathies, rests upon very flimsy evidence. The only medical testimony that supports it is the statement of Dr. Boyle, a Southern physician, strongly opposed in politics to Sumner and very friendly to both Senator Butler and Preston Brooks. Even if Dr. Boyle had been an unprejudiced observer, his testimony as to Sumner's superficial wounds, lack of fever, etc., would have only limited medical value, for it was given on May 27, before septicemia was apparent. In his frequently overlooked testimony on the following day, Dr. Boyle added that Sumner had begun to run a fever, that infection had set in, and that he had prescribed opiates. If Dr. Boyle's testimony is accepted in its entirety, it proves only what no one ever denied; that Sumner seemed to be recovering quite satisfactorily during the first few days after the assault, but that infection set in on the evening of May 27.

Opposed to Dr. Boyle's slight evidence are elaborate, sworn statements by the four physicians who were in charge of Sumner's case from May 27 until the end of the year. Dr. Harvey Lindsly declared that when he came on the case, Sumner was unable to resume his public duties, and that he had urged him to go to the seashore or to the mountains to recuperate. Dr. Caspar Wister, of the eminent Philadelphia family of physicians, opposed in politics to Sumner, made an early diagnosis that Sumner's recovery depended upon his "entire abstraction from all excitement" and, on re-examining him in late September, held that he was "still an invalid," requiring constant medical care. Dr. R. M. Jackson, who was a Democrat, swore that Sumner was "still extremely unwell" when he came to the Pennsylvania mountains and that he left Cresson prematurely, "still an invalid." Dr. Marshall S. Perry, one of the most respected doctors in Boston, was positive that Sumner was so badly injured that mental or bodily exertion would cost him his life.

There is a notable lack of evidence to support the theory that Sumner was pretending to be ill. Certainly not one word he ever uttered or wrote, even to his closest friends and to his brother, could be interpreted as lending support to such a charge. If there was a plan to have Sumner feign sickness until after the 1856 elections, somebody must have been in on the plot. But there is not a known scrap of evidence, in the correspondence of any of his friends, in the papers of any Republican leader, or even in any belated reminiscence, which lends credence to the theory. If there was a plot, it was one of the best kept secrets in American history. Those who charged Sumner with shamming relied upon logic as defective as their evidence. If he was pretending invalidism in order to aid the Frémont campaign or to promote his own re-election to the Senate—and there is no question but that his illness was skillfully exploited for both purposes—surely by January 1857 the game should have been over and Sumner should have resumed his seat. In fact, Southerners were puzzled at his failure to do so. Recognizing that after 1856 neither Sumner nor the Republican party had anything to gain by continuing a charade of this kind, proslavery men changed their attack and, during the next two years, attributed Sumner's absence from Washington to embarrassment at having been detected in his sham or to cowardice.

If the charge that Sumner was malingering must be dismissed as illogical theorizing upon insubstantial evidence, it must be admitted that the precise nature of Sumner's ailment was mysterious.[5] He looked well in the face, his voice was as firm and manly as usual, his intellect was bright and strong; but, when he tried to rise from his chair, he had to reach out for support, and he "walked with a cane and quite feebly, instead of his peculiarly vigorous stride." His progress toward recovery was disturbingly unpredictable. "Sometimes I think at last it has come," he wrote in January 1857, "and then before the day is over I am admonished that I can do but little."

Disturbed over these setbacks, he postponed returning to Washington until late February, when Massachusetts businessmen demanded that he vote on the new tariff bill. Republican colleagues greeted Sumner warmly as he resumed his seat, as did the two Democratic senators from Rhode Island; the rest, including Douglas, Toombs, Slidell, and Cass, "passed and repassed Mr. Sumner's seat and neither gave nor received a look of recognition." After casting the deciding vote against a proposed increase in import duties on raw wool, a proposal naturally opposed by Massachusetts woolen manufacturers who desired cheap raw materials, Sumner felt too unwell to continue in his place. "I have sat in my seat only one day," he reported to Theodore Parker on March 1. "After a short time the torment to my system became great, and a cloud began to gather over my brain. I tottered out and took to my bed."[6]

He decided to go to Europe for his health. Delaying in Washington only long enough to be sworn in on March 4, the beginning of his second Senate term, he sailed from New York three days later. Though he was seasick, his other symptoms began to disappear. By the end of the voyage he could rise from a seat without difficulty, and, aided only by a cane, he walked the decks for hours.

Landing at Le Havre on March 21, Sumner spent the next seven months in an exhausting round of visiting and sight-seeing. The twenty years that had passed since his first trip to Europe had dimmed none of his enthusiasm for historic sights or his admiration for eminent persons. Though some of the friends he had made on his former visit were dead, there were still many who remembered him and who flooded him with calls and invitations. Guizot, Lamartine, Drouyn de Lhuys, Michel Chevalier, Tocqueville, and Turgenev welcomed him in Paris. In London he had barely registered at Maurigy's Hotel, in Regent Street, when Lord Brougham and Lord Chancellor Cranworth called. The Duchess of Sutherland entreated him to make Stafford House his home; her daughter, the Duchess of Argyll, took a fond interest in Sumner's health, and, with her husband, persuaded him to pay a visit to Inverary. Nassau Senior, George Grote, Henry Reeve, Charles Kingsley, William Makepeace Thackeray, and Thomas Babington Macaulay entertained him. He met Lord Palmerston, who "seemed to have the gift of perpetual youth," lunched with Lord John Russell, and dined with William E. Gladstone. He renewed his acquaintance with Richard Cobden and met John Bright for the first time.

During the entire trip Sumner kept up a rigorous schedule of sight-seeing which would have exhausted a man half his age. Despite a cold that persisted for the two months he remained in Paris, he saw everything and everybody in the French capital. On May 24 he went on a tour of the French provinces and visited Orleans, Blois, Chambord, Tours, Angers, Nantes, La Haye, Poitiers, Bordeaux, Bayonne, Toulouse, Lyons, and Dijon—as well as a number of intervening places—in something less than three weeks. Then followed two months of frenzied social life and sight-seeing in London. Returning to the Continent, Sumner then went to Rheims, Strasbourg, Basle, Berne, Lucerne, Turin, the Hospice of St. Bernard, Geneva, Heidelberg, Frankfurt, Cologne, Amsterdam, the Hague, and Brussels, all within a month and without missing one of the starred attractions in his Baedeker. Returning to London for a week in September, during which he had five dinner engagements, Sumner then traveled to Manchester, Leeds, Edinburgh, Glasgow, Aberdeen, and Llandudno before sailing from Liverpool on November 7.

The mere recital of this exhausting peregrination is enough to prove that Sumner, while in Europe, was not severely troubled by the effects of the Brooks assault. Though he occasionally complained that his health was "not yet firm" and that he had "a morbid sensibility of the spinal system," everybody reported that he looked remarkably well. Young Henry James never forgot his disappointment when Sumner turned up in Paris "with wounds by that time rather disappointingly healed," and not even the senator's "visible, measurable, unmistakable greatness" could quite compensate for that defect.

Toward the end of his European tour, however, Sumner's health received a setback, which was of psychological rather than physiological origin. Convinced that he had received "injuries to the brain" during Brooks's assault, he was uncertain about whether he should resume his place in the Senate when the new session of Congress began in December. Instead of asking the advice of any of several distinguished British physicians, he solicited the opinion of George Combe, whose writings on phrenology he had at a much earlier day admired. Combe, who was not a doctor and who was nearly seventy years old, wrote out an account of what he took to be Sumner's symptoms and submitted them to Sir James Clarke, the Queen's physician. Clarke, without making any examination himself—indeed, without even seeing Sumner—gave as his considered judgment: "I have no hesitation in affirming, that, if he returns to mental labor in less than a year from this time he will soon become a permanent invalid, if he does not lose his life." Passing the diagnosis along to the senator, Combe added his personal opinion that Sumner's "brain, although apparently functionally sound, . . . would give way under the pressure of public life in America."[7]

Bearing these medical warnings always in mind, Sumner returned to America torn between conflicting desires. With all his conscious will he wanted to reappear in the Senate and further to expose the villainies of the slavocracy. From the very day after the Brooks assault he had expressed "the constant wish . . . that he might be speedily restored so as to take his seat again in the Senate, from which . . . he had never before been absent for a single day." Compelled to be silent during the 1856 presidential campaign, he vowed on the day of his re-election to the Senate that he would return to Washington and "paint in its true colors, that institution, whose barbarism had with its own peculiar instrument enforced silence upon him." He told Theodore Parker that he expected to deliver an oration "in the Senate which shall tear Slavery open from its chops to its head—from its bully chops down to its coward heel!" "If I ever get back to Washington," he promised Thomas Wentworth Higginson, "the speech that I shall make when I do get there . . . will be to my last speech in the Senate of the United States as first proof brandy to molasses and water."[8]

Perhaps the very frequency and intensity of such statements suggest the inner reluctances that Sumner also felt about returning to the Senate. The more Sumner committed himself to delivering another powerful attack on slavery, the less he could forget the likely consequences. All along he had been convinced that a new attempt would be made against his life. He believed such letters as that signed by "A South Carolina Plug Uglie," who wrote "to say if you value your life not to visit Washington the coming session. . . . You may take the whole of Boston as your body guard but it wont make a damn bit of difference I am willing to sacrifice my life for the honor of my native state." "I suppose I shall be shot," Sumner told Higginson as he talked of going back to his seat. "I don't see what else is left for them to do." Now to these fears the English physicians added another and, in his eyes, even greater danger—one that had never been entirely absent from his thoughts—the likelihood that if he returned to the Senate, it would be "at the peril of his intellect."[9]

When the new session of Congress opened in December 1857, Sumner was able to force himself to attend, but he could not take much interest in politics. The feud between President Buchanan and Senator Douglas over the Kansas question, which threatened to split the Democratic party, attracted only his most cursory attention; like any other invalid, he was concerned chiefly with his own health. He found that listening to the Senate debates jangled his nervous system. After only a few days of attendance he felt "the weight spreading over his brain." He thought that it might help if he kept away from the Senate, though remaining within call if his vote was needed, but still he grew no better.

Tense and worried by his absence from duty during the day, he now spent sleepless nights, for a bladder condition, probably prostatitis, obliged him to rise three or four times during each night. Sumner connected this new affliction—quite incorrectly, and contrary to Dr. Perry's very sound diagnosis—with the injuries produced by Brooks's assault. Here was just one more bit of evidence that the English doctors had been correct, and he began worrying even more about having "paralysis or softening of the brain." "I cannot work with the mind, except in very narrow limits," he wrote the Duchess of Argyll in despair. "To sit in the Senate is exhausting, even though I renounce all special interest in the debate and leave every thing to others. This is hard—very hard. It is hard to be so near complete recovery and still to be kept back."[10]

On December 20 Sumner left Washington, and he remained away during most of the next five months. As soon as he left the "vileness and vulgarity" of the capital, he noted a considerable improvement in his health. To occupy his time he started studying engravings, a large collection of which had just been presented to Harvard College, and his enthusiasm and energy in his new recreation exhausted his friends. "Verily, he goes thoroughly through the work," Longfellow complained. "For my part I cannot take in so much at once." But, guided by Dr. Louis Thies of Harvard, Sumner examined every engraving at the college. Then he studied private collections, first in Boston, then in New York and Philadelphia.

Once Sumner was away from Washington, his interest in public affairs picked up. He longed to show that the continuing "injustice, cruelty and meanness" of Buchanan's Kansas policy was "the natural fruit of slavery—which makes men unjust, cruel and mean." He yearned also to denounce William Walker's filibustering expedition against Nicaragua as a new attempt to spread slavery. He worried fretfully over Southern schemes to seize Cuba. In letter after letter he urged the Duchess of Argyll and his other English friends to have the British government persuade Spain to emancipate the slaves in Cuba, for such an action would end the illegal

American slave trade, stop filibustering in the Caribbean, and "humble forever the whole slave-interest in the United States." When Lord Napier, the British minister in Washington, failed to agree with Sumner, but instead fraternized with the Southern Democrats, Sumner pungently reported his deficiencies to English friends. When Napier was recalled in 1858, the American press gave Sumner the credit.

Every time Sumner had to go to Washington, all his old symptoms returned. In February 1858 Wilson summoned him to the capital for a few days to vote against Buchanan's Army Bill, "giving soldiers to a wicked Government" for use in Kansas, but, though Sumner tried to spend most of his time in the Smithsonian Institution and in the Library of Congress, the strain was too great and he had to return to New York. Brought down again in April, he arrived too late to give his vote for the free-state cause in Kansas, but, during the several days he remained, the tense bitterness of the Senate debates once again affected him. Without warning his old enemy struck. While reading in the stacks of the Library of Congress, he was called to the Senate to cast a vote. Perhaps he rose too quickly or walked too rapidly to the Senate chamber, for the afternoon found him prostrate with exhaustion. For the next three or four days he suffered back ailments and could rise from his chair only with great difficulty. At Wilson's insistence, he again left Washington. "All my plans are clouded," Sumner gloomily wrote Howe. "I had hoped to do something—indeed to strike a blow before this session closed." "Two years gone already! How much more!"

Dr. Wister, whom Sumner consulted again in Philadelphia, found his condition serious and warned that he "must resolutely renounce all idea of doing any thing till next winter." The advice confirmed Sumner's fears. "The English physicians understood my symptoms better than I did," he once more began to think. There must be a "deep-seated disease," the softening of the brain and the paralysis suggested by Sir James Clarke.

"Never before was I so uncertain what to do or where to go," Sumner lamented. He had no faith in his American doctors. Dr. Perry's diagnosis that his symptoms were caused by his "generous diet and little exercise," by his urinary complaint, and by that "depressing passion," fear, which acted "sadly upon the nervous system," seemed shallow to him. Both Dr. Perry and Dr. Wister advised him to go abroad again, but, after all, he had tried that remedy. "Where shall I go? What do?" he desperately queried. "Europe? where in Europe? baths there? water-cure there? extensive travel there? Switzerland and baths there? . . . the Pyrenees, and baths there? . . . Spain? Russia? . . . Where shall I go and what do? I know not, nor can I divine."

When Sumner sailed again for Europe on May 22, 1858, all his friends and most of his enemies were convinced that his senatorial career was closed. People said that his case was hopeless; the fact that, on the train from Washington, he allowed his pocket to be picked of a $2,000 note of Longfellow's suggested that "his mind was somewhat weakened." Shedding hypocritical tears over "Mr. Sumner's physical infirmity," the Boston *Courier* joined the Boston *Herald* in demanding that a senator so incapacitated should resign.

Sumner's appearance at this time justified the most ominous forebodings. He walked only with the greatest difficulty. "When he tried to move forward he was compelled to push one foot slowly and gently forward but a few inches, and then drag the other foot to a level with the first, holding his back at the same time to diminish the pain that he had there." Only after moving about for fifteen minutes or so in this slow and stiff fashion did the pain abate, so that he would walk more easily. More disturbing was the fact that "he could not make use of his brain at all. He could not read a newspaper, could not write a letter. He was in a frightful state as regards the activity of the mind, as every effort there was most painful to him. It seemed to him at times as if his head would burst; there seemed to be some great force within pushing the pieces away from one another."[11]

His physicians did not agree on the causes of these distressing complaints. After some hesitation, Dr. Wister finally concluded that there was "no evidence of organic disease." Sumner suffered, he thought, from "extreme nervous prostration"; "the injuries he originally received on the floor of the Senate had been aggravated by the peculiar condition of his nervous system at the time, a condition induced by severe mental and nervous tension from the loss of sleep for several consecutive nights, also by the peculiar susceptibility of his temperament, which is highly nervous." Dr. Jackson, on the other hand, was certain that Brooks's blows had caused "either congestion, or concussion followed by congestion, or positive inflammation of the brain or its investing membranes" and that Sumner's "brain and spinal cord had been the seat of a grave and formidable lesion." Though not so positive, Dr. Perry also believed "that the base of the brain, as well as the spinal cord, has been the seat of some serious lesion." But, when Sumner was examined in Paris, his physician was emphatic in declaring that he "never had a brain affection" and that he "had no paralysis."

It is difficult to appraise the medical validity of these conflicting statements. Unfortunately Sumner never had a complete neurological examination, for he never consulted Dr. S. Weir Mitchell, of Philadelphia, the one specialist in the United States competent to make such a study. As Sumner's friends refused to permit an autopsy of his brain and spinal cord after his death in 1874, the question of his injuries can never be settled with absolute certainty. Fortunately, however, Sumner kept such elaborate records of his health, his physicians' opinions, and even his medical prescriptions that modern neurologists and brain specialists can agree on the nature of his affliction.

These physicians declare that Sumner's reactions during the first few days after the Brooks assault were precisely what they would expect in a patient who had received a nasty blow on the head.[12] He did not have either a fractured skull or a concussion, for he did not suffer the severe headaches, changes in state of awareness, and somnolence which accompany brain traumas; instead, his condition was feverish and excited. Septicemia developed in his wounds and left him considerably debilitated, perhaps suffering from anemia. The symptoms of which he subsequently complained—pressure on the skull, weakness of the spine, difficulty in walking—could not, from a neurological point of view, possibly have been the results of blows he received on his head or even of a spinal lesion. The urinary condition that caused Sumner so much distress had no medical connection with the Brooks assault. At the same time no physician who has studied the voluminous medical documents in Sumner's case has the least suspicion that Sumner was malingering; his sufferings were intense and genuine.

The diagnosis, then, is that Sumner was not shamming, but that his ailments were not, neurologically, the result of Brooks's beating. Cases of this sort are far from rare in medical history, and modern specialists classify Sumner's illness as "post-traumatic syndrome," in which numerous symptoms without objective causes follow a traumatic experience, such as an accident (physical trauma) in which the patient is not seriously injured. The precise nature of such a post-traumatic syndrome is not entirely clear; most neurologists believe it to be largely psychogenic. Patients suffering from such symptoms have great difficulty in reassuming their obligations to their families, their friends, and their employers.

In Sumner's case it is clear that the Brooks assault produced psychic wounds that lingered long after the physical injuries had disappeared. The pressure he felt on his head was a mental reenactment of the beating. Bearing in mind that the attack occurred in 1856, one is not so puzzled that he felt the weight on his skull to be precisely fifty-six pounds. The pain in his thighs was reminiscent of his tearing up his desk as he sought to rise under Brooks's lashing. It is at least suggestive that the senator who had for years been demanding a political party with "Backbone" should suffer mysterious spinal complaints. All these symptoms occurred chiefly, though not exclusively, when Sumner turned his mind to public affairs or tried to return to his Senate duties. The incredibly unprofessional and unscientific warnings of his English physicians that mental exertion might permanently impair his brain added to his tension on these occasions, as did his strong belief that the Southerners would shoot him. Hitherto Sumner had driven himself with his inflexible will to maintain impossibly high standards, despite overwork and mental strain; now he was faced with rebellion on the part of his body and of an unconscious segment of his mind.

As the ordinary remedies of rest and exercise were ineffectual for a malady of this sort, Sumner did not know what further steps to take for recovery; he was ready for desperate measures. In June 1858 an American merchant residing in Paris suggested that he visit Dr. Charles Edward Brown-Séquard, the French-American physician who was already famed for his pioneer work in the dissection of the spinal cord and for his discovery of the vasomotor nerves. Though Brown-Séquard was not then in general practice, he welcomed a case so interesting and important as Sumner's. "There is," he wrote the senator, "hardly a single human being,— my own family included,—whom I would so heartily rejoice to relieve from pain or disease, as Mr. Charles Sumner."

On June 10 Brown-Séquard gave Sumner a three-hour examination. After noting his more obvious symptoms, the doctor tested the sensitivity of Sumner's spine, first with ice, then with boiling water, and finally with an esthesiometer, and he repeated his experiments again and again to ascertain the precise range of the disease in the spine and the neck. He found two "exquisitely tender" spots on the spine, one "situated at the junction of the cervical and dorsal regions, the other at that of the dorsal and lumbar." The brain itself he declared "free of any serious remaining injury," though there was still "an effusion of liquid about the brain and . . . a slight degree of congestion, chiefly if not only confined to the membrane around the brain."

Sumner had instant and complete faith in this "most careful, skilful, learned and devoted physician," whose every word was reinforced by his worldwide reputation. He felt enormously relieved to be assured, by such an authority, that his brain was unaffected. He could easily accept Brown-Séquard's explanation in simple, everyday language, of the symptoms from which he suffered. His back ailments, the doctor told him, were "the effect of what is called *contre-coup*. Mr. Sumner being seated and inclined over his desk at the time of the assault, the blows on his head took effect by *counter-stroke*, or communicated shock in the spine." "It is the nature of this disease," he added, "that, when the blow is struck upon the head, especially when the person struck is in a sitting posture, that the shock follows the spinal column until it reaches what is termed the point of resistance. Here the shock stops, and at this point there arises the germ of future trouble." It was, Brown-Séquard explained, just like trying to drive a nail into very hard wood; the blow of the hammer bent not the head of the nail, but the weakest spots in its shaft. So, the thick bones of the skull had protected Sumner's brain, but the shock had injured the spine at the two points that were now so sensitive. The upper irritation was "the cause of the whole mischief as regards the function of the brain"; the lower "caused the pain which gave the appearance of paralysis" in the legs.

Having diagnosed the case, Brown-Séquard proposed a cure. "Fire" was his remedy. If he applied counter-irritants to the two sprains, these would "produce the absorption of the excess of fluid effused about the brain, and diminish the congestion of the membranes of this organ," and would thus lessen "the degree of pain, if not altogether render the sensibility normal, so as to allow walking and other movements to take place without pain." The most effective counter-irritant, Brown-Séquard told his patient, was the moxa, a treatment of Japanese origin, in which the naked skin was burned with inflamed agaric (*amadou*), cotton wool, or some other very combustible substance. The medical records do not show which form of moxa Brown-Séquard favored, but the standard one in use at the time was formed of "cotton, rendered downy by carding, and made into a roll an inch long, and from half an inch to two inches in diameter." The treatment, Brown-Séquard warned, would be most painful, but without it Sumner must remain "a permanent invalid, always subject to a sudden and serious relapse."

Brown-Séquard's "examination and report gave me such confidence," Sumner wrote Howe, "that I put myself at once in his hands." He asked the doctor when he could apply the first moxa.

"To-morrow, if you please," said Brown-Séquard.

"Why not this afternoon?" countered Sumner eagerly.

The doctor prepared to give his patient chloroform to ease the pain. Sumner objected: "If you say positively that I shall derive as much benefit if I take chloroform as if I do not, then of course I will take it, but if there is to be any degree whatever of amelioration in case I do not take it, then I shall not take it." Believing that the greater Sumner's pain, the better his chance of recovery, Brown-Séquard did not give him the anesthetic, but burned the moxa on his bare back.

During the next thirteen days Brown-Séquard gave Sumner the moxa treatment five additional times, each time without anesthetic. "I have never seen a man bearing with such fortitude as Mr. Sumner has shown, the extremely violent pain of this kind of burning," he declared at the time, and many years later he still felt that he had submitted Sumner "to the martyrdom of the greatest suffering that can be inflicted on mortal man." Sumner bore the pain stoically. "The torment is considerable," he wrote Howe, in marked understatement, "but that is over in 5 or 10 minutes. But then come the annoyances and inflammations which . . . are incident to burns. Of course, I walk with pain; lie down with pain, rise with pain."

After six moxae Brown-Séquard gave his patient a two month

respite from burning, but, in the ninety-degree heat of Paris, Sumner got little benefit from the rest. The six open suppurating wounds resulting from his burns kept him in torment. "For 5 weeks," he lamented, "I have not been able to lie on my back or to turn over in my bed." He began complaining that the fire had driven his pain into one of his legs, which was "sadly disabled."

On July 20 the meaning of that last symptom appeared. In the middle of the night "neuralgic, constringing and oppressing" pain in his chest woke him up. He could neither lie down nor stand up. Finally he managed to prop himself up with cushions in a chair, so as to get a little relief. Alone in his hotel, unattended except by servants, he had to wait in this position from four o'clock in the morning until six in the evening, when Brown-Séquard arrived. Finding the pain "almost without precedent," the doctor attributed it to "the original concussion" of the Brooks assault and rather proudly decided that Sumner's case was "one of the most interesting in the history of science." Giving Sumner opiates for immediate relief, he prescribed belladonna and decided to postpone indefinitely further moxa treatments.

Sumner was apparently entirely satisfied with Brown-Séquard. If he had any doubts about his treatment, they were dispelled when George Hayward, a Boston physician then practicing in Paris, not only endorsed it, but reported that four of "the most eminent medical authorities in England," Sir Benjamin Brody, Sir James Clarke, Sir Henry Holland, and Dr. Lawrence, also approved it. Many of Sumner's American friends, however, were very dubious about Brown-Séquard and his remedies. Dr. Perry was sure that "a life of perfect repose would be more beneficial . . . than the application of hot irons." Howe, who was a doctor himself, thought that his friend had fallen into hands of quacks who were "certainly tormenting and injuring him, in the pursuit of a baseless theory."

From a medical point of view, Brown-Séquard's critics were entirely correct. His neurological examination of Sumner had been wholly inadequate, and his diagnosis of spinal sprains brought about by *contre-coups* was medical nonsense. The moxa treatment was, therapeutically, no treatment at all; it was merely a terribly painful experience. Application of moxae could no more give permanent benefit to a brain or spine injury than could a strong liniment. Brown-Séquard's theory that the constrictive pressure in Sumner's chest was somehow an extension of the spinal injury "through the avenue of the nearest network of veins . . . from the spinal column to the heart" is anatomically ridiculous. In fact, Sumner had his first attack of angina pectoris, perhaps brought on by—though not caused by—the shock and discomfort of the moxa treatment; Brown-Séquard quite properly prescribed belladonna for it.

If from a physiological point of view Brown-Séquard's treatment—which, it must be remembered, was in keeping with the most advanced medical thought of the time—was worse than worthless, it is possible that it benefited Sumner in other ways. His sufferings, which were widely publicized in American newspapers, gave the lie, once and for all, to charges that he was shamming; moreover, the same very real and demonstrable pain freed Sumner himself from his worried sense of guilt at being absent from his post of duty. He even gained some psychic income from his torture. While his back was being burned, he allowed his mind to wander, and he "thought sometimes of St. Lawrence on the gridiron—sometimes of Prometheus with the vulture at his liver, and also of many others in the list of fire-sufferers." Identifying himself with the martyrs of the past, he erased any unconscious doubts about the correctness of his course; never again in the future would he feel lost without the unstinted approbation of his peers. Having, as Prescott observed, enjoyed "quite contrary to usage—the crown of martyrdom during his own lifetime," Sumner came to be, even in his own eyes, less a fallible human being than a symbol of a righteous cause. He found it easy to suppress any expression of resentment against Preston Brooks, who, in this new mood, seemed only "the unconscious agent of a malign power." Not even the death of the South Carolina congressman of an agonizing disease in March 1857 evoked a bitter word from Sumner. "The Almighty has settled this," he told a friend, "better than you or I could have done."

Secure in his faith that his and the Almighty's ways were identical, Sumner began to mend. Gradually the sores on his back healed, and he could ride comfortably in a carriage. His "neuralgia," as Brown-Séquard persisted in calling his angina pectoris, was an ever present danger; on a little excursion to St. Germain in August he suffered "those terrible pains" in his chest four times. Still he could now receive callers, make occasional visits, and listen to lectures. At the end of the summer he went to Aix-en-Savoie to try the famous mineral baths. After his experience with Brown-Séquard, he found the treatment of hot and cold douches a positive luxury. The regimen palled after about a month, and he "rushed through Switzerland," visited Milan, Verona, Padua, and Venice all too briefly, and then came north by way of Vienna, Prague, Dresden, and Berlin. "All my time," he explained, "has been devoted simply to regaining my lost health."

Notes

1 *Cong. Globe*, 34 Cong., 1 Sess., Appendix, 625. Cf. *ibid.*, 806.

2 Boston *Courier*, June 21, 1856; Boston *Post*, Aug. 21, 1856; Washington *Union*, and Philadelphia *News*, quoted in *The Liberator*, XXVI (July 25, 1856), 118, and XXVI (Nov. 28, 1856), 189.

3 Sumner to Mrs. Hamilton Fish, Sept. 27, 1856, Fish MSS.

4 New York *Atlas*, quoted in *The Liberator*, XXVIII (July 2, 1858), p. 105.

5 In the following discussion of Sumner's medical problems, I have been fortunate to secure the advice of two leading specialists, Dr. Bronson S. Ray, of the Cornell Medical Center, and Dr. Julia L. Schneider, of the Neurological Institute of New York. Giving generously of their time, both Dr. Ray and Dr. Schneider read through a 30-page memorandum I had prepared, listing in objective fashion Sumner's symptoms and the treatments prescribed for them. The judgments of these two eminent specialists, made quite independently and without any consultation between themselves, coincided at every point.

6 W. B. Spooner to Sumner, Feb. 24, 1857, Sumner MSS.

7 Sumner to Bird, Sept. 11, 1857, Bird MSS.

8 Harvey Lindsly to Wilson, Sept. 22, 1856, Sumner MSS.

9 Adams, Diary, Nov. 20, 1857, Adams MSS.

10 M. S. Perry to Sumner, Dec. 10, and 18, 1857, Sumner MSS.

11 Dr. Charles Edward Brown-Séquard, in New York *Tribune*, Mar. 18, 1874.

12 Sumner's remarkably complete medical record includes diagnoses by Drs. Boyle, Wister, Lindsly, Jackson, Perry, Brown-Séquard, and George Hayward; prescriptions and medical instructions given Sumner by Brown-Séquard, Hayward, Perry, and Jackson; and elaborate day-by-day accounts of Sumner's appearance and symptoms by Sumner himself, by interested friends, and by political and personal opponents.

6

THADDEUS STEVENS

CARL SANDBURG, IN HIS *Abraham Lincoln, The War Years*, DE-scribes Thaddeus Stevens thusly: "Scholar, wit, zealot of liberty, part fanatic, part gambler, at his worst a clubfooted wrangler possessed of endless javelins, at his best a majestic and isolated figure wandering in an ancient wilderness thick with thorns, seeking to bring justice between man and man—who could read the heart of limping, poker-faced old Thaddeus Stevens?"

In her biography of Stevens, Fawn M. Brodie attempts to do just that. Thaddeus Stevens, congressman from Lancaster, Pennsylvania, father of the Fourteenth Amendment, staunch abolitionist, fighter for Negro suffrage and schooling, one of the main prosecutors in the impeachment trial of Andrew Johnson, and chief architect of Reconstruction after the Civil War, is still perhaps the most controversial figure in American history. For the Southern white man, he is considered a malevolent Caliban who has left for himself an immortality of hate and infamy. But for every white Southerner who detested Stevens, there was the counterpart of a Northern white man who looked to him as a great champion of freedom and democracy. As for the Negro, he was considered a hero second only to Lincoln.

Mrs. Brodie's biography suggests what may have been the basis of Stevens' extraordinary capacity for hatred, which was an energyzing force for good as well as evil. His radicalism was an outgrowth of his own desperate inner needs. While Sumner's favorite quotation was King Lear's "Nothing will come of nothing," Stevens' favorite line was from Alexander Pope's *Essay on Man*, "A being darkly wise and rudely great," which may well characterize the man and give a clue to his inner torments.

Stevens' reputation remains many-sided, writes Mrs. Brodie, "partly because his character and history were full of paradoxes and contradictions. He was a humanitarian lacking in humanity; a man of boundless charities and vindictive hates; a Calvinist convinced that all men are vile who nevertheless cherished a vision of the Promised Land where all men should be equal before the law; a revolutionary who would carve up the estates of the 'bloated aristocrats' of the South, but in the same breath offered to defend Jefferson Davis in his trial for treason. He was an equalitarian who would pinion the Southerner for his racial bigotry and caste prejudices, but who for twenty years would live with a colored woman as his mistress, apparently content with a relationship common in the Southern aristocracy, and one that Northern abolitionists generally pointed to with horror."[1]

How to account for such spectacular pendular ambivalences? Thaddeus, the second of four sons, born with a clubfoot like his brother before him, first saw the light of day on April 4, 1792, on an impoverished Vermont farm. His father, an unsuccessful farmer and part-time shoemaker, surveyor and wrestler, sought escape in liquor and flight. He twice abandoned his family, the second time disappearing altogether when Thaddeus was a young adolescent. The desertion left an ineradicable scar on the boy's psyche. "Whether in later life it was the defection of friends from his political party, or the desertion of Southern states from the Union, he responded with explosive protest and a sense of acute, personal betrayal."[2] The implacable, aggressive hatred that marked Stevens' entire life in all probability stemmed from the corroding hostility of his childhood and hatred of his father.

---

1 Brodie, Fawn M. *Thaddeus Stevens. Scourge of the South.* New York: W. W. Norton & Co., 1959, p. 20.

2 *Ibid.*, p. 24.

He most likely overcompensated for this hatred through his love for his mother. Sarah Morrill Stevens, "a woman of great energy, strong will, and deep piety," taught her sons to endure failure, to fight it and eventually overpower it. Stevens considered his mother an extraordinary woman, for whom he had an abiding and deep affection. It is perhaps significant that Stevens never married, although he had, some thought, the deserved reputation of a rake.

As if abandonment and the inflexible and severe Calvinist tradition in which he was raised were not enough, the boy had to live with the prevailing superstition that the clubfoot was a mark of the Devil and to endure, as well, the torment and cruelty of his peers. Like many cripples, Stevens tried desperately to compensate for his twisted foot: he became an expert swimmer, horseman and weightlifter. He identified with other crippled people, helping handicapped youngsters generously. "A lame man is a minority of one wherever he walks, and there was in fact, no persecuted minority in America for whom Stevens did not at some time speak out. Over and over again in his speeches the words 'branded' and 'marked' crop up like specters that will not be exorcised."[3]

Another compensatory mechanism used by Stevens was a shrewd wit and verbal skill. These he developed at Dartmouth College into formidable weapons of defense and attack. Brodie cites one other physical difficulty which Stevens experienced and which made him even more defensive and tormented. At the age of thirty-nine, an apparent attack of typhoid fever left him completely bald. His obvious wig soon became the object of ridicule, and combined with his saturnine, forbidding and dour face, with its piercing, hooded eyes, all conjured up for his many enemies the appellations, "Robespierre" and "Caliban."

In the following pages, Mrs. Brodie describes the role of father surrogate Stevens played to his brother's sons and suggests some of the causes which prompted the congressman to behave so reprehensibly to members of his own family while behaving so generously to friends and strangers.

---

3 *Ibid.,* p. 26.

The Tyrant Father

FAWN M. BRODIE

When you have passed through the romantic period of your existence, and found your warm sympathies and ardent hopes all chilled or blasted; and the milk of human kindness which flows in your breast is in danger of being curdled by the cold ingratitude of those upon whom you have continually bestowed nothing but benefactions, you will learn to appreciate the truth of the remark "that he is a happy man who has one true friend; but he is more truly happy who never has need of a friend."

Thaddeus Stevens

THIS BITTER note, unsigned and undated, was preserved among Thaddeus Stevens' papers in the Library of Congress. He did not destroy it, as he did many letters and documents before his death; it is written in his characteristic impatient and almost indecipherable scrawl—a handwriting so confused and tortuous that one cannot but wonder if it betrayed contempt for his correspondents or a deep-seated fear of discovery. The note is melancholy enough in itself, but coming from the pen of a man who kept no diary, and who wrote letters that were usually remarkably free of self-revelation, it is poignant evidence of his continuing loneliness.

Stevens seems to have kept a barrier always between himself and his friends. Even his law students, his stoutest defenders, stood somewhat in awe of him long after they left his office. He had always attracted students, and when after 1842 he temporarily abandoned politics and concentrated on his law practice in order to reduce his debts, they swarmed to him. He had the best law library in the region and a distinguished collection of books on politics and history, all of which he loaned freely. Before long his office became the acknowledged "law school" of southern Pennsylvania. To a new student, asking the cost of reading with him, Stevens would reply: "Two hundred dollars. Some pay; some don't." The fact was, as one student observed later, "there were . . . two recommendations which never failed to procure an entrance into his office: ambition to learn, and inability to pay for the privilege."

His students, several of whom became Congressmen, repaid him with admiration and devotion that continued until his death. One of them, Alexander H. Hood, later wrote a warm and sympathetic biography. This was an important counterweight to the vitriolic memoir published by Alexander Harris, a Lancaster historian who detested Stevens. Harris, it was said, met Stevens on a narrow path one day and refused to give him the space to pass, saying, "I never stand aside for a skunk." Stevens hesitated, then bowed and stepped to one side, replying with gravity, "I always do."

Stevens became especially fond of one student, Simon Stevens, who, though not a relative, he came to treat almost like a son. The letters from Simon Stevens which have been preserved show an enduring friendship. "Can't you go to Vermont this summer when I go in June," Simon wrote to him on April 25, 1865. "Come what do you say? . . . You are uncle to us all." Thaddeus Stevens helped him financially, made him a law partner, took a paternal interest in his wife and son—who was named Thaddeus in his honor—and remembered him in his will.

During the Civil War, Simon became embroiled in some unsavory ammunition deals, and was accused on the floor of Congress of purchasing defective guns already rejected by the U.S. Army, and of selling them, after retooling, to the Army of the West for an exhorbitant profit. Thaddeus Stevens, obviously pained by the scandal, pointed out in Congress that Simon Stevens was not his kin but a former law student. He defended his character with slight mockery as being "as unimpeachable as anyone in his law office," and got the expected laugh from the House in reply. But he did not gloss over the charges. "It was a speculation which may not be very pleasant to look at," he said, "but it was a legitimate business transaction, and involves no officer of the Government."

When accused by one Congressman of taking "good care of his bantling," Stevens replied brusquely: "I take care of nobody; I do not care much for anybody." It was a characteristic denial and retreat. However deeply committed, he could not admit his affections. But Simon Stevens' reputation, at least in the Lancaster area, remained somewhat unsavory, and it is quite possible that he was one of many whose "cold ingratitude" chilled Stevens into ever deeper moroseness and pessimism.

Thaddeus Stevens saw little of his brothers, but he sent them money and befriended their children. His niece, Lizzie Stevens, who lived in Indianapolis, was a lively, warmhearted girl who sent him affectionate letters. But she died in 1867 before reaching the age of twenty. Her brother, Thaddeus, who became a physician, seems to have visited his uncle seldom. The other two nephews, however, came to live with him in Lancaster after the death of their father, Abner Stevens, in Vermont in 1847.

With these youths, Alanson and Thaddeus, Stevens was demanding and uncompromising in a fashion that did not carry over to his students. From his own kin he expected much, and though he acquired these substitute sons late in life, he was feverishly intent on seeing them become successful men. Thaddeus Jr.—as he was called to distinguish him from his uncle—after graduating from an academy in Pennsylvania, was sent in 1854 to the University of Vermont, where it was expected that he would be under the supervision of his aged grandmother, Sally Stevens. His academic record in Pennsylvania had been bad, and Stevens wrote him a stern letter which revealed both his ambitions for the boy and his apprehensions:

. . . Mere meditating should not be your ambition. Be first in your class. You can if you will. It will take intense application, but the prize is worth all the toil. . . .

Knowledge cannot be had per order when you want to use it, as you can order dinner at a restaurant. Not only your classic, but general information should be mastered. History, biography, the whole circle of knowledge should be traversed while in college.

I fear indolence is your besetting sin for sin it is. But now in the midst of stimulants to effort, I trust you will raise your energies, and do honor to yourself. You need not partake of your grandmother's fear that you will be injured either in body or mind by close study. I have never known such a case.

Let strict morality guide all your actions, or your acquirements will be a curse. *Never* taste intoxicating drink—a little is folly—much is crime.

This is a fascinating letter on many counts, not the least of which is the suggestion of a troubled relationship between Thaddeus Stevens and his mother. When he wrote: *You need not partake of your grandmother's fear that you will be injured either in body or mind by close study,* could he have been indicating that she, who had given so many years of toil to provide for his education, was now bitter because this schooling, instead of producing an upright minister, had resulted instead in a lawyer-politician slandered by charges of fornication and atheism? It was said that he visited her almost annually. Still she would write begging him to visit her instead of going "to them Hote Springs." She did not go south to visit him, and it may have been that her resentment, such as it was, stemmed rather from the feeling that her most promising son, like her husband, had abandoned her.

Thaddeus Stevens Jr. failed at the University of Vermont, and was expelled four times from Dartmouth College. One of his penitent letters has been preserved in the Library of Congress. Significantly enough, it was addressed to "Mrs. Smith," and not his uncle. ". . . I have been here nearly 3 months and Mr. Carpenter the man with whom I have been studying has expressed his willingness to give me testimonials of good behaviour at any time. He even offered to write to the faculty of the college and try and get me back at the commencement of the spring term but I told him that I thought it would be of no avail. . . . I will go to Peachem and fix my things there and try and be there when Uncle arrives let him know how all my affairs stand he knows the worst part of them. . . ."

The letters Stevens wrote to his nephew in college show a growing exasperation. "I fear also you love rum and sometimes drink it," he wrote. "If so, the sooner you are abandoned the better, as there is no hope for one who ever tastes strong drink." Later he wrote an angry ultimatum:

I have read your letter with pain. It is grievous to lose your near relatives by death. But it is still more painful to see them disgraced and worthless men.

I foresaw that your indolence and habits would lead you to ruin unless reformed. It seems that instead of reforming, you have continued them, and they have produced the natural result . . .

I must say that until you have redeemed yourself from disgrace, I have no desire ever to see you.

Yet Stevens softened when Thaddeus Jr. within a month left college and came back to Lancaster to throw himself upon his uncle's mercy. He took him into his office as a law student, and the two seem to have worked out an uneasy truce. Thaddeus Jr. became a lawyer and helped his uncle in the management of the Caledonia Ironworks. Stevens had him appointed Assistant Clerk of the House for a time, which brought down upon him the charge of nepotism.

Still their relationship continued to be subtly poisoned. This became clear after Stevens' death with the publication of the provisions of his will. He made it specific that Thaddeus Jr. would inherit his estate only if he "abstained from all intoxicating drinks." He was to be given $800 a year for five years, and if during that time he remained a teetotaler he would inherit one fourth of the estate. At the end of a second five years without liquor he was to be given another fourth. After a third five-year period he would inherit the remainder. If, however, he went back to his rum, the estate was to be used for the endowment of an orphanage.

Then Pennsylvania Supreme Court opinion on the will said pointedly: "It is clear that he did not intend that his estate should go to his heirs as such." Whether out of contempt for his uncle, or because as a real alcoholic he was incapable of living up to the stipulated pledge we do not know, but Thaddeus Jr. had no part of his uncle's property. When he died on June 1, 1874, only six years after the elder Stevens, he had received nothing.

Stevens seems to have found it impossible to disentangle the uses of money from the uses of affection. He gave money lavishly to utter strangers and went on his way fortified by their surprise and gratitude. To his nephew he could not give without exacting something in return. But using his purse as a weapon resulted only in alienation and failure. Still he could not cease manipulating the youth's life, and trying to make his decisions for him.

When his second adopted nephew, Alanson, was killed in the Civil War, he took measures at once to bring Thaddeus Jr. home from the battle front and had him made provost-marshal in Lancaster, well out of reach of Confederate guns. Like so many well-meaning parents he would save the life but relentlessly punish the spirit.

In his early years Thaddeus Stevens had been a convivial drinker and had belonged to a club where the members drank regularly when they met to play cards. Late one night a member of the club, a bank cashier, left the party very drunk and died shortly after reaching home. Stevens, it was said, was so shocked he went down into his cellar, carried up his wine and whisky barrels and demolished them with a hatchet in the middle of the street. The sight of so much liquor running down the cobblestones made a great impression on the townspeople, who seem also to have heard the thunderbolt.

From this moment forward, according to local legend, he refused to touch alcohol altogether. Like so many of his antislavery friends, he formally joined the temperance movement which had mushroomed in the late 1830's, and for a time worked for anti-liquor legislation in Pennsylvania. But unlike many temperance crusaders, he was a practical politician, and soon became disillusioned with the whole notion of legislating against liquor. "I should be glad if legislation would cure intemperance," he said in Congress in 1864, "but I have seen it tried, and tried in vain. . . . When I was a young man, and I would not object to being so again, I was in a State Legislature, and moved that the sale of liquor should be prohibited in my district, and the motion was carried. I did not find that I thereby made one drunkard the less—they would only drink the more when they had a chance."

Stevens eventually owned a brewery and a tavern. In a genial debate on liquor taxes in Congress he defended the beer-drinkers of Pennsylvania as honest and industrious, though admitting that the effects of his own lager beer were "sometimes eccentric and amusing." Mindful of his beer-loving German constituents, Stevens argued to keep the liquor taxes low. "The gentleman from Maine," he said, "says he wants the wages of sin to be as high as possible.

I want them to be low. I think the bill makes the price of sin as high as it ought to be. . . . Now, how high does the gentleman suppose the price of sin ought to be?"

Congressman Rice answered him adroitly: "If the gentleman is a better judge upon that subject than I am—"

Whereupon Stevens neatly interrupted; "Well, sir, the gentleman places it higher than I do." And he urged the end of the debate. "I think our thirsty friend had better *dry* up upon this subject. This is not a law to prohibit the sale of liquor or to correct the morals of the country. We should never attempt that in Congress."

Urbane and realistic though he may have sounded here, Thaddeus Stevens clearly had a different set of rules for his nephews and himself. True to the logic if not the theology of his Calvinist upbringing, he demanded from himself and those he loved behavior becoming to the Lord's élite, and counted the rest of the world beyond saving in any case. His renunciation of alcohol was real, and lasted nearly to the end of his life, when under doctor's orders he began to drink small quantities of brandy and wine as a stimulant for his failing heart. His years of self-denial apparently gave him a bitter pleasure, and filled a deeper need than the best Bourbon or Madeira. Unhappily and futilely he chose to exact from his nephew the same kind of self-denial. It is even possible that the smoldering memories of his father's drunkenness were at work here, and in humiliating his nephew he was unwittingly working off an ancient hate.

Stevens' relations with his nephew Alanson were no less uneasy than with Thaddeus Jr., and at the end took on the coloring of tragedy. For a time Alanson read law with his uncle, but soon gave it up and went to work as a clerk in the Caledonia Iron Works. Soon the foreman, John Sweeney, brought Stevens word that his nephew had "taken up housekeeping" with a fourteen-year-old girl, Mary Jane Primm. In describing this occasion years later Sweeney said: "Mr. Stevens said it was very bad behavior on the place; that was all that was said on the subject, and Mr. Stevens remarked as we parted, 'Charge him with whatever he gets.' "

Mary Primm in 1859 bore Alanson a son who died at the age of nine weeks. There was no public funeral for a child born out of wedlock; the neighbors simply stood at their windows to watch the parents weeping together on the way to the graveyard. Mary Primm, suing later to collect money from Alanson's inheritance, insisted that she had been married to him in Harrisburg. The couple did in fact go to Harrisburg on April 19, 1861, a few weeks before their second child, Alanson Jane, was born. When they returned, Alanson said to Jacob Tuckey in Caledonia: "Now we are married, and it's nobody's damn business." But it is clear from the court records and several letters that actually there had been nothing in Harrisburg but a generous exchange of promises.

Mary Primm could never produce a marriage certificate to make good her claim as Alanson's widow, although she maintained stoutly that it had been burned by the rebels during the raid on Caledonia. Many of her old neighbors testified that she had never been known as anything but Mary Primm. One witness, Mary Rea, stated in court that Mary Primm had told her Alanson had promised to marry her when he came back from the war. "She told me if Alanson would marry her the old gentleman would disinherit him—meaning Thaddeus Stevens."

So Stevens emerges again in the role of a harsh and uncharitable father. He wrote a letter to Alanson at the battle front May 22, 1863, which said in part:

... I am glad you remained well. I could wish you were safely back. . . . I think when you come we'll have to take the management of the works. . . . I must say to you . . . you are bestowing the money you send here on a very worthless, dissolute woman—Stage, hack drivers and others speak freely of it—

This is all I intend to say as I have made no inquiry into the subject.

> Y uncle
> Thaddeus Stevens

The cruelty of this letter is easy to see. Stevens was not only repudiating Alanson's mistress—while clinging to his own—but also by implication repudiating their illegitimate child. And he was bargaining again with his purse, saying in effect: "Give up this dissolute woman and her child and you may be manager of Caledonia."

When Alanson received this, and other apparently more detailed letters from neighbors, he wrote a tortured letter to Mary Primm accusing her of entertaining "persons of very low caracter" and neglecting their daughter, Jennie. She replied angrily:

. . . Lance I think you must of been drunk when you wrote this letter for I dont think you could meane it after living with me one year and knowing me as long as you have. . . .

Yours truely untill death

M J P

Shortly after their bitter exchange, the youth was killed in the Battle of Chickamauga. Mary Primm, now eighteen, was left with the two-year-old Jennie and no claim to honorable widowhood save a slip of paper signed by Alanson Stevens which said: "I hereby acknowledge Mary Primm to be my lawful wife, as I go forth to battle." She took the paper to the foreman, John Sweeney, and begged him to help her obtain a pension as Alanson's widow.

"She showed me a paper and asked me what I thought of it," Sweeney said at the trial. "I just laughed and treated it as a joke. She made no claim to be his wife." Nevertheless Sweeney admitted signing affidavits to help her obtain the pension. However, with her extraordinary incapacity for holding on to the last shreds of respectability, Mary Primm lost even this evidence.

She continued to insist that she was Alanson's legal widow, and used the title in 1866 when trying to enter Jennie in school. When the school superintendent asked Thaddeus Stevens about the relationship, he coldly disavowed her. Lydia Smith, distressed over the child's plight, wrote a delicate letter to Thaddeus Jr.: "Mary Primm has been applying to this district," she said, ". . . to get her child in representing herself the widow of Alanson Stevens and Mr. Burrowes inquired of your uncel about it and he told them that thair was no such widow. Mr. Stevens have you seen the child . . ."

But young Thaddeus, too, hardened his heart against the girl. Alanson had inherited $2,400 from his father, which Mary Primm tried to collect. It was in the form of a promissory note, made payable on demand, and signed by Thaddeus Stevens, who had invested the money for his nephew. When Mary Primm learned that the note had been found among Alanson's possessions, she went to Thaddeus Stevens in Lancaster and begged the money on behalf of her child. Later she testified in court "that Thad Stevens told her his nephew Thaddeus had the note and she would have to look to him for it. But that he would do all he could; that he meant he would do right by me; that he would try and see that young Thaddeus would do right by me; that it was out of his hands entirely."

When, however, she approached Thaddeus Jr., he refused to give it to her. The note remained among his papers, mute reminder of a formidable unkindness. Young Thaddeus could not bring himself to collect on the note for his own pocket, and old Thaddeus retained an uncomfortable memory of the whole matter. According to Simon Stevens, he mentioned the note shortly before his death, expressing surprise that it had never been presented for payment because Alanson had left a widow and child. "Simon," he said, "you know all about this note; that I hold the money in a fiduciary capacity, and if it is ever presented you can explain that it must be paid to the legal holder."

The girl Jennie died at the age of eleven, and Mary Primm drifted from one man to another. In 1894, twenty years after Thaddeus Jr.'s death, the note was found by Simon Stevens, and on behalf of Mary Primm, then Mrs. Clason, he tried to collect the money from the Thaddeus Stevens estate. The suit was lost, not because the court decided against the legality of the claim, but simply because according to the statute of limitations the note had been permitted to expire.

So ends the story. No one of the characters emerges untarnished, least of all Thaddeus Stevens, whose role as the tyrant parent was ugly from the beginning.

7

ULYSSES S. GRANT

ULYSSES S. GRANT'S PERSONALITY WAS SO FULL OF NEGATIVE ELEMENTS that it is difficult to understand how he ever achieved the rank of general and the position of President of the United States on merit. Dumb luck and presence in the right place at the right time seem to account for his rise more than any other factor, according to one school of thought, while others believe he was the child of genius.

Jesse Grant, Ulysses' father, a tanner by trade, has been characterized as a compulsive talker, aggressive, eccentric, amiable and boastful. He had an eager, inquisitive mind but was disputatious and opinionated. He was extremely affectionate toward his boy, indulging in much fulsome, fatuous praise about him to his tittering neighbors. Ulysses' mother, on the other hand, was a silent, retiring, even-tempered, pious and unselfish woman, but toward her son was unaffectionate and apparently unperturbed by the ridicule to which he was subjected and its effect on him.

It is hard to tell whether the boy became the victim and prey of neighboring children because of his father's unabashed and fantasied boastings or because of his own colorless, negative personality. Probably both contributed to the torment, ridicule and hateful ribaldry to which he was subjected. Ulysses was soon rechristened

"Useless." He became the butt of jokes, reacting to them with stolid silence. Compensation was effected by conforming to his parents' wishes, by hard work and by mastery over horses. Another defense mechanism he incorporated was flight: he took long, solitary trips as a boy through much of Ohio and Kentucky. Later on, as a young adult, separated from his family and hopeless of the future, he was to turn to drink to escape his hardships and the depressing evidences of failure on all sides. Up to and through his teens, Grant gave the impression of stupidity and mediocrity, but his perseverance, at least, in completing four years at West Point is a manifestation of a mind at work, and not quite as slothful and dull as the outward evidence would have us believe.

Undoubtedly the mechanism most frequently and successfully used by Grant was repression. The hurt boy became the hurt man. Even during his presidency he was comparatively friendless, remaining ill-at-ease at social affairs, reticent but given to tedious, detailed monologues to his coterie. It was only in his wife's understanding presence that he was entirely at ease. Towards his children, too, he was affectionate. But the restrictive, inward mask he acquired as a child was the pose he presented to the public.

As Hesseltine, the author of the following chapter writes, "To look into the years of Grant's failure for an explanation of his successes seems quite futile. His repressed boyhood, his lackadaisical acquisition of the rudiments of an education at West Point, his inconspicuous years in the army, and his succeeding seven years of failure apparently contributed nothing which could account for his achievements. By those years his personality was moulded into one adapted to a life of failure. At the end of the war, as at the beginning, Grant was timid, silent and shy. These, however, were now but the superficial aspects of his personality. In the fires of war he developed aggressiveness, a willingness to take responsibility, clear judgment, and an obstinate will. These were qualities which, in time of peace, he had never tried. Whatsoever of genius shone in Grant's character was a composite of these new qualities. Good fortune placed him where he could opportunely use his abilities." [1]

---

1 Hesseltine, William B. *Ulysses S. Grant: Politician.* New York: Frederick Ungar Publishing Co., 1957, pp. 19–20.

Forty Years of Failure

WILLIAM B. HESSELTINE

THE STORY of the first forty years of Ulysses S. Grant's life is one of dismal failure. Thereafter, the story is one of sudden success, of numerous rewards, and of unexpected honors. However, the forty years of adversity had no uses. They did not give rise to the twenty succeeding years of accomplishment, nor did they serve as an adequate preparation for glory. These two periods—Grant's entire career—were so neatly severed from each other by the Civil War that they might easily have been the careers of two separate individuals. Except for a few idiosyncrasies of manner and habit which Grant the general and Grant the President shared with the ante-bellum Grant, the careers were practically without connection. Had it not been for an occasional ghost of the first, rising to haunt the second, even Grant himself might have forgotten his first four decades of futile existence.

A life thus segmented could have been possible only to a man whose personality was essentially colorless. Strong personalities, possessions of men who roughhew their own destinies, seldom conform to the rules in the copybooks. Their success or failure is absolute and final. In achieving it, they mould themselves. Only a plastic person, following purblindly conventional axioms of his day, could experience both failure and success. Only a person devoid of dramatic characteristics, of dynamic force, and of any definite direction could emerge so calmly from years of adversity and as inertly proceed to years of success. The negative elements in Grant's nature very positively conditioned his career. Ambition was foreign to his makeup. He evinced no desire to hold political office or to rise beyond his appointments. Once having tasted sweets, however, he clung to them with stubborn tenacity. Essentially, Grant's was a submerged personality—an unimaginative, albeit sensitive soul

193

which shrank from contacts with the world, and hid its sensitiveness under an impervious and taciturn shell.

To a large extent this suppressed personality was a result of parental influences. Unfortunate in his parents, neither of whom possessed characteristics which he cared to imitate, Grant inherited no abilities toward adjustment in the world from either his verbose, aggressive, and eccentric father, or his silent, pious, and shrinking mother. Rather, he was temperamentally different from each and attuned to neither.

Jesse Root Grant, the father, is variously described by his contemporaries as a shrewd Yankee and a fool. Actually, he seems to have possessed clear title to both designations. As a child he had been deserted by his ne'er do-well-father and taken into the home of Judge Todd in upper Ohio. Here he learned the trade of a tanner. After working for the father of the famed John Brown, he set up for himself at Ravenna. In a few years, he married and moved to Point Pleasant, in Clermont County, where Ulysses was born.

Although his opportunities for an education were limited, Jesse became a voracious reader. According to his son, his "thirst for education was intense," and he studied all that he read. Certain it is that he possessed an inquisitive mind and made excellent use of the information which he gleaned in disputatious argument with his neighbors. Strongly opinionated and vigorously contentious, he quarreled frequently with his associates, and found himself involved in numerous lawsuits. He was inordinately proud of his erudition and displayed his literary talents by writing letters to the newspapers. One stanza of a poem which he wrote will suffice to illustrate his literary abilities:

> "Dame Fate with me, though need not flirt,
> For I'm not poet enough to hurt!
> The World, 'tis said, owes all a living,
> What can't be bought, then, must be given;
> And though I have not much to spare,
> I can at least supply a pair—
> Or leather for a pair—of shoes,
> That you may sally forth for news.
> And when another pair you want,
> Just drop a note to
>
> J. R. GRANT."

Hannah Simpson, whom Jesse had married in June, 1821, was the antithesis of her husband in every respect. Silent and retiring where he was verbose and aggressive, reticent where he was boastful, amiable where he was contentious, she won and retained the regard of neighbors who would not tolerate Jesse. Contemporaries remembered her even temper, her unselfish kindness, and her modesty; and biographers of her son have been prone to ascribe the reticence of Ulysses to his mother's influence. [1] Loyal without stint to her Methodist Church, she was earnestly pious. Her only extant letter, written in old age after her son had been President, is a letter of exultation that a grandson, who had long been "under conviction," had at last "been converted." [2]

For the son whom she bore on April 27, 1822, Hannah Grant gave no evidences of affection. Yet, in a formal sense, she was a good mother. She used no rod to keep young Grant from spoiling, but there is evidence that she otherwise admonished him according to the codes of the age. When childhood ailments overcame him, she administered castor oil, put him to bed, and continued about her work, trusting, according to a neighbor, "in the Lord and the boy's constitution." The neighbors could not understand this imperturbability, nor could they understand the quiet confidence in providential protection which she manifested when anxious women of the neighborhood rushed to her with the news that Ulysses was swinging on the tails of the horses in the barnlot. "Oh, 'Lyss will be all right," was her only comment. Throughout his career she maintained her indifference and seemed to take no pride in his successes. When campaign biographers, at a later date, besought her for significant incidents of his babyhood, she remembered nothing; and when fatuous admirers praised him in her presence, she silently left the room. Praise of her children, aver the biographers who knew that the mother of a great man must herself be great, she considered akin to self-praise—a thing she regarded with "unmitigated horror."

But if Ulysses suffered from a lack of solicitous affection from his mother, his father made up the deficiency. From the time of the boy's birth, Jesse enjoyed in him the pride of a self-made man in his possessions. He looked upon this ten and three-quarter pound addition to his household as a superior child, and carried the infant about in his arms to point out his extraordinary qualities to any

who would look and listen. The Simpson family in solemn convo-
cation had drawn the names of Hiram and Ulysses out of a hat and
given them both to the defenceless baby. However, such an extraordinary child could not be called by the ordinary name of Hiram;
so Ulysses he became. This name the neighbors soon converted into
"Useless"; and the Hiram, never used, was forgotten and eventually
lost in the mazes of governmental red-tape.

Paternal pride, of the variety his father manifested, was only a
handicap to Ulysses. In Georgetown, Ohio, where Jesse moved in
the fall of 1823,[3] the father's aggressive contentiousness soon
turned town ridicule on the son. Biographers of Grant have ascribed
Jesse's unpopularity to his abolitionist tendencies, but he would
have been obnoxious to his neighbors even if he had not flaunted
his whiggery in their democratic and pro-slavery faces. Soon the
children of the community, catching the spirit of their elders, transmuted adult dislike into the barbed ridicule of youth. Always they
were "laying for" Ulysses, making him the butt of their jokes, and
proving, to the smug satisfaction of their parents, that the intelligent
boy of whom Jesse had boasted was a surpassing dolt.

With sordid glee the residents of Georgetown rolled under their
tongues the story of Ulysses and his purchase of a horse. Told in
many versions, the one given by Ulysses himself is probably the
most accurate. The story is that, at the age of eight, Ulysses wanted
a horse for which a neighbor asked twenty-five dollars. Ever eager
to gratify Ulysses' wishes, Jesse told him he might have the horse,
but directed him to offer less before paying the amount demanded.
Delighted with the prospect, and inexperienced in the ways of the
economic world, Ulysses rode to the neighbor, saying, "Papa says
I offer you twenty dollars for the colt, but if you won't take that,
I am to offer twenty-two and a half, and if you won't take that to
give you twenty-five." The story was of peculiar pungency in a
day when the ability to dicker over a horsetrade was a social asset,
and it confirmed the suspicions of the community that the lad
was stupid.[4]

Not even Jesse's story of how Ulysses, sent into the woods for a
load of logs and finding no one there to load his wagon, "snaked"
the logs up an inclined tree-trunk and on to his wagon, could overcome the impetus which the legend of Ulysses' stupidity had received. The neighbors continued to scoff, and eventually came to

believe that Ulysses was indeed stupid.[5]

Under such a shower of ridicule, many boys would have become belligerent, fighting their way into the respect of their fellows; but Ulysses, despite his sturdy build, was not pugilistically inclined. The victim of a persecution which he could not comprehend, he adopted a protective coloring. To the disapprobation of the community and the barbed sneers of his contemporaries, he presented a shell of stolid silence. Learning early that his actions and his words would bring mockery upon him, he became a silent and slothful youth. The silence and the sloth, palpable proof of the community opinion, served but to make him the target for more ribaldry. His fear of ridicule soon made him wary, barring him from social games, and excluding him from the play world of make-believe which would have exercised his imagination and laid the foundations of ambition. Throughout his life, Ulysses was to fear ridicule, and when, in his dying days, he wrote his *Memoirs,* the most distinct memories of his childhood were those of the heartaches caused by the jokes played upon him.

The result of public disapprobation was that Ulysses sought compensation in fields other than social. Some compensation was found in the comparative freedom which he enjoyed at home. He grew into an honest and truthful boy, working well at his chores, and causing his parents no trouble. He was seldom scolded and never whipped. Conformity to rules became easier than their violation, especially as that violation would obtain for him no sympathy from his fellows. For thus conforming, he was commended—a welcome change from the scorn he had endured. Another compensation he found in horses. These he learned to control almost as soon as he could sit astride one. Of farm work and teaming, occupations which enabled him to demonstrate his mastery over horses, the boy was fond; and Jesse, proud of his abilities, gave him a team for his own at an age when most boys were not permitted to hold the reins of a plug. Ulysses went into the teaming business for himself, hauling passengers sometimes for long miles, and making occasional trips to visit his maternal grandparents fifteen miles away.[6]

Compensation came, too, in wider travels. In an age and community where the horizon of most boys was limited to a few miles from the homestead, Ulysses soon acquired the distinction of being the best traveled boy in Georgetown. Several times he went to

Cincinnati, frequently to Maysville, Kentucky, and once he drove the seventy miles to Chilicothe. Once he went to Louisville on an errand for his father.[7]

These travels, and his ability with horses, served somewhat to avert the hated mockery of the village boys; and, so long as he maintained his stolid and silent exterior, Ulysses avoided many heartaches. Colorless mediocrity as well as genius has its rewards, and these rewards Ulysses reaped. In school, the masters of the birch rods refrained from singling out Ulysses for either especial rewards or punishments. And Ulysses, as if to protect himself, gave no opportunity for an embarrassing distinction. He learned readily enough, but he evaded any necessity of demonstrating superior qualities; and, secure among the middle masses, he avoided the extremes of his class, although one teacher did remember him as being *somewhat* above the average in mathematics.

As Ulysses passed into adolescence, his father faced the problem of his son's future. For the work of his father's farm Ulysses showed aptitude, if not liking, but for the tannery, which was Jesse's main source of income, the boy had a positive distaste. With a less ambitious parent than Jesse, Ulysses might have become a farmer, but Jesse's pride and ambition for his son brought about a different destiny. Alert to every possibility, Jesse took advantage of a favorable opportunity to get an appointment for Ulysses at West Point.

A series of fortuitous circumstances brought about Ulysses' appointment. First, after a visit to the neighboring Mrs. Bailey, Mrs. Grant brought home the news that the Baileys' son had just been dismissed from the United States Military Academy. The Baileys, injured in pride, had told no one until Hannah Grant came to call. Realizing the news was not known in Georgetown, Jesse perceived the opportunity for quick action. Unfortunately, Jesse had quarreled with the Congressman from his district, and had to proceed by indirection. Accordingly, he wrote to Senator Thomas Morris, who without sympathy for Jesse's squabble with Congressman T. L. Hamer, told him to write to the Congressman. Ambitious for Ulysses, Jesse swallowed his pride with what humility he could muster, and wrote to Hamer that "in consequence of a remark from Mr. Morris . . . I was induced to apply to the Department, through him, for a cadet appointment for my son, H. Ulysses. . . . I have thought it advisable to consult you on the subject, and if you have no other person in mind for the appointment, and feel willing to consent to the appointment of Ulysses, you will signify that consent to the department."[8]

Although this was hardly a frank statement of the case, Congressman Hamer was too busy with other things to bother with an investigation into the merits of the applicant. Jesse's letter, the only one making application for the place, arrived on March 3, 1839. On the next day, Hamer's term in Congress expired, and, not averse to doing a favor even for a Whig constituent, he immediately sent Ulysses' appointment to the War Department. In his haste, he made a mistake in the name of the appointee, endowing Ulysses with the middle name of Simpson, and consequently with initials of peculiar significance.[9]

In Georgetown, the news of Ulysses' luck was accorded indignation and ridicule. Fathers, whose sons might have had the appointment had they but imitated Jesse's celerity, criticized Hamer; and one, in neighborly congratulations, voiced his astonishment that Hamer "did not appoint someone with intellect enough to do credit to the district." They consoled themselves, however, with the knowledge that Ulysses was too stupid to pass the examinations.

Probably only Jesse believed that Ulysses would make a success at the Academy. Certainly Ulysses, who had a high conception of the standards of West Point, did not share the paternal confidence, but demurred at the idea of taking the examination. However, he bought an algebra, which he could not understand, in order to prepare himself for the ordeal. In the early summer, when he reluctantly departed from Georgetown, he told himself that he was going to visit the cities enroute, and would soon be home. In this way he prepared himself to bear the shock of his failure.

As bitter experience had taught him precaution, he made one other preparation to avoid humiliation. On the trunk he was taking with him, an artistic workman had formed his initials, "H.U.G." with bright tacks. Ulysses could hear himself dubbed "Hug" by his fellow cadets. Such a thought would have been frightful to any adolescent; to the sensitive Ulysses it was harrowing. He persuaded the workman to transpose the letters, and as "U.H.G." he set forth, only to find, when he arrived at the Academy, that Congressman Hamer had already changed his name. With relieved feelings, Ulysses accepted the new appellation.[10]

The career of Ulysses at West Point, as undramatic as his earlier life had been, sufficed, nevertheless, to give the lie to his Georgetown detractors. More than that, it surprised Ulysses himself. Expecting to fail the entrance examinations, he was astonished at the announcement that he had been admitted. At each examination period he expected dismissal, but while seventy of those who had been admitted with him were dropped from the rolls in four years, he found himself among the thirty-nine who remained. And yet he did not study. French he found difficult, mathematics came easily. In later years he remembered that "I never succeeded in getting squarely at either end of my class, in any one study, during the four years. I came near it in French, artillery, infantry and cavalry tactics, and conduct." Never reading a lesson more than once, he found thereby time to enjoy the novels of Scott, Bulwer, and Cooper. Although this demonstrates that he was more than a dolt, there is no evidence that he received any intellectual stimuli from his academic career.

In an atmosphere supercharged with patriotism, the never belligerent Ulysses gained no enthusiasm for military life. Soon he was watching with hopeful interest a bill in Congress which bore promise of abolishing the Academy, and, when that failed, he looked forward to graduation, with martial glory playing no part in his ambitionless dreams. Instead, he hoped to be detailed as instructor in mathematics at the Academy, to be followed by a career as professor in some "respectable" college. The fear of failure, with its attendant ridicule, was driving him to seek asylum, and with judgment as shrewd as when he transposed the initials on his trunk, he perceived that the academic cloister would protect him.

Before he entered the Academy, fear of failure had grown to the dimensions of an obsession. In his mind any turning back was a symbol of failure. As Grant told it, he had a "superstition" which made him keep on with any task he attempted. He relates that even when he was going to a new place, depending upon inquiries along the road to find it, and passed his destination, he continued until he came to a road which would bring him in by another route.[11] This strange obsession, rather than any military lessons, furnished the dogged determination which opened the road to Vicksburg and flanked Lee into Richmond.

Ulysses' classmates at West Point remembered him as a quiet and unassuming lad. Among his intimates he was regarded as frank and generous, lazy in his studies, careless in drill, but possessed of quick perception, and a judgment tempered with common sense. "Uncle Sam," or Sam, names inspired by his newly acquired initials, seemed to fit him well. One cadet remembered him as an "uncle-ish" sort of boy. But the circle of his intimates was small. From the Southern society leaders he was excluded by his Western crudities. By the intellectual leaders he was generally ignored. Yet, in 1843, he was President of the Academy's only literary society.[12] Aside from the literary society, Grant was a member of the Twelve in One, a typical adolescent secret society whose mystic name was hidden behind the letters "T.I.O." Among these twelve, Rufus Ingalls, who was to be commissary-general during the war; Simon Buckner, who was to make Grant's initials signify "Unconditional Surrender"; and Fred Dent, who was to become a brother-in-law, were his closest associates. None of these, however, recognized any genius in their friend. W. B. Franklin, who led the class, remembered that Grant "was a good fellow and no dullard," but had no premonition that he would eventually serve under his classmate.[13] Grant's only achievement at West Point was in horsemanship with the record for the high jump.

The class of 1843 was considered by the faculty the poorest ever turned out by the institution. Under the system of making appointments, the best men in a class were commissioned to the engineers, the poorest to the dragoons. Grant, who stood twenty-first in the class of thirty-nine, requested appointment to the dragoons, but received an appointment as brevet second lieutenant in the Fourth Regiment of Infantry. The appointment was a tribute to his mediocrity.

Yet, despite his aspect of mediocrity, he had accomplished something. With no love for the military life and no pronounced mental ability, he had succeeded where many had failed. He returned to Georgetown with a feeling that he had vindicated his father's confidence. However, the neighbors of Jesse Grant did not recognize the success but continued to ridicule the silent son of an unpopular father. Unfortunately Jesse's ebullient pride inspired again the snickers and jeers of the neighborhood, and Hannah Grant's indifference to her offspring raised no bulwark to buffet a rising tide of scorn. Deeply hurt by the community's attitude, the young lieutenant, hoping to impress his neighbors favorably, hastened to order the regalia of an infantry officer. But with this, as with most of his bids for social approbation, the hope of impressing anyone was destined to failure. When the uniform arrived, Grant donned it, and rode proudly to Cincinnati. There a street urchin, shrewdly spotting the newness of both lieutenant and uniform, shrilled out: "Soldier, will you work? No, Sir-ee, I'll sell my shirt first." Crestfallen, he returned home, only to find that the stableman at the village tavern was strutting about with cotton stripes sewed down the seams of his blue pantaloons. "The joke was a huge one in the minds of many people," Grant remembered in later years, "but I did not appreciate it so highly." From that day, the uniform of the army made no appeal to him, and he was eventually to have a reputation for slovenliness in dress. His modesty and simplicity, later to be lauded so highly, were born of disappointment and heartache.

Late in the summer of 1843, Lieutenant Grant reported to his regiment at Jefferson Barracks in St. Louis. The sixteen companies stationed in the barracks made this the largest army post in the country, but the young lieutenant found life little different from that at West Point. There were drills and inspections, but there was no urgency to study and little zeal in discipline. Time hung heavy on the hands of a young lieutenant, and Grant might have been bored had not Fred Dent, his roommate at West Point, invited him to the family estate, "White Haven," where, after meeting his friend's seventeen-year-old sister, he became a frequent visitor. The Dent family were none too well pleased with the colorless youth, who, properly chaperoned by a younger sister, went walking with the eldest daughter.[14]

As the visits became more frequent and the walks longer, young Grant fell into difficulty. Frequently he was late to the officers' mess—a crime involving the fine of a bottle of wine. Captain Robert Buchanan, presiding officer of the mess, and a military martinet of the highest order, enforced the rules with tactless impartiality. Three times in ten days Grant's visit to White Haven brought fines upon him. On a fourth occasion, as he entered the mess hall, Buchanan roared, "Grant, you are late as usual: another bottle of wine, Sir."—The sensitive youth arose. "Mr. President," he said, "I have been fined three bottles of wine within the last ten days, and if I am fined again, I shall be obliged to repudiate." —"Mr. Grant," roared back the martinet, "young people should be seen and not heard, Sir."[15] Under ordinary circumstances the incident might have been merely unpleasant; as it turned out, it was tragic. Eventually, as a result of it, Grant left the army. Even when dying, Grant remembered the incident and bore sarcastic tribute to the unnamed Buchanan as he recalled that "it did seem to me, in my early army days, that too many older officers, when they came to command posts, made it a study to think what orders they should publish to annoy their subordinates and render them uncomfortable. I noticed, however, a few years later, when the Mexican war broke out, that most of this class of officers discovered that they were possessed of disabilities which entirely unfitted them for active field service. They had the moral courage to proclaim it, too. They were right, but they did not always give their disease the right name."

However, Grant did not intend to remain long in the army. His professorial ambitions were still upon him, and he wrote to the professor of mathematics at West Point with a request for a detail as an instructor. Awaiting the transfer, he devoted what time he could spare from White Haven's fair attraction to a course of study. He reviewed mathematics and read history and an occasional novel as a preparation for an academic life.[16]

Yet a nation's needs take precedence over a lieutenant's ambitions. The Mexican War interfered with a potential professor's career. In May, 1844, Grant obtained leave to visit his home in Ohio. During his absence, his regiment received orders to go to Louisiana. "I now discovered that I was exceedingly anxious to get back to Jefferson Barracks," said Grant; "and I understood the reason without explanation from anyone." At the end of his furlough, reporting at St. Louis, he received orders to go to Louisiana. But he got permission to visit White Haven before departing. Although a swollen stream crossed his path, Grant's "superstition" against turning back stood him in good stead. He plunged through the stream, borrowed a dry suit from a prospective brother-in-law, and rode on to offer his hand and heart to Julia Dent. She accepted. They would be married after the war.[17]

Grant had little knowledge of and less interest in the political events which preceded the Mexican War. In his *Memoirs,* written after he had done much to bring about friendly relations with Mexico, he remembered that he had been "bitterly" opposed to the war, and regarded it as "one of the most unjust ever waged by a stronger against a weaker nation." There is no contemporary evidence, however, that Grant's attitude was other than one of indifference.[18] Certainly there was nothing in his conduct to indicate disapproval. He worked steadily at his assigned task as regimental quartermaster—a job of detail involving neither danger nor the opportunity for heroism. Yet he participated in the fighting, riding to the front to do duty as a combatant. At Monterey he volunteered to carry a message through streets lined with snipers, and rode at breakneck speed through the enemy riflemen. At Cerro Gordo, in order to shell the enemy, he mounted a cannon in the spire of a church. For both of these acts he was commended, but in a war that gave military reputations to Lee, Jefferson Davis, and Albert Sidney Johnston, no one recognized ability in Grant. Having been transferred from Taylor's to Scott's army, he was in every battle of the war except Buena Vista. He emerged a full lieutenant—with a beard—who might be trusted with the duties of a quartermaster in charge of the mules.[19]

When the war closed, Grant received a leave of absence, and on August 22, 1848, was married at White Haven to Miss Dent, with "Pete" Longstreet serving as best man. In November, after a visit to Jesse, in Ohio, Grant took his bride to his new post at Detroit.[20] To this bride Grant remained devoted throughout his life. Besides his father, she was the first human being to show him affection. His youth had been one of suppressed emotions, and on Julia, and the four children she bore him in the next decade, Grant lavished the affection of an emotionally starved man. There is not even an intimation, in all the writing about him, that there was ever an unpleasant word between them. Only the most insanely bitter of his partisan opponents would accuse him of infidelity.

Personally, Julia was not especially attractive. A cast in her left eye caused her to squint, and marred one side of her face. Intellectually, she bore the disadvantages of middle-class women of her day. Her letters show her inept in spelling and unfamiliar with the niceties of grammar—deficiencies she shared with her husband. But she was gifted with intuitive kindliness, and she understood her husband. She returned his affection, bore his children and cared for them devotedly, and sustained him in the dark years of his adversity. Throughout the Civil War she followed him, enduring the hardships and ofttimes the dangers of headquarters camps in order to be near him.

In the spring of 1851, three years after Grant had married, the Fourth Infantry was ordered to the Pacific coast. The order brought consternation to the Grant household, for another baby was expected, and the pay of a lieutenant would not support a family in the golden west. Reluctantly, they parted. Julia took their young son Frederick Dent to Ohio, where Ulysses Simpson, Jr., thereafter known as "Buck," was born. Grant went to the coast, hoping to send for his family as soon he could afford the cost.[21]

Of the three routes to the newly acquired Pacific coast, the one across Panama was shortest, but hardly less difficult than the long journey around the Horn or over the rugged trails of the Rockies. By Panama the troops were sent, arriving on the isthmus in the midst of the rainy season and during an epidemic of cholera. As quartermaster, it was Grant's duty to look after the baggage, and bring up the rear of the march with the sick and with such families as had dared the migration. After his regiment had departed for the rainsoaked march to the Pacific shore, Grant found himself alone with a problem. Unable to procure mules in the cholera-infested region, the contractor, hired to haul regimental supplies, was unable to transport Grant's charges. In the emergency, Grant took the initiative, made a new contract, and personally supervised, amid considerable hardships, the mountainous trip. One third of the people who were with him on the arduous journey were lost, and one seventh of his entire regiment succumbed to disease. The experience had revealed unsuspected reserves of energy and decision in the lieutenant, but no one appreciated him, and he was almost censured for departing from the rules.[22]

Assigned to Fort Vancouver, in Oregon Territory, Grant found himself in another typical army post, even less attractive than the others had been. Prices on the Pacific coast, with flour at twenty-five cents a pound, potatoes at sixteen, and onions thirty-seven and a half, precluded any possibility of sending for his family. Accordingly, with Rufus Ingalls, friend of West Point days, and two other officers, he ventured into business. The four planted a crop of potatoes, dreaming of success as profiteers, but the Columbia River rose and ruined part of their crop. When they came to sell they found that everyone had been growing potatoes and the bottom had fallen out of the market. The entrepreneurs then chartered a ship and loaded it with ice for San Francisco, but when the ship neared the Golden Gate, an ice-boat from Sitka preceded it into the harbor. The pay of a lieutenant could not stand such losses; and Grant's family was as far away as ever.[23] The life of the post was monotonous. In desperation born of hopeless boredom, Grant took to drink.

Concerning Grant's drinking so much has been said that the truth is almost lost in the maze of legend. That Grant drank, there is no question; to have drunk as much as his enemies allege would have been impossible. There is evidence that Grant drank little, but that that little was of great effect. To a man of Grant's suppressed emotional nature, a little liquor could do a great deal. Under its influence, the silent shell of reticence was temporarily broken, and another personality emerged. Grant drunk was a very different person from Grant sober. To drive three horses tandem at breakneck speed while the three buggies trailed behind—it was local tradition at Fort Humboldt—would have been impossible for Grant in his sober moments. Grant drunk was so much more interesting than Grant sober, that his colorful drunken moments have been remembered while the gray haze of oblivion has obscured his years of sobriety. On the whole, there is authentic evidence for only a few sprees.[24]

In the fall of 1853, Grant was promoted to a captaincy, and ordered to Fort Humboldt in California.[25] As a captain's salary was but little better than a lieutenant's his family could not yet be brought to the post. His duties at Fort Humboldt, although less onerous than those of a quartermaster, were more strict and distasteful. Grant continued to drink. Under ordinary circumstances the drinking would not have been noticed; but the commander of the fort was Brevet Lieutenant-Colonel Robert Buchanan, erstwhile President of the officers' mess at Jefferson Barracks. That worthy, still a martinet, remembered as clearly as Grant the incident of the fine and its protest. In consequence, when he learned of Grant's departures from sobriety, he demanded that Grant reform or resign. According to some accounts, Buchanan insisted that Grant stand a court martial or hand in his resignation to be used when next he imbibed too freely. Friends urged Grant to stand the trial, assuring him of a lesser penalty, but Grant would not have Julia know that he had been tried on such a charge. He resigned.[26]

Without money, and without definite plans, Grant started home. In San Francisco he stopped in the cheapest of lodging houses. Finally, Major Robert Anderson, the local army quartermaster, obtained money to pay a forty-dollar claim which Grant had against the government, and arranged for the Captain to travel free to Panama. In New York, Grant borrowed money from Simon Buckner for his trip to Ohio.[27]

In Ohio, Jesse received him grimly—the self-made Jesse had small sympathy with failure. With the prescience which had made him a shrewd trader and a successful man, he perceived the bitter truth that Ulysses would be a greater failure in civil life than he had been in the army. When he learned of the resignation, Jesse wrote Jefferson Davis, Secretary of War, pointing out pitifully that "I never wished him to leave the servis," and requesting that the resignation be changed to a six-months' leave to visit his family. But Davis coldly replied that Captain Grant had given no reason for his resignation, and it had been accepted. Mournfully, Jesse turned to his other sons, Orville and Simpson, saying, "West Point has ruined one of my boys for business."[28]

The next six years gave proof to Jesse's forebodings. The fear of failure, which had followed Grant from childhood, became a reality. Never a fighter against circumstances, he sank lower and lower, unable to pull himself from the slough. Colonel Dent, who would not see his daughter suffer, kept him through the first winter, and in the spring gave Julia a farm near St. Louis. During 1855, Grant built a cabin—"Hardscrabble" he called it in bitter humor—on the farm, and for three years they lived there. Liking farm work, Grant labored hard in the fields and in bad weather hauled wood to peddle on the streets of St. Louis. Again failure attended his efforts. His crops were not good; money was not available. In 1857, following the death of Mrs. Dent, Grant managed the larger "White Haven" farm, but he was no more of a success with better land and equipment. In 1859, he sold his farm and moved to St. Louis, where a cousin of the Dents had promised him a job in a real estate house. Here too he failed: he could not collect the rents. For a month he held a position in the custom house; but the collector died, and Grant lost his job. He made application for a surveyorship in the county, but failed to receive it because he was nominally a Democrat. He looked longingly at a vacant mathematics professorship in Washington University, but was too aware of his own unfitness to apply. His clothes became ragged; his shoulders drooped more than usual; poverty found him pawning his watch the night before Christmas in 1858 in order to bring cheer to his family, which now, with the addition of Nellie and Jesse, numbered four.[29]

These dismal days of failure were borne by Captain Grant with that same silent stolidity which had ever masked his inner feelings. Doubtless the realization of failure was no worse than fear of it had been. To his army comrades, whom he occasionally met, he gave the appearance of having deteriorated to a considerable extent, but he drank with them, and laughed, albeit hollowly, at his misfortunes. To them it was evident that he was not fitted to succeed in the world of business. To his family it was equally evident. In the fall of 1859 he wrote to his brother a letter which indicated that he could never succeed in a world of harsh realities. "I have been postponing writing to you," he said, "hoping to make a return for your horse; but as yet I have received nothing for him. About two weeks ago a man spoke to me for him and said that he would try him the next day, and if he suited give me one hundred dollars for him. I have not seen the man since; but one week ago Saturday he went to the stable and got the horse, saddle and bridle; since which I have seen neither man nor horse. From this I presume he must like him. The man, I understand, lives in Florisant, about twelve miles from the city. . . . The man that has your horse is Captain Covington, owner of a row of six three story brick houses in this city; and the probabilities are that he intends to give me an order on his agent for the money on the first of the month, when the rents are paid. At all events, I imagine the horse is perfectly safe." [30]

To brothers Orville and Simpson, managers for Jesse of a leather store in Galena, Illinois, the economic incompetence manifested in this letter must have been pitiful. At Jesse's intercession, they offered their brother a clerkship in their store. The wages were fifty dollars a month. Gratefully accepting it, Grant removed his family to Galena.

During the year in the leather store, Grant exhibited no ability to adjust himself to civil life. Consciousness of failure made him more silent than before. Clad in an army overcoat of faded blue, smoking a clay pipe, silently puttering about a store in which he could not remember the prices, Grant escaped the notice of his fellow townsmen. Scarcely three people in the town knew him. Occasionally he went collecting, spending as much for horse and buggy hire as he collected. Even as a clerk he was a failure.

In those seven years of failure Grant was too busy looking after his family to concern himself with the affairs of the nation. The bitter battles over Kansas and the virulence of the slavery controversy left him a passive spectator. In 1856, because he remembered the army's dislike of Fremont, he voted for Buchanan, and thereby became nominally a Democrat. On slavery he seems to have had no opinions. His father was bitterly anti-slavery, and his father-in-law an equally vehement supporter of the peculiar institution. On the constitutional question of the right of a State to secede, he had definite convictions. He wrote a friend in St. Louis that it would be criminal for Missouri to secede, and he made indignant remarks about Buchanan—"our present granny of an executive." Not until Lincoln had been elected and Fort Sumter fired upon did Grant take more than a passing interest in the national crisis.[31]

When Lincoln, the day after the fall of Fort Sumter, called for volunteers, Galena shared with the country an outburst of military enthusiasm. A meeting was planned to raise a company of troops, and the civic leaders looked about for a man who could tell them something of military affairs. Captain Grant, they learned, was the only citizen of the town who had an intimate acquaintance with such matters. They persuaded him to preside at the meeting, which he did awkwardly enough, but his quiet seriousness impressed the enthusiastic assembly. They asked him to drill the company which was raised, and even offered him the captaincy. He refused, hoping against hope that some better offer would come to him. Perceiving the need for trained men, he hoped for a commission in the regular army. But none came, and Grant decided to apply at Springfield.

When the company he had drilled departed for the State capital to be mustered into the service, Ulysses S. Grant, carpet-bag in hand, swung on to the rear of the train enroute to fame. From the depths of failure began the road to Appomattox.

Notes

1 Albert D. Richardson, *Personal History of U. S. Grant,* 68; Hamlin Garland, *Life of U. S. Grant,* 56.

2 MS. Letter in Library of Congress.

3 U. S. Grant, *Personal Memoirs of General Ulysses S. Grant,* I, 24.

4 U. S. Grant, *Memoirs,* I, 29. The story, as told later by campaign biographers, adds the clause, "but since I have seen the horse, I shall not offer more than twenty."

5 A. D. Richardson, *Personal History of U. S. Grant,* 40–41.

6 Hamlin Garland, *Life of U. S. Grant,* 13–15; U. S. Grant, *Memoirs,* I, 26–29.

7 U. S. Grant, *Memoirs,* I, 21 ff., 29.

8 Hamlin Garland, *Life of U. S. Grant,* 25–26.

9 U. S. Grant, *Memoirs,* I, 32–36; A. D. Richardson, *Personal History of U. S. Grant,* 74–5.

10 Hamlin Garland, *Life of U. S. Grant,* 31.

11 Grant, *Memoirs,* I, 50.

12 A certificate of membership in the Dialectic Society, made out to J. A. Hardie, later a General in the Civil War, and signed by Grant as president of the society is in the possession of Col. U. S. Grant, 3d. The certificate is signed "U. H. Grant." Cf., also, Garland, *Grant,* 46. Winfield Scott Hancock was secretary of the society.

13 For Grant's career at West Point see his *Memoirs,* I, 38–43; Richardson, *Personal History,* 90 ff.; Henry C. Deming, *Life of Ulysses S. Grant,* 34 ff.; Frank A. Burr, *A New Original and Authentic Record of the Life and Deeds of General U. S. Grant,* 185 ff.; Henry Coppée, *Life and Services of General U. S. Grant,* and Adam Badeau, *Military History of Ulysses S. Grant.*

14 Grant, *Memoirs,* I, 46–51.

15 Burr, *Life and Deeds of Grant,* 91–92.

16 Grant, *Memoirs,* I, 51–52.

17 *Ibid.,* I, 50–51.

18 Grant, *Memoirs,* I, 53.

19 *Ibid.,* I, 61–180; Richardson, *Personal History,* 120–127; Garland, *Life of Grant,* 65–92.

20 Grant, *Memoirs,* I, 193.

21 Garland, *Grant*, 109–114; Grant, *Memoirs*, I, 193 ff.; Richardson, *Personal History*, 131.

22 Grant, *Memoirs*, I, 194–199.

23 Grant, *Memoirs*, I, 203.

24 Richardson, *Personal History*, 148 ff. Richardson says "with his peculiar organization a little did the fatal work of a great deal." Garland collected much similar testimony from Grant's associates; cf., *Life of Grant*, 124 ff.

25 Grant, *Memoirs*, I, 207.

26 Grant, *Memoirs*, I, 210; Garland, *Grant*, 127; Richardson, *Personal History*, 149.

27 Garland, *Grant*, 128; William Henry Barnes, *Grant, A Study*, 9–10.

28 Garland, *Grant*, 126–128.

29 Walter Barlow Stevens, *Grant in St. Louis, passim*.

30 M. J. Cramer, *Ulysses S. Grant, Conversations and Unpublished Letters*, 26–27.

31 Garland, *Grant*, 152.

8

ROBERT E. LEE

In this penetrating article, Dr. Fox raises the pointed question, "Since the utter futility of making the third day assault at Gettysburg was so heart-sickeningly clear to Longstreet, what force compelled Lee, rated as one of the Great Captains of history, stubbornly to disregard the heated protests of his trusted and experienced senior Corps Commander and adamantly to insist on launching a frontal attack on the center of the numerically larger and heavily gunned Union Army entrenched on Cemetery Ridge?"

Mr. Fox's answer is predicated on the Freudian postuate of the defense mechanism of identification in the relationship between the group and the group leader: that Lee's previous string of military successes presented him and his rank and file with the delusion of invincibility; that one valorous Confederate soldier was worth two Yankee peddlers; and that "only men obsessed with overwhelming confidence in their own powers and in their commander who ordered it could have so gallantly faced the fiery ordeal of that charge and carried it forward so far as they did." Evidence is presented of General Lee's loss of contact with military realities because he had become the victim of the subtle operation of group psychology.

Was General Lee a Victim
of Group Psychology?

EZRA G. BENEDICT FOX

By THE MORNING of the third day at Gettsyburg the Union Army of the Potomac under General Meade was fully concentrated and solidly entrenched behind stone walls along the crest of Cemetery Ridge with its right flank anchored on Culp's Hill and its left flank protected by the dominating Little and Big Round Tops. Its battle-hardened infantry was supported by some 200 guns. Not only did they outnumber the guns available to General Lee, but the Union artillery was recognized as superior in quality to that of the Confederates. The bulk of Lee's Army of Northern Virginia was at that time drawn up along Seminary Ridge, parallel to, and a little over a mile to the west of, the Union lines.

On the first day of the battle the Confederates had attacked the Federal right. While gaining some local successes, they had failed to take Culp's Hill. On the second day, two divisions of the First Corps, supported on their left by four brigades of Anderson's division, had advanced up the Emmittsburg Road against the Federal left. They had smashed the main body of the Federal Third Corps which had been sent forward into the Peach Orchard, well in advance of the remainder of the Union army, by the Tammany Hall Major General, the "incredible" Dan Sickles, contrary to orders from General Meade, the Army Commander. Nevertheless, the men in gray had been unable to pierce the main Federal lines along Cemetery Ridge.

As his next move General Lee determined upon a massed frontal attack on the Federal center. Lieutenant-General Longstreet, Lee's experienced senior Corps Commander, favored reverting to the defensive, thereby shifting the burden of attacking to General Meade. As an alternative, he urged General Lee to manoeuvre his army to

214

its right so as to get between Meade and the capital at Washington and thus force the Union army to abandon its fortified position at Gettysburg. Lee summarily rejected both these alternatives and with supreme confidence ordered the frontal attack to be made in accordance with his own plan.

Early in his career as commander of the Army of Northern Virginia, General Lee had launched a frontal assault on heavily-gunned entrenchments of McClellan's army at Malvern Hill and had suffered a bloody repulse. The lesson of Malvern Hill had later been underscored by the heavy casualties sustained by the Federal army in its frontal attacks on Lee's defensive positions at Antietam. Only the year before, the extreme hazards inherent in a direct frontal assault in the face of the greater firepower and longer range of the then newly developed weapons were demonstrated by Lee's defeat of General Burnside at Fredericksburg. There the Federal divisions had bravely and doggedly stormed up the slopes leading to the heights occupied by the Confederates, only to be driven back with heart-breaking losses. Despite these examples within his personal knowledge, General Lee on the third day of Gettysburg, over the vehement objections of battlewise Lieutenant-General Longstreet, reverted to the same tactics he had employed at Malvern Hill and ordered a frontal assault on the Federals entrenched on the crest of Cemetery Ridge.

The attack was made by Pickett's division of the First Corps, supported on its left by two divisions from the Third Corps—a total of 15,000 infantry directed at the center of an army of some 70,000 veterans in fortified positions, supported by some 200 well-served guns. Merely to reach the first stone-walls of the enemy's lines, over a mile distant, the attackers had to descend the uncovered slopes of Seminary Ridge, cross the fenced-in farm lands in the intervening valley and then ascend the slopes of the higher Cemetery Ridge on the crest of which the Union infantry and guns were massed. It was a day of July heat (87 degrees in the shade) and high humidity.

The infantry attack was preceded by an hour and a half cannonade from a concentration of massed Confederate guns under Colonel Alexander. Due to the supply of artillery ammunition running low, they had to cease their fire before the Federal guns were silenced.

On receipt of word from Colonel Alexander that it was now or never, Pickett, calling on his men to "remember old Virginia," gayly sang out the fateful order: "Forward! Guide center. March." The men in gray, who had been lying down just over the crest of the hill to avoid Federal observation, rose up, formed solid ranks and marched down the slope and into the open fields of the valley as if on parade. Veteran Brigadier-General Garnett, sick though he was, rode ahead of the advancing line, wrapped in his old blue overcoat buttoned up to the neck. Abreast was Kemper's brigade, its fife corps shrilling "Dixie." Next marched Armistead's Virginia brigade in perfect alignment with flags flying while on its left the Third Corps divisions—chiefly North Carolinians—under Generals Trimble and Pettigrew moved steadfastly forward at shoulder arms. The Federal batteries redoubled their fire and, as the Confederate lines drew closer, changed from solid shot to explosives and then to canister. Especially destructive was the fire from the Federal guns on Little Round Top off on the exposed Confederate right flank.

The men in gray, however, closed up the gaps torn in their lines by the steady hail of shot and shell and forged on up the slope. General Garnett, waving his old black hat with its silver cord, rode along his line cheering his men on even while cautioning them: "Don't double-quick. Save your wind and ammunition for the final charge." As he drew near to the stonewall on the crest, he suddenly slumped forward in his saddle and then went down with his black horse. General Kemper was already out of action, critically wounded. Somehow the gallant Armistead, holding his hat aloft on his sword point for all his brigade to see, actually managed, together with about 150 of his men, to get over the first stonewall and lay his hand on a Federal gun before he fell mortally wounded riddled by a hail of bullets. Off on the left, "Old Man" Trimble with some of his North Carolinians also penetrated the first line of Federal rifle pits. But the flanking fire, as well as direct fire from the second Union line, mowed down the men in these two shallow salients. The other decimated waves of advancing grey finally faltered, first on the exposed flanks and then all along the line, and at long last turned and stumbled exhausted back down the slopes and across the valley. At the muster call of Pickett's division only 800 of the 4800 who started for Cemetery Ridge responded and many of these had been wounded.

As General Bosquet had said of the equally futile charge of the Light Brigade at Balaklava: *"C'est magnifique, mais ce n'est pas la guerre."*

Even though General Longstreet had vehemently and repeatedly protested to Lee against making this frontal assault, the latter imposed on his "old War Horse," as Lee had affectionately dubbed him for his previous services, the task of co-ordinating the divisions from the two separate Corps and of timing the charge. Battle-hardened though he was from First Bull Run on to that fateful day almost three years later, Longstreet flinched at the prospect which was clear to his professional mind. Contrary to all military regulations, he tried to shift the decision for the exact moment at which to start the assault to Colonel Alexander in charge of the artillery preparation. However, the latter's note to Pickett was received by him in the presence of Longstreet. Pickett later described the ensuing scene:

He looked at me for a moment, then held out his hand. Presently, clasping his over mine without speaking, he lowered his head upon his breast. I shall never forget the look in his face nor the clasp of his hand when I said: "General, I shall lead my division on." . . . The stern old War Horse, God bless him, was weeping for his men. . .

On a visit to the battlefield years later, Longstreet himself told a news reporter:

I could not speak. I merely gave a nod of assent, and then the tears rushed to my eyes as I saw those brave fellows rush to certain death.

Since the utter futility of making the third day assault at Gettysburg was so heart-sickeningly clear to Longstreet, what force impelled Lee, rated as one of the Great Captains of history, stubbornly to disregard the heated protests of his trusted and experienced senior Corps Commander and adamantly to insist on launching a frontal attack on the center of the numerically larger and heavily gunned Union Army entrenched on Cemetery Ridge? The answer would seem to lie in the observations made by Dr. Franklin S. Klaf in his paper, "Napoleon and the Grand Army of 1812: A Study in Group Psychology," in the Fall 1960 issue of

Psychoanalysis. He there wrote (p. 75):

Freud has emphasized the importance of the mechanism of identification in the relationship between the group and group leader. We suggest that the group leader, exercising a type of paternalism with the group, succeeds in reviving the early ego identifications of childhood with all their emotionally charged ambivalent potential. In one stage of ego development the child conceives of the father as omnipotent. Benedek has recently pointed out that, "The normal parent, in spite of his insight into his realistic limitations, embraces the gratifying role of omnipotence." The child, Benedek shows, is able to exert a profound effect on the parent, reactivating in the parent the omnipotent fantasies of his own childhood. This reciprocal reactivation of omnipotent fantasies between child and parent has wide implications for group psychology.

The power of the group leader may arise from his basking in the glory of the omnipotent fantasies of the group-members and feeling himself as powerful as he is imagined to be. The danger inherent in this relationship is that members of the group, bound to the leader by a tie that depends on primitive ego functioning, continues to exert a profound influence on the leader. The group members, unfettered by reality testing, influence the developed reality sense of the leader and may impel him to actions that sweep him along to his destruction.

The personality of General Lee and his relationship to the group making up the Army of Northern Virginia fulfill exactly the conditions described by Dr. Klaf.

At age 56 Lee was older by a decade or more than the majority of the generals serving as his subordinates and was more than a generation separated from the impressionable and romantically oriented Southern youths comprising the bulk of his army. In addition, his inherent dignity, his grave mien and grey beard, his aloof reserve, and his fatherly concern with the welfare of his troops, all these combined to create a patriarchal aura, the more potent because natural and unaffected. Like the Father of Our Country, General Lee was not a man whom another man would ever in camaraderie slap on the back. The prideful veneration of "Marse Robert" by the rank and file became almost idolatry.

Moreover, even as early as the outbreak of the war, the feeling was generally prevalent throughout the Confederacy that one

Southerner could lick any two Yankee tradesmen and mechanics. This satisfying egotistical belief was nurtured and seemingly confirmed in the Army of Northern Virginia by an almost unbroken series of brilliant victories under Lee's daring generalship. Within a few days after he took command from General Joseph E. Johnston under whom the Confederate army had retreated into the defenses of Richmond, General Lee lifted the siege of the city and forced the lavishly equipped Federal hosts under General McClellan back to the mouth of the James River. A few months later at Second Bull Run his inspired combinations had routed and driven pell-mell back to Washington the numerically larger forces under the bombastic General Pope, who had come East with a high reputation from his successes at Fort Pillow and Island No. 10. At Antietam he had repulsed the massed attacks of the Federals and had marched his army back into Ole Virginia unmolested. At Fredericksburg he had hurled back the Grand Divisions commanded by General Burnsides and left that general bogged down and completely stymied. Only a few months before Gettysburg he had achieved a brilliant victory at Chancellorsville over "Fighting Joe" Hooker.

This succession of successes created in the Army of Northern Virginia a delusion, not merely that it was the superior of its oft-defeated opponent, the Army of the Potomac, which it again faced at Gettysburg, but that, under Lee's leadership it was actually invincible, in other words, militarily omnipotent.

It should also be borne in mind that General Lee's personal situation materially differed from that of modern army commanders. Today they operate within the insulation afforded by headquarters located far behind the lines of battle. Lee, on the contrary, lived in the midst of his troops, rode with them on their marches and directed the battles from a command post close to the front lines.

It was while subject to the pervading and cumulative influence of the group psychology described above that Lee almost brusquely brushed aside the repeated and reasoned objections of his experienced senior Corps Commander and made his solely personal decision of attacking the Federal center entrenched on Cemetery Ridge. Tough-minded realist that he was, Longstreet remonstrated that, under such a plan, the Confederates would have no advantage over their Yankee opponents. "But in courage, General" is supposed to have been Lee's rejoinder. Bluntly, Longstreet warned him "that the fifteen thousand men"—the force assigned by Lee for the assault —"who could make successful assault over that field had never been arrayed for battle." He also pointed out that "the conditions were different from those in the days of Napoleon when field batteries had a range of six hundred yards and musketry about sixty yards." Repressing memory of his early failure under similar conditions at Malvern Hill, Lee was supremely confident that Southern valor, particularly the dashing bravery of his fellow-Virginians who made up Pickett's division which he designated to lead off the charge, could accomplish what the Yankees had failed to achieve with larger forces at Antietam and again at Fredericksburg. So fortified, he chose to storm the heights of Cemetery Ridge. Only men obsessed with overwhelming confidence in their own powers and in their commander who ordered it could have so gallantly faced the fiery ordeal of that charge and carried it forward so far as they did. This is patent.

One other factor requires mention. For several days prior to, and during, the battle of Gettysburg Lee suffered from diarrhea. Many Southern writers attribute it to his presumably having over-eaten of fresh fruit in the fertile Pennsylvania countryside. It seems more probable, however, that it was psychosomatic, caused by his manifested worry over absence of any word for several weeks from the missing Jeb Stuart and his cavalry upon whom General Lee had grown to rely as the eyes and ears of his army. Conceivably, his debilitated physical condition made him all the more susceptible to psychic influences.

SUMMARY

On the basis of the foregoing, it is submitted that the above-quoted observations of Dr. Klaf are wholly apposite here and that, in making his fatal decision on the third day at Gettysburg, General Lee lost contact with military realities because he had become the victim of the subtle operation of group psychology.

Notes

BIBLIOGRAPHY

FREEMAN, D. S.: *Robert E. Lee.* New York: Chas. Scribner's Sons, 1934.

——: *Lee's Lieutenants.* Chas. Scribner's Sons, 1942.

KLAF, FRANKLIN S.: Napoleon and the Grand Army of 1812. *Psychoanalysis and the Psychoanalytic Review,* Vol. 47, No. 3, Fall 1960. p. 69.

LONGSTREET, LT.-GEN. J.: *From Manassas to Appomattox.* Philadelphia: J. B. Lippincott Co., 1896.

PICKETT, GEORGE: *Soldiers of the South; Letters of Gen. Pickett,* Boston: 1928.

PRATT, FLETCHER: *Ordeal by Fire,* New York: Harrison Smith & Robert Haas, 1935.

TUCKER, GLENN: *High Tide at Gettysburg.* Indianapolis: The Bobbs-Merrill Co., Inc., 1958.

9

WALT WHITMAN

ONE OF WALT WHITMAN'S FRUSTRATED AMBITIONS WAS TO WRITE A history of the Civil War, which he had observed and participated in as a male nurse in military hospitals, in the Army Paymaster's division in Washington, and in two extended visits near the battle lines. He published the most famous collection of Civil War poems, *Drum-Taps*, and some vivid war reminiscences in *Specimen Days*; his poems, letters, diaries and newspaper articles provide some of the best contemporary descriptions and emotional records extant.

Whitman's persistent attempts to absorb himself in the entire cosmos, merging everything and everyone into his self, and his endless insistence upon the first person singular in his search for a personal identity, are particularly revealed in the letters of *The Wound-Dresser*. They reveal, too, his hypochondriasis, for he was oppressed by headaches and worried about his overweight. These letters show, as well (as do his other writings), his preoccupation with his homosexuality, for Whitman was titillated by the beautiful young soldiers so touchingly maimed. As Fiedler points out,[1] Whit-

---

1 Fiedler, Leslie A. Images of Walt Whitman, in *An End to Innocence*. Boston: Beacon Press, 1952, p. 155.

man's body was quite simply the book—to be slipped into the blouses of young men, to lie next to their flesh in innocence.

"Or if you will, thrusting me beneath your clothing,
Where I may feel the throbs of your heart or rest
upon your hip."

In Whitman's great hymn of self-affirmation, the "Song of Myself," there is an exaltation of the bodily and psychological ego which sounds like a song of liberation but which really illustrates the poet's narcissistic-megalomaniacal overcompensation. In the William James excerpt on the Religion of Healthy-Mindedness, a portion of which is incorporated here, we see Whitman imagining himself as the Source of Radiant Health, exuding a strength and health he does not possess. Lewisohn has pointed out that the poem, "Whoever You Are Holding Me Now in Hand," with its curious "Lilliputian" fantasy (see Ferenczi's acute solution of the Swift mystery in reference to his Lilliputian hallucinations), throws doubt on Whitman's robust aggressiveness even as a homosexual, and tells the whole story, revealing the man's nature and appetite. A contemporary picture of Whitman's physical longings is given by John Aldington Symonds, who also touches on the myth Whitman invented for himself of siring six bastards after he had been accused of homosexual practises.

Bychowski, in an essay on Whitman's use of the defense mechanism of sublimation, states that the poet could not reconcile himself with the existence of the outward world separately and independently from his ego, and this was closely interwoven with the anguish of love. "With Whitman's early longing for a return to mother, it is easy to understand that not only outward reality must have appeared as something vague but the same must have been true for his ego, never completely freed from its prenatal fixation. Therefore, since the boundaries of his ego were unusually fleeting, it was either yearning for and actually merging with its place of origin or in self-defense and compensation trying to assert itself in glory and importance."[2]

---

2 Bychowski, Gustav. Walt Whitman. A study in sublimation, in Roheim, Géza (Ed.), *Psychoanalysis and the Social Sciences*, Vol. III. New York: International Universities Press, 1951, p. 228.

D. H. Lawrence, in his essay on Whitman, mercilessly lampoons the good, grey poet. "Your Moby Dick must be really dead. That lonely phallic monster of the individual you. Dead mentalized. Your mainspring is broken, Walt Whitman. The mainspring of your individuality. And so you run down with a great whirr, merging with everything."[3] Like Bychowski, Lawrence believes that Whitman sublimated his sexuality. "You have mentalized your deep sensual body, and that's the death of it."[3] The poet's merging of his self with everything into One Identity creates "mush, not a woven thing. A hotch-potch, not a tissue . . . Oh, Walter, Walter," Lawrence cries out derisively and somewhat sadly, "What have you done with [your self]? With your own individual self? For it sounds as if it had all leaked out of you, leaked into the universe."[3]

Asselineau, in giving us some background to Whitman's family, establishes the basis for Whitman's flight from home at the age of fourteen and his subsequent remarkable flights into narcissism, autism and attempts to lose self-identity. "The elder Walter Whitman was . . . a hasty and violent man, soured by failure, somber and morose. The mother was perfect in Whitman's eyes and he adored her, but she was often ill, and being illiterate, could not understand his ambitions. Edward, his youngest brother, born in 1815, was a congenital idiot, and the oldest, Jesse, was syphilitic and was to die in an insane asylum. Andrew, who was probably also infected, tried to forget his troubles by drinking and soon became a habitual drunkard. He later married a woman not much better than himself. After he died of tuberculosis or cancer of the throat, his widow sent their children out to beg in the streets and herself became a prostitute. Hannah, one of his sisters, after her marriage, became neurasthenic and probably showed signs of instability even during Whitman's youth. No wonder that he felt the need to escape and this flight for a time was his salvation."[4]

The following four chapters take up Whitman's physical case history, his advocacy of the Body Electric, his homosexuality, and his infantile fixation and unresolved Oedipal conflict. They tend to depict a man ridden by anxiety, impotency, desire and guilt.

---

3 Lawrence, D. H. Whitman, in *Studies in Classic American Literature.* Garden City, N.Y.: Doubleday Anchor Books, 1955, p. 177.

4 Asselineau, Roger. *The Evolution of Walt Whitman: The Creation of a Personality.* Cambridge, Mass.: Harvard University Press, 1960, p. 25.

Walt Whitman—A Case History

JOSIAH C. TRENT, M.D.

WALT WHITMAN, THE "GOOD GRAY POET," THE "POET OF DEMOC-racy," has been the center of many controversies since the publication of his *Leaves of Grass* in 1855. Although Walt was the prophet of the perfect body—"I sing the body electric"—the last 30 years of his life were dogged by ill health. He finally died 2 months before his 73rd birthday, a veritable pathological museum. Although there are many references to the state of Whitman's health, particularly during the later period of his life, these are largely superficial and subjective. Examination of the available records, however, has allowed us to reconstruct, at least in outline, the tremendous struggles waged by one of our literary giants against physical and mental deterioration.

Walt Whitman was born at West Hills, Long Island, on May 31, 1819, the second of 9 children. His father, Walter Whitman, was a farmer and carpenter. When Walt was 4 years old the family moved to Brooklyn, then a village of about seven thousand inhabitants. He was educated in the common schools of Brooklyn and at 13 left school and began work as an errand boy in a doctor's office. Before reaching 15 he became an apprentice typesetter in the printing office of the *Long Island Patriot;* at 18 he tried teaching for a time in Long Island country schools, but in 1839 he turned again to printing, now as publisher of his own newspaper, *The Long Islander,* in Huntington. After a year or two he gave up the paper and returned to Brooklyn, where in 1841 he became editor, briefly, of the *Daily Aurora,* at the same time writing essays, stories, and poems for other newspapers and magazines. In 1842, he wrote a temperance novel, *Franklin Evans.* All these productions, whether prose or verse, show very little of the distinctive manner that was to mark Walt's later writings; they show, in fact, very little merit of any kind.

With frequent vacations on rural Long Island, Whitman remained in Brooklyn and New York until early in 1848 when, having lost his post as editor of the Brooklyn *Eagle*, he set out for New Orleans to become editor of a newly established paper there. After a few months he returned to New York, where he continued to work as editor and writer and, for a time, as carpenter. In the spring of 1855, at the age of 36, at a Brooklyn printing house, he began to set type for a book of poems he had written, and in July the first edition of *Leaves of Grass* appeared.

This amazing publication, utterly different from almost all he had earlier published, met for the most part with indifference or contempt in the literary world. Praise came chiefly from Emerson, who wrote in a letter to Whitman: "I find it the most extraordinary piece of wit and wisdom that America has yet contributed. I greet you at the beginning of a great career. . . ." The most truly appreciative reviews were written by Whitman himself.[1]

Further editions of *Leaves of Grass* appeared in 1856 and in 1860, the latter from a Boston publishing house, which collapsed with the coming of the Civil War. Walt's brother George enlisted promptly when the war began, while Walt stayed quietly in Brooklyn, writing poetry and visiting sick and disabled stage drivers in the hospitals. In December of 1862, when word came that George had been wounded, Walt left for the front. He found George nearly recovered, but encountered many sick and helpless soldiers who needed his care; accordingly, he stayed in Washington to serve as volunteer nurse in the hospitals. This activity he carried on for 3 years, meanwhile holding various government positions and corresponding with New York papers. In the summer of 1863, when the hospital work appeared to be affecting his health, he decreased somewhat the number and length of his visits, but by the end of the war he computed that he had made six hundred visits, seeing over eighty thousand sick and wounded soldiers.

After the war Whitman stayed on in Washington, working as a clerk in government offices and writing and publishing new editions of *Leaves of Grass*. In 1873, at the age of 54, he suffered a severe paralytic stroke. When he had partially recovered, he set out for the Jersey coast to avoid the summer heat of Washington, but broke down in Philadelphia and was taken to the home of his brother George in Camden. In this town he spent the greater part of his remaining years, at first with George, then in his own home on Mickle Street. Here he prepared further editions of the *Leaves*, the chief being those of 1881-1882 and 1891-1892. For long periods he was an invalid, confined to his room; at times he was stronger and able to travel, to the West, to Canada, to Boston and New York. During these years his literary reputation, which had received its first real impetus from his recognition by English literary lights in the sixties, grew ever wider, though his poetry was not to receive general acceptance until the twentieth century. He had a small coterie of fervent admirers, among whom was the Canadian physician, Richard Maurice Bucke, who first visited Whitman in July, 1877, and became one of the poet's closest friends as well as his principal medical adviser. After an illness of four months' duration, Whitman died on the 26th of March 1892.

CASE HISTORY

Family History (5)

Father. Walt Whitman (1789-1855). Died after an exhausting illness of nearly 3 years from paralysis. His death was "easy and unconscious."

Mother. Louisa Van Velsor Whitman (1795-1873). Her letters to Walt in the sixties complain often of "lameness in the right arm," which was "swollen and painful" (arthritis?), also of "dizziness in my head," "soreness and distress in my side," and "bad coughing" (November 19, 1867). Cause of death unknown.

Brother. Jesse Whitman (1818-1870). Had cardiovascular and central nervous system syphilis. In the last few years of his life became violent and was judged insane. He was confined to King's County Lunatic Asylum, Brooklyn, New York, where he died of "rupture of an aneurism."

Sister. Mary Elizabeth Whitman Van Nostrand (1821-1899). Had arthritis. Cause of death unknown.

Sister. Hannah Louisa Whitman Heyde (1823-1908). Was considered psychoneurotic. In 1892 had a mild paralytic stroke. Died in her 85th year of "pulmonary edema, mitral insufficiency, valvular disease of the heart and chronic nephritis."

Infant. Born April, 1825—died September, 1825. Cause of death unknown.

Brother. Andrew Jackson Whitman (1826-1863). Had a chronic disease of the "throat and bronchia" which probably was tuberculosis. Walt lived in the same house with Andrew until shortly before he left for Washington in 1862.

Brother. George Washington Whitman (1829-1901). In 1865 after George returned from the Army he was very sick for a time with "lung fever." During 1865 he had "headaches and face was bloated for a time." He also had rheumatic pains in his legs and hips. In 1899 George was sick and paralyzed.

Brother. Thomas Jefferson Whitman (1833-1890). Died of "typhoid pneumonia" (tuberculosis?). Jeff married Martha E. Mitchell (1859), who died in 1873 of tuberculosis. Walt had close contact with Jeff and his wife until he left for Washington.

Brother. Edward Whitman (1835-1892). Eddie was never normal. Apparently he had a birth injury which left him with a "crippled left hand and a paralyzed leg." "At the age of three he had scarlet fever which left severe after effects." He was also feeble-minded and an epileptic. He died in Blackwood Sanatorium, New Jersey, of "valvular heart trouble."

Marital history

Walt never married although, according to his own statement, he had several illegitimate children (3, 14).

Past history

In his youth Walt presumably had no serious illnesses. "I develop'd (1833-4-5) into a healthy, strong youth (grew too fast, though, was nearly as big as a man at 15 or 16.)" "The years 1846, '47, and there along, see me still in New York city, working as writer and printer, having my usual good health. . . ." (16). His "usual good health" continued until about 1858 when he suffered from a "sunstroke" (17); the details of this illness are unknown but it probably was the first of a subsequent series of minor strokes. He recovered, apparently uneventfully, and continued well except for colds. In April, 1863, he wrote his mother, "I weigh about 200, and as to my face (so scarlet) and my beard and neck, they are terrible to behold. I fancy the reason I can do some good in the hospitals among the poor languishing and wounded boys, is, that I am so large and well—indeed like a great wild buffalo, with much hair" (19).

Except for numerous colds accompanied by slight deafness, Walt remained fairly well until June, 1863, when he complained of "quite an attack of sore throat and distress in my head" (18). In July, 1863, while assisting at the amputation of a gangrenous limb of a Virginia Union soldier to whom he was much attached, he sustained a cut of the right hand. His hand became inflamed and swollen, and red streaks ran up to the shoulder (10). The infection subsided in approximately 4 to 5 weeks but left him so extremely weak and debilitated that he was advised to desist from his hospital visits for a while. He improved rapidly and on August 11, 1863, was again able to write his mother that he felt better than he had in 6 weeks. "About the wound in my hand and the inflammation, etc., it has thoroughly healed. . . ." (19). During the summer of 1863 Walt began to complain that the sun affected him, causing "aching and fulness on the head" (17). He resumed nursing the soldiers, however, and in January, 1864, was "well and fat" and weighed "about 206." He continued to complain of "fullness of the head," particularly in hot weather, and "spells of deathly faintness." He was again advised that he had "continued too long in the hospitals" and that he should not go "inside the hospitals for the present" (19). His spells continued with increasing frequency until finally, in July, 1864, he was "prostrated." Following this rather severe attack the "unconscious and perfect health" he "formerly had" was gone. It was his "first appearance in the character of a man not entirely well" (14). His spells persisted and in August and September, 1869, he had another severe attack which left him "prostrated and deadly weak," with little use of his limbs (13). He recovered satisfactorily and except for numerous severe colds remained well apparently until 1872, when he began to complain again of those "spells in the head" which had troubled him at intervals since 1864, and on January 24, 1873, he awoke to find himself paralyzed on the left side. He was placed under the care of Dr. W. B. Drinkard[2] of Washington, D. C., who gave him general supportive treatment, followed later by electric stimulation to his paralyzed side. After he had recovered sufficiently Walt started for the New Jersey shore to recuperate but broke down in Philadelphia and had to be taken to the Camden home of his brother George (10). Apparently Walt asked Dr. Drinkard to send his case report[3] to Dr. Matthew Grier[4] of Philadelphia, whom he saw several times.[5]

Under Dr. Grier's care[6] Walt improved gradually, but in July, 1885, had another attack which left him a year later "scarcely able to get up and down stairs" (3). It was at about this time that Dr. William Osler at Dr. Bucke's request paid Walt a professional visit. The poet had recovered from his paralytic attack of 13 years before and had only a slight residual weakness in his left leg. After a careful examination Osler told Walt that "the machine was in fairly good condition considering the length of time it had been on the road" (12, 7).

Whitman's fairly frequent "sick spells" during the late seventies and early eighties culminated in June, 1888, in another severe paralytic stroke. Bucke, who happened to be in Philadelphia at the time, took Osler with him to see Walt. They "found him in bed, conscious but mentally confused and with the speech slightly blurred and indistinct. There was no fever and the pulse was good. He had had one or possibly two attacks of transient unconsciousness with difficulty in speaking such as we now know are not uncommon with sclerosis of the arteries of the brain. For a week or more the condition looked doubtful, but he gradually improved and recovered without any permanent paralysis or loss of speech" (7).

Although Walt appeared to have recovered from this attack satisfactorily, his course continued down hill. In addition to his usual complaints of headache, lassitude and inertia, for the first time he began to complain of "indigestion" and "bladder trouble" (see Review of Systems). On March 18, 1891, Dr. Bucke asked Dr. Daniel Longaker[7] of Philadelphia to see Walt professionally. He found Walt an old man who complained of constipation, lack of energy, "inertia," urinary frequency and urgency. His apparent age was greater than his real years. Remote memory was better than recent. He moved about awkwardly with the aid of his cane. Muscular strength in the upper extremities was normal and sensation was not impaired. Heart and lungs were in good condition with little sclerosis of temporal or radial arteries.

Walt was treated expectantly with massage, laxatives, and catheterization[8] but continued in poor health until the onset of his Present Illness in December.

Review of Systems

Head. See Past History.

Eyes. Walt did not wear glasses and apparently had good vision until late in life.

Ears. Except for occasional episodes of deafness associated with severe colds, hearing was good.

Nose, pharynx, tonsils. Frequent colds and sore throats: see Past History.

Mouth. Negative.

Teeth. No record of his ever having visited a dentist.

Heart. Negative.

Lungs. During the years 1863 to 1865 while nursing the sick and wounded in Washington, Walt was constantly exposed to "lung diseases" (19). In April, 1890, he had a "severe attack of the grip" which "sometimes almost strangles me" (3). In March, 1891, he had some slight trouble in his upper respiratory tract which he called his "old attack of grip" (4). At no time did he complain of cough, dyspnea, wheezing, hemoptysis, or chest pain.

Abdomen. See Present Illness.

Gastrointestinal. In December, 1873, at the age of 54, Walt complained of "head troubles, & stomach troubles, & *liver* troubles —the doctor thinks the latter the seat & basis this time of all, or nearly all—head-swimming, faintness, vomiting, &c." (14). On May 22, 1874, "my being disabled and want of exercise for 16 months, (and many other wants too) have saddled me with serious dyspepsia and what the doctor calls gastric catarrh, very obstinate, causing me really more suffering and pain than my paralysis." In December, 1875: "these troubles" ["feeling of death and dizziness"], in the doctor's opinion "are from a very serious and obstinate *liver affection*—not from head, lungs, heart. . . ." (13). March, 1876: "I still have this baffling obstinate, apparently chronic affection of the stomachic apparatus and liver. . . . appetite sufficiently good, eat only very plain food. . . . digestion tolerable. . . ." (2). Jan. 21, 1891: "head, belly and bladder matters all in a bad way." March 16, 1891: "Ostinate long-continued horrible indigestion" (3). May 23, 1891: "The fiendish indigestion block continued" (14). Walt complained of obstinate constipation until onset of present illness. There is no mention of jaundice, characteristic gall-bladder pain, or intolerance to fatty foods.

Genitourinary: Dec. 3, 1888: "My physical trouble has veer'd quite entirely lately, or (more truly) added to, and is now that senile botheration from prostate or enlarged or inflam'd gland (bladder business, diabetes) or other worse or less form of ailment. Dr. Osler was here this afternoon and is to bring over a surgeon on the 5th P.M., for more concise examination.[9] It has resulted the last four nights in quite no sleep. . . ." Dec. 4: "The gland suffering or whatever it is (the distressing recurrent stricture-like spasms, ab't from three to ten minutes almost continuously, the last five days and nights) has let up" (3). Jan. 21, '91: "head, belly and day, nocturia, dysuria. (See Past History)

Venereal. Negative.

Neuromuscular. See Past History.
Extremities. See Past History.
Personal habits. In person Whitman was large and tall, above six feet. "He was in no sense a muscular man, an athlete. His body, though superb, was curiously the body of a child. One saw this in its form, in its pink color, and in the delicate texture of the skin. He took little interest in feats of strength, or in athletic sports. He walked with a slow, rolling gait, indeed, moved slowly in all ways; he always had an air of infinite leisure"(1).

His usual weight was 200 pounds or more, but at the onset of the present illness was only 140 pounds. Although temperate in the use of alcohol, he was not a total abstainer. He was inclined to eat excessively. He did not use tobacco.

Present Illness (4, 6)

Walt was in his usual health until the afternoon of December 17, 1891, when he had a severe shaking chill followed by a rise in temperature (102°). This was accompanied by slight hoarseness and a cough productive of mucopurulent sputum. There was complete loss of appetite and marked prostration.

Course of illness. Dr. Longaker saw the patient 24 hours after the onset of the illness. At that time he found areas of dullness over both lungs, particularly on the right. The following day, the third of his illness, the areas of dullness had increased, especially over the right lung. It was thought he had a widely diffused bronchopneumonia. The lungs were poorly aerated and there were "hints of heart failure." On the fourth day Dr. Alexander McAlister of Camden was called in consultation so that a doctor could be immediately available in case of a sudden change for the worse. Walt showed no improvement and a tracheal rattle and cyanosis were noted. On December 22nd irregularity of the pulse developed. The following day the irregularity was more marked. Somnolency and cyanosis continued. Dec. 24: Extensive involvement of the left lung was found, with the right practically useless. There was marked cyanosis, labored respirations, and a rapid weak, and irregular pulse. Dec. 26: Walt appeared semi-conscious but could be roused easily. The heart was still irregular and intermittent. Dec. bladder matters all in a bad way." Mar. '91: Frequency, 20 times a 27: A careful examination of the chest revealed some resonance on percussion and faint breath sounds, bilaterally posteriorly. The "left side [was] more impaired than we had believed." The respiratory movements were rapid and entirely abdominal. Mucopurulent expectoration continued. The cough, prominent from the beginning, was greatly accentuated when Walt lay on his right side. There was little if any fever. Weight loss was evident. By December 29th, when it became clear that the illness was to be protracted, a professional nurse, Mrs. Elizabeth Keller, was engaged.

Slight improvement occurred and continued, and by January 7, a normal pulse and respiration ratio was re-established, 72/18. During the previous year "the pulse [was] very uniformly at sixty-four." All alarming symptoms abated, and Walt settled down to a routine of life little varied to the end. He frequently complained of pain and soreness in the left side, splenic region, and later severe pain in the left foot. On January 20 a fine rash was discovered on his abdomen and chest. On March 9th Longaker records: "P-90, R-20 rather shallow and when lying on back almost entirely abdominal. Traubel informs me that immediately the position on the right side is assumed he has a profuse expectoration attended by cough. Probably a bronchiectatic cavity which partly empties." And on March 11th: "P-80 R-22 mostly abdominal. Making a superficial examination of anterior surface of chest I found mucus râles on left side—vesicular murmur on right side scarcely audible—bronchial breathing instead. Heart sounds at apex faint, first scarcely heard—over aortic cartilage and pulmonary the second sound only can be heard. Impairment of resonance on right side—good on left."

Hiccough began shortly after onset of the present illness and except for brief intervals was a persistent symptom until the end. Night sweats occurred only late. After the initial attack fever, "if present at all," was very moderate. There was persistent weight loss. If Walt lay on his left side he had severe pain in that side and if on the right side he coughed constantly and the "phlem choked him." Hourly or oftener he would ring or call the nurse to change his position. Soon it was possible for him to lie on the left side only, and finally even this tortured him. Toward the end he had occasional urinary and fecal incontinence. A few days before his death an ecchymotic area was found over his left flank.

On March 23, 1892, his dyspnea increased and his pulse again became faint and irregular. He died quietly on March 26th.

Autopsy

The account of the autopsy given by Dr. Longaker (4) may be quoted at length: "The following are the notes of the post-mortem

performed on the body of Walt Whitman, March 27, 1892, by
Henry W. Cattell, demonstrator of gross morbid anatomy, University of Pennsylvania. The autopsy was made in the presence of Dr.
Daniel Longaker, Prof. F. X. Dercum, Dr. Alexander McAlister, and
Horace L. Traubel.[10] The brain was removed by Dr. Dercum, and
is now, after having been hardened, in the possession of the American Anthropometric Society.[11] This Society, which has been organized for the express purpose of studying high-type brains, intends
to first photograph the external surfaces and then make a cast of
the entire brain. After this, careful microscopic observations will be
made by competent observers.[12]

"Both the head and the brain were remarkably well formed
and symmetrical. The scalp was thin, and practically no blood was
lost when the incisions were made. The calvarium was white and
the muscular tissue pale. The dura mater was very adherent to the
scull cap and showed recent pachymeningitis on both sides, but especially on the right. The blood in the longitudinal sinus was fluid.
The bone was well ossified, and there was little or no diploid substance remaining. The pia and arachnoid were very oedematous,
and considerable cerebrospinal fluid escaped during the removal
of the brain. Numerous milky patches, especially over the vertex,
were seen, but no military tubercles were discernible. The membranes were not adherent to the cortex, and the brain substance was
excessively soft. The blood vessels of the circle of Willis were very
slightly atheromatous. The brain weighed forty-five ounces, two
hundred and ninety-two and one-half grains avoirdupois. . . .

"The body was emaciated, postmortem lividity was slight, and
there was no rigidity. On attempting to remove the skin of the left
side a little to the left of the median line at the sixth rib laudable
pus escaped. On careful examination there was found here an
elevated area the size of a fifty-cent piece, which was situated over
but slightly to the left of the center of the manubrium and had
eroded that bone to the extent of a twenty-five cent piece. The abscess had burrowed into the pectoralis major and had commenced
to erode the superficial fascia. It had not broken inwardly, though
it could be plainly seen from the posterior surface of the sternum.

"About half an ounce of pericardial fluid was found. The heart,
which weighed about nine ounces, was very flabby and well covered with epicardial fat, except a small portion in the center of the
right ventricle. The pulmonary valves were slightly thickened but
competent. Aortic valves in good condition, closing completely. The
mitral valves good, the tricuspids perfectly good.

"There were three and one-half quarts of serious fluid in the left pleural cavity, and the lung, the size of the hand, was completely pressed against the mediastinum, so that it was absolutely impossible for air to enter. A few bands of recent lymph extended across an injected pleura, which was hemorrhagic in spots.[13] On the pleural surface at a point just below the nipple was an abscess the size of a hen's egg, which had completely eroded the fifth rib, the longest diameter of the abscess being in the vertical direction. There was no external mark on the skin to lead one to suspect the presence of the abscess, though there was some bulging and distinct fluctuation, and the two ends of the rib could be plainly felt grating against each other. Only about one-eighth of the right lung was suitable for breathing purposes. The upper and middle lobes were consolidated and firmly bound down to the pleura. There were about four ounces of fluid in the cavity. Large tubercular nodules and areas of catarrhal pneumonia were everywhere to be found. Those portions of the lung not tubercular were markedly emphysematous, this being especially marked at the free edges of the lung.

"The spleen was soft and weighed about eight ounces, the capsule thickened and fibrous; on section pulpy. It was matted down to the diaphragm and showed only peritonitis and perisplenitis. Numerous tubercles occupied this region, extending to the anterior wall of the stomach and to all of the neighboring viscera. The diaphragm was pushed downward by the fluid.

"The kidneys were surrounded by a mass of fat. The left suprarenal capsule was tubercular and contained a cyst the size of a pigeon's egg. In this was found a darkish fluid. The capsule strips readily; the kidney weighed about six and one-half ounces, and showed some parenchymatous change. The kidney substances were soft, red, and swollen, and somewhat granular. The right kidney was a little the smaller and the better of the two.

"The liver was about normal in size, though fatty and contained an extra fissure near the center. Some tubercles were observed.

"A huge gall stone almost entirely occupied a rather small gall bladder to which it was firmly adherent. The outer surface of the stone was covered with a whitish deposit.

"The pancreas was hemorrhagic. The common iliacs were but very slightly atheromatous.

"Over the whole of the mesentery, especially in its lower portion, were hundreds of minute tubercles varying in size from that of a fine needle-point to the head of a good-sized pin. These whitish points were surrounded by a hemorrhagic base. The serous surface of the intestines was injected and dotted with tubercles. The bladder was empty and the walls thickened. The prostate was enlarged. The rectum was swollen and filled with semi-fluid feces. A few hardened masses were found in the transverse colon. The stomach was small. The vermiform appendix was two inches long and patulous, containing two small hardened fecal masses of an irregular outline. The sigmoid flexure was unusually long.

"The above macroscopic lesions of the various organs were confirmed by microscopic sections.

"It would seem very probable that the extensive adhesion of the dura mater to the calvarium was due to an old sun-stroke.

"The cause of death was pleurisy of the left side, consumption of the right lung, general miliary tuberculosis and parenchymatous nephritis. There was also found a fatty liver, gallstone, a cyst in the adrenal, tubercular abscesses, involving the bones, and pachymeningitis."

COMMENT

The autopsy is exasperatingly incomplete, and from the available facts it is difficult to reconstruct the exact sequence of events which led to Walt's death. However, it is sufficiently inclusive to allow us to revise the diagnosis to conform with our present-day concepts of pathology.

Did Whitman really have tuberculosis? Could he have had cancer of the prostate with terminal spread or a primary cancer of the lung? Tuberculosis was well recognized by 1892[14], however, and since the autopsy was performed by some of the best American pathologists of the day, we are reasonably safe in accepting their diagnosis.

Judging from the extensive involvement of the right lung, "the upper and middle lobes were consolidated and firmly bound to the pleura," the tuberculous process was of long duration, probably years. Unfortunately, no mention is made of the left lung other than that "it was completely pressed against the mediastinum." The apparent long duration of the pulmonary lesion with no antecedent history of cough, dyspnea, chest pain or hemoptysis is nothing short of remarkable. Walt was exposed to members of the family with tuberculosis for several years before he left for Washington in 1862, at the age of 43, but it was precisely at this time that he was proclaiming his excellent health. During his Washington hospital days, also, he must have been exposed to much tuberculosis among the soldiers. However, in his frequent references to illnesses of this period there is no mention of pulmonary complications. The tuberculous pleural effusion on the left probably had been present some months before his terminal illness and could have been secondary to extension through the parietal pleura of the chest wall abscess or the rupture of a small tuberculous node.

At the onset of his last illness the infected pleural fluid, which could have been responsible for the sudden chill and fever, must have ruptured into a bronchus, for there was profuse expectoration of mucopurulent sputum at the onset, something entirely new for Walt. This profuse expectoration, which was greatly accentuated when he lay on his right side, persisted until his death. Sufficient drainage of the left chest through the bronchus must have occurred to produce the slight symptomatic improvement noted early in the course of his last illness. The fluid on the left was not diagnosed antemortem because the doctors did not wish to subject Walt to the discomfiture of a complete examination. The presence of a bronchopleural communication on the left is further borne out by Dr. Longaker's examination of the anterior surface of the chest on March 11th, when he found "impairment of resonance on right— good on left," indicating that there was air in the left pleural space and not in the lung, since the autopsy showed the lung to be collapsed against the mediastinum.

The tuberculous abscesses of the sternum, rib and chest wall and foot were old but their exact duration is difficult to estimate.

Numerous tubercles occupied the area around the spleen extending to the anterior wall of the stomach and all neighboring viscera including the left adrenal gland. No tubercles were found in the splenic pulp, and only a few were observed in the liver. The mesentery and intestine, particularly the lower portion, were covered with minute tubercles. This certainly is not the picture of a miliary spread via the blood stream but rather that of a direct dissemination probably from an old focus around the spleen, a lesion which may have been of the same vintage as the abscesses described above and which undoubtedly accounted for the hiccough and severe pain in his left side.

The left adrenal cyst indicated an old process and may have

been in part responsible for the "lassitude and inertia" Walt complained of for many years. No mention was made of the right adrenal gland.

Since careful examination of the brain was not carried out we have no record of old areas of destruction which might have been present, but we do have the autopsy findings of extensive cerebral atrophy. In spite of marked wasting of the brain described at the postmortem examination, Walt's mind continued active and keen to the last[15] although his memory had begun to fail.

His long-standing symptoms of indigestion, nausea, and constipation can be attributed to the chronic cholecystitis and cholelithiasis.

His urinary symptoms arose from the urethral obstruction secondary to hypertrophy of the prostate.

Did Walt have hypertension or perhaps a labile blood pressure secondary to vasospasm? This, of course, would have been an antemortem diagnosis if his blood pressure could have been measured.[16] In favor of such a condition are his ruddy complexion, frequent severe headaches and feeling of fulness in the head, and the numerous slight to severe cerebral insults suffered after 1858. However, in hypertension of such long standing we should expect more advanced arteriosclerosis and cardiac hypertrophy.

Our revised and final diagnosis should read, then: Pulmonary tuberculosis, far advanced, right, atelectasis of left lung; tuberculous empyema, left; bronchopleural fistula, left; disseminated abdominal tuberculosis; tuberculous abscesses of sternum, fifth rib and left foot; cyst of left adrenal gland; chronic cholecystitis and cholelithiasis; cerebral atrophy; cerebral arteriosclerosis; benign prostatic hypertrophy; pulmonary emphysema; cloudy swelling of kidneys; history of hypertension(?).

In an age of psychiatry no discussion of Whitman's medical history would be complete without some mention of that very controversial subject of his sexuality. Was he homosexual? At this late date an unassailable answer is unlikely, although after a study of his life, personality, habits, and writings, one fact stands out clearly: by no standards could Whitman's attitudes and behavior toward sex be considered "normal." Yet the charge of homosexuality has never been proved. John Burroughs, a friend of long standing, described Walt as in "no sense a muscular man, an athlete. His body, though superb, was curiously the body of a child. One saw this in its form, in its pink color, and in the delicate texture of the skin" (1). Perhaps this is the real clue to the personality of the man who embraced all mankind, man and woman alike. Could he have been eunuchoid?

Notes

1 He published anonymously several reviews one of which began: "An American bard at last! One of the roughs, large, proud, affectionate, eating, drinking, and breeding, his costume manly and free, his face sunburnt and bearded, his postures strong and erect, his voice bringing hope and prophecy to the generous races of young and old. . . . If health were not his distinguishing attribute, this poet would be the very harlot of persons" (18).

2 William Beverly Drinkard (1842–1877) was born in Williamsburg, Virginia, the son of William R. Drinkard, Assistant Secretary and later acting Secretary of War under Buchanan. He received his education at Georgetown College, Washington, D.C., and the Lycée Imperiale, Orleans, France. In November, 1861, he began the study of medicine at Paris. Here he assisted in Desmarres Clinic where he studied principally diseases of the eye. He studied also under such other eminent teachers of the times as Velpeau and Flourens. In July, 1865, he went to London for several months and in the autumn of the same year returned to Washington where he entered the National Medical College, from which he received the M.D. degree in March, 1866. In 1872 he was elected professor of anatomy at the National Medical College, a post he held until his premature death 5 years later. Although trained in ophthalmology he did not confine himself to this specialty but engaged in the general practice of medicine. He was one of the founders of Washington Children's Hospital. (8)

3 Dr. W. B. Drinkard to Dr. Matthew Grier; Washington City, July 24, 1873; autograph letter in the Trent Collection, Duke University Library (15). The letter reads as follows:
My dear Doctor—
I am informed by Mr. Whitman, lately a patient of mine; now on a visit to Camden, that he intends to avail himself of your counsel and treatment before returning to this city: and he requests me to let you have a short statement of the history of his case up to the present time. It may be briefly stated, thus: On the 23d of January—? February—last Mr. W.—previously in good health—was attacked with left hemiplegia, presenting all the symptoms of such conditions, though none of them very marked at any time. Speech was hardly appreciably impaired: facial distortion very slight, & deviation of tongue just perceptible: left upper extremity never wholly useless: left

lower showing the paretic condition more than any other part or organ. Constipation, slight at onset of attack, has required little attention subsequently.

Under the influence of rest, and such incidental treatment as was demanded from time to time, his general condition has slowly improved: locomotive power having, however, been only imperfectly regained. His principal annoyance has been a recurrent headache, with tendency to nausea—never actually reaching the latter point [preceding ten words cancelled by Drinkard].

After subsidence of everything like active manifestations I commenced, cautiously, the use of the induced Current—with Gaiffe's battery,—and continued it for a number of weeks, without apparent result, beyond a decided improvement in nutrition of the lower limb. When he was on the point of leaving, I suggested to him the *possible* benefit to be derived from the use of the continued current: and I think it is with reference to that more particularly that he wishes to consult you.

Mr. Whitman's physical mould, his habits of life, tastes & mental constitution, are, I think, the most *natural* I have ever encountered: and as far as those things go, he has all in his favour. Beyond this, the prognosis is, of course, of the stereotyped uncertainty characteristic of such cases. He has occasionally taken pot. bromide & sod. bromide for his headaches: for a short time took the phosphates of iron, quinia & strychnia: Semi-occasionally, a mild laxative:—no other drugs that I recollect.

Hoping that you may be able to help Mr. Whitman in regaining the bodily independence on which his usual mental hopefulness very much depends, I am, my dear Doctor,

Very truly Yours

Wм. Bev. Drinkard

4 Matthew J. Grier (1838–1900) was born in Philadelphia of Scotch-Irish ancestry. He received his M.D. degree from the University of Pennsylvania in 1863 (8).

5 An incomplete manuscript note by Whitman (15) concerning a visit to Dr. Grier is of interest here: "June 2, '74 visited Dr. Grier again today at 312 S. 12th st. Phil. for consultation.

"He reiterated his theory that my sufferings (later ones), come nearly altogether from gastric, stomachic, intestinal, non-excretory, &c. causes, causing flatulence, a very great distension of the colon, fill'g of passages, weight on valves, crowding & press'g on organs, (heart, lungs, &c) and the very great distress & pain I have been under in breast left side, & pit of stomach, & thence to my head, the last month. Advised me by all means to begin the use of an injecture syringe, (Fountain No. 2, tepid water for clysters)—was favorable to my using whiskey—advised assaf [oet]ida pills. 292—Kneading the bowel."

6 The following notes (15), written by Dr. Grier, indicate the treatment administered to Whitman:

R/Syr Calc lactophosph 3 1/10
Sig ½ teaspoonful after
breakfast & dinner
8-1-73   Grier
R/40153
Sodae lactatis 3p
Glycerineae 3 T
M. Sig Teaspoonful after
each meal
5-6-74   Grier

descending secondary currents of Electro-Magnetism to lower limbs—none to the upper. *treat each* muscle separately, For the brain—Inverse constant current say about 6 to 10 Daniells cells from each sciatic N. to sacrolumbar region, *not any higher under any circumstances. Every other days.*

7 Dr. Longaker is still living in Philadelphia. In a personal letter to the author Dr. Longaker reminisces about Walt's last illness but cannot recall any details not already recorded in his article, "The Last Sickness and Death of Walt Whitman" (4).

8 Dr. Longaker showed Walt how to catheterize himself with a soft rubber catheter. "He. . . . expressed surprise that the operation was so easy and painless. No arguing or coaxing was required, as is almost always necessary when this procedure is instituted" (4).

9 On his next visit Osler brought with him a Dr. Wharton; there is no record of their joint opinion on the case (11).

10 "Mrs. Davis, Walt's housekeeper, was much opposed to the postmortem examination of Mr. Whitman's body. Of course, she had no legal right to object. Mrs. George Whitman was consulted as to this, and, it was understood, consented. During the postmortem (it was in the back parlor), I detected the odor of a fearful pipe. It might have been from the street and it might not have been. Mr. Whitman was not smoking, I was sure" (2).

11 "The American Anthropometric Society was established in 1889 at a meeting which took place at the residence of . . . . . The founders were: Harrison Allen, Francis Xavier Dercum, Joseph Leidy, William Pepper and Edward Charles Spitzka. The chief object of the society was the preservation of the brains of its members. . . . In the order of acquisition, the list of brains in the collection included the following: (1) Joseph Leidy, (2) Philip Leidy, (3) J. W. White, Sr., (4) Andrew J. Parker, (5) Walt Whitman, (6) Harrison Allen, (7) Edward D. Cope, (8) William Pepper" (9).

12 The brain of Walt Whitman, together with the jar in which it had been placed, was said to have been dropped on the floor by a careless assistant. Unfortunately, not even the pieces were saved. . . ." (9).

13 "This pleurisy was due to deposit in the membrane of tubercles, the same as were found about the spleen and the peritoneum of the left side of the abdomen in general" (Longaker's comment).

14 Koch's work on the tubercle bacillus was done in 1882.

15 Last revision of *Leaves*, 1891-92.
16 Sphygmomanometry was introduced in the late 19th century.

BIBLIOGRAPHY

BURROUGHS, JOHN. Walt Whitman, a Study. Boston and New York: Houghton, Mifflin & Co., 1896.

DONALDSON, THOMAS. Walt Whitman the Man. New York: F. P. Harper, 1896.

KENNEDY, W. S. Reminiscences of Walt Whitman. Paisley and London: A. Gardner, 1896.

LONGAKER, DANIEL. The Last Sickness and Death of Walt Whitman, in In Re Walt Whitman. Philadelphia: D. McKay, 1893, pp. 393–411.

MOLINOFF, KATHERINE. Some Notes on Whitman's Family. New York: the author [1941].

Notes W. W. Last Sickness. A collection of manuscript notes by Mrs. Elizabeth Keller, Dr. Daniel Longaker, Dr. Alexander McAlister, and Dr. R. M. Bucke; December 23, 1891 to March 26, 1892. In the Trent Collection, Duke University Library.

OSLER, SIR WILLIAM. Walt Whitman—An Anniversary Address with Personal Reminiscences (delivered at the Schools, Oxford, to Sir Walter Raleigh's Class in English Literature). Manuscript in the Osler Library, McGill University.

SILVER, ROLLO G. Personal communication.

SPITZKA, E. A. Trs. Am. Phil. Soc., 1908, n.s., 21:176.

TRAUBEL, HORACE. Walt Whitman at Date, in In Re Walt Whitman. pp. 109–147.

Idem. With Walt Whitman in Camden. New York: Mitchell Kennerley, 1914–1915, 3:240.

WHITE, WILLIAM. Am. Lit., 1939, 2: 73–77.

WHITMAN, WALT. Calamus. Boston: L. Maynard, 1897.

Idem. Complete Poetry & Selected Prose and Letters. London: The Nonesuch Press [1938].

Idem. June 2, '74 visited Dr. Grier again today. Autograph manuscript, bound with autograph letter from Dr. Drinkard to Dr. Grier and three prescriptions by Dr. Grier. In the Trent Collection, Duke University Library.

Idem. Specimen Days & collect. Philadelphia: R. Welsh & Co., 1882–83.

Idem. Walt Whitman and the Civil War. Philadelphia: University of Pennsylvania Press, 1933.

Idem. U. S. Review, 1855, 5: 205–212.

Idem. The Wound Dresser. Boston: Small, Maynard & Co., 1898.

The Religion of Healthy-Mindedness

WILLIAM JAMES

IF WE WERE to ask the question: "What is human life's chief concern?" one of the answers we should receive would be: "It is happiness. How to gain, how to keep, how to recover happiness, is in fact for most men at all times the secret motive of all they do, and of all they are willing to endure. The hedonistic school in ethics deduces the moral life wholly from the experiences of happiness and unhappiness which different kinds of conduct bring; and, even more in the religious life than in the moral life, happiness and unhappiness seem to be the poles round which the interest revolves. We need not go so far as to say with the author whom I lately quoted that any persistent enthusiasm is, as such, religion, nor need we call mere laughter a religious exercise; but we must admit that any persistent enjoyment may *produce* the sort of religion which consists in a grateful admiration of the gift of so happy an existence; and we must also acknowledge that the more complex ways of experiencing religion are new manners of producing happiness, wonderful inner paths to a supernatural kind of happiness, when the first gift of natural existence is unhappy, as it so often proves itself to be.

With such relations between religion and happiness, it is perhaps not surprising that men come to regard the happiness which a religious belief affords as a proof of its truth. If a creed makes a man feel happy, he almost inevitably adopts it. Such a belief ought to be true; therefore it is true—such, rightly or wrongly, is one of the "immediate inferences" of the religious logic used by ordinary men.

"The near presence of God's spirit," says a German writer,[1] "may be experienced in its reality—indeed *only* experienced. And the mark by which the spirit's existence and nearness are made irrefutably clear to those who have ever had the experience is the utterly incomparable *feeling of happiness* which is connected with the nearness, and which is therefore not only a possible and altogether proper feeling for us to have here below, but is the best and most indispensable proof of God's reality. No other proof is equally convincing, and therefore happiness is the point from which every efficacious new theology should start."

In the hour immediately before us, I shall invite you to consider the simpler kinds of religious happiness, leaving the more complex sorts to be treated on a later day.

In many persons, happiness is congenital and irreclaimable. "Cosmic emotion" inevitably takes in them the form of enthusiasm and freedom. I speak not only of those who are animally happy. I mean those who, when unhappiness is offered or proposed to them, positively refuse to feel it, as if it were something mean and wrong. We find such persons in every age, passionately flinging themselves upon their sense of the goodness of life, in spite of the hardships of their own condition, and in spite of the sinister theologies into which they may be born. From the outset their religion is one of union with the divine. The heretics who went before the reformation are lavishly accused by the church writers of antinomian practices, just as the first Christians were accused of indulgence in orgies by the Romans. It is probable that there never has been a century in which the deliberate refusal to think ill of life has not been idealized by a sufficient number of persons to form sects, open or secret, who claimed all natural things to be permitted. Saint Augustine's maxim, *Dilige et quod vis fac,*—if you but love [God], you may do as you incline,—is morally one of the profoundest of observations, yet it is pregnant, for such persons, with passports beyond the bounds of conventional morality. According to their characters they have been refined or gross; but their belief has been at all times systematic enough to constitute a definite religious attitude. God was for them a giver of freedom, and the sting of evil was overcome. Saint Francis and his immediate disciples were, on the whole, of this company of spirits, of which there are of course infinite varieties. Rousseau in the earlier years of his writing, Diderot, B. de Saint Pierre, and many of the leaders of the eighteenth century anti-christian movement were of this optimistic type.

They owed their influence to a certain authoritativeness in their feeling that Nature, if you will only trust her sufficiently, is absolutely good.

It is to be hoped that we all have some friend, perhaps more often feminine than masculine, and young than old, whose soul is of this sky-blue tint, whose affinities are rather with flowers and birds and all enchanting innocencies than with dark human passions, who can think no ill of man or God, and in whom religious gladness, being in possession from the outset, needs no deliverance from any antecedent burden.

"God has two families of children on this earth," says Francis W. Newman,[2] "*the once-born* and *the twice-born*," and the once-born he describes as follows: "They see God, not as a strict Judge, not as a Glorious Potentate; but as the animating Spirit of a beautiful harmonious world. Beneficent and Kind, Merciful as well as Pure. The same characters generally have no metaphysical tendencies: they do not look back into themselves. Hence they are not distressed by their own imperfections: yet it would be absurd to call them self-righteous; for they hardly think of themselves *at all*. This childlike quality of their nature makes the opening of religion very happy to them: for they no more shrink from God, than a child from an emperor, before whom the parent trembles: in fact, they have no vivid conception of *any* of the qualities in which the severer Majesty of God consists.[3] He is to them the impersonation of Kindness and Beauty. They read his character, not in the disordered world of man, but in romantic and harmonious nature. Of human sin they know perhaps little in their own hearts and not very much in the world; and human suffering does but melt them to tenderness. Thus, when they approach God, no inward disturbance ensues; and without being as yet spiritual, they have a certain complacency and perhaps romantic sense of excitement in their simple worship."

In the Romish Church such characters find a more congenial soil to grow in than in Protestantism, whose fashions of feeling have been set by minds of a decidedly pessimistic order. But even in Protestantism they have been abundant enough; and in its recent "liberal" developments of Unitarianism and latitudinarianism generally, minds of this order have played and still are playing leading and constructive parts. Emerson himself is an admirable example.

Theodore Parker is another,—here are a couple of characteristic passages from Parker's correspondence.[4]

"Orthodox scholars say:

'In the heathen classics you find no consciousness of sin.' It is very true—God be thanked for it. They were conscious of wrath, of cruelty, avarice, drunkenness, lust, sloth, cowardice, and other actual vices, and struggled and got rid of the deformities, but they were not conscious of 'enmity against God,' and didn't sit down and whine and groan against non-existent evil. I have done wrong things enough in my life, and do them now; I miss the mark, draw bow, and try again. But I am not conscious of hating God, or man, or right, or love, and I know there is much 'health in me'; and in my body, even now, there dwelleth many a good thing, spite of consumption and Saint Paul." In another letter Parker writes: "I have swum in clear sweet waters all my days; and if sometimes they were a little cold, and the stream ran adverse and something rough, it was never too strong to be breasted and swum through. From the days of earliest boyhood, when I went stumbling through the grass, . . . up to the gray-bearded manhood of this time, there is none but has left me honey in the hive of memory that I now feed on for present delight. When I recall the years . . . I am filled with a sense of sweetness and wonder that such little things can make a mortal so exceedingly rich. But I must confess that the chiefest of all my delights is still the religious."

Another good expression of the "once-born" type of consciousness, developing straight and natural, with no element of morbid compunction or crisis, is contained in the answer of *Dr. Edward Everett Hale*, the eminent Unitarian preacher and writer, to one of Dr. Starbuck's circulars. I quote a part of it:—

"*I observe, with profound regret, the religious struggles which come into many biographies,* as if almost essential to the formation of the hero. I ought to speak of these, to say that any man has an advantage, not to be estimated, who is born, as I was, into a family where the religion is simple and rational; who is trained in the theory of such a religion, so that he never knows, for an hour, what these religious or irreligious struggles are. I aways knew God loved me, and I was always grateful to him for the world he placed me in. I always liked to tell him so, and was always glad to receive his suggestions to me. . . . *I can remember perfectly that when I was coming to manhood, the half-philosophical novels of the time had a deal to say about the young men and maidens who were facing the* 'problem of life.' I had no idea whatever what the problem of life was. To live with all my might seemed to me easy; to learn where there was so much to learn seemed pleasant and almost of course; to lend a hand, if one had a chance, natural; and if one did this, why, he enjoyed life because he could not help it, and without proving to himself that he ought to enjoy it. . . . A child who is early taught that he is God's child, that he may live and move and have his being in God, and that he has, therefore, infinite strength at hand for the conquering of any difficulty, will take life more easily, and probably will make more of it, than one who is told that he is born the child of wrath and wholly incapable of good."[5]

One can but recognize in such writers as these the presence of a temperament organically weighted on the side of cheer and fatally forbidden to linger, as those of opposite temperament linger, over the darker aspects of the universe. In some individuals optimism may become quasi-pathological. The capacity for even a transient sadness or a momentary humility seems cut off from them as by a kind of congenital anaesthesia.[6]

The supreme contemporary example of such an inability to feel evil is of course Walt Whitman.

"His favorite occupation," writes his disciple, Dr. Bucke, "seemed to be strolling or sauntering about outdoors by himself, looking at the grass, the trees, the flowers, the vistas of light, the varying aspects of the sky, and listening to the birds, the crickets, the tree frogs, and all the hundreds of natural sounds. It was evident that these things gave him a pleasure far beyond what they give to or-dinary people. Until I knew the man," continues Dr. Bucke, "it had not occurred to me that any one could derive so much absolute happiness from these things as he did. He was very fond of flowers, either wild or cultivated; liked all sorts. I think he admired lilacs and sunflowers just as much as roses. Perhaps, indeed, no man who ever lived liked so many things and disliked so few as Walt Whit-man. All natural objects seemed to have a charm for him. All sights and sounds seemed to please him. He appeared to like (and I be-

lieve he did like) all the men, women, and children he saw
(though I never knew him to say that he liked any one), but each
who knew him felt that he liked him or her, and that he liked
others also. I never knew him to argue or dispute, and he never
spoke about money. He always justified, sometimes playfully,
sometimes quite seriously, those who spoke harshly of himself or
his writings, and I often thought he even took pleasure in the opposition of enemies. When I first knew [him], I used to think that he
watched himself, and would not allow his tongue to give expression to fretfulness, antipathy, complaint, and remonstrance. It did
not occur to me as possible that these mental states could be absent
in him. After long observation, however, I satisfied myself that
such absence or unconsciousness was entirely real. He never spoke
deprecatingly of any nationality or class of men, or time in the
world's history, or against any trades or occupations—not even
against any animals, insects, or inanimate things, nor any of the
laws of nature, nor any of the results of those laws, such as illness,
deformity, and death. He never complained or grumbled either at
the weather, pain, illness, or anything else. He never swore. He
could not very well, since he never spoke in anger and apparently
never was angry. He never exhibited fear, and I do not believe he
ever felt it."[7]

Walt Whitman owes his importance in literature to the systematic expulsion from his writings of all contractile elements. The
only sentiments he allowed himself to express were of the expansive
order; and he expressed these in the first person, not as your mere
monstrously conceited individual might so express them, but vicariously for all men, so that a passionate and mystic ontological emotion suffuses his words, and ends by persuading the reader that
men and women, life and death, and all things are divinely good.

Thus it has come about that many persons to-day regard Walt
Whitman as the restorer of the eternal natural religion. He has
infected them with his own love of comrades, with his own gladness that he and they exist. Societies are actually formed for his
cult; a periodical organ exists for its propagation, in which the
lines of orthodoxy and heterodoxy are already beginning to be
drawn;[8] hymns are written by others in his peculiar prosody; and
he is even explicitly compared with the founder of the Christian
religion, not altogether to the advantage of the latter.

Whitman is often spoken of as a "pagan." The word nowadays means sometimes the mere natural animal man without a sense of sin; sometimes it means a Greek or Roman with his own peculiar religious consciousness. In neither of these senses does it fitly define this poet. He is more than your mere animal man who has not tasted of the tree of good and evil. He is aware enough of sin for a swagger to be present in his indifference towards it, a conscious pride in his freedom from flexions and contractions, which your genuine pagan in the first sense of the word would never show.

"I could turn and live with animals, they are so placid and self-contained,
I stand and look at them long and long;
They do not sweat and whine about their condition.
They do not lie awake in the dark and weep for their sins.
Not one is dissatisfied, not one is demented with the mania of owning things,
Not one kneels to another, nor to his kind that lived thousands of years ago,
Not one is respectable or unhappy over the whole earth."[9]

No natural pagan could have written these well-known lines. But on the other hand Whitman is less than a Greek or Roman; for their consciousness, even in Homeric times, was full to the brim of the sad mortality of this sunlit world, and such a consciousness Walt Whitman resolutely refuses to adopt. When, for example, Achilles, about to slay Lycaon, Priam's young son, hears him sue for mercy, he stops to say:—

"Ah, friend, thou too must die: why thus lamentest thou? Patroclos too is dead, who was better far than thou. . . . Over me too hang death and forceful fate. There cometh morn or eve or some noonday when my life too some man shall take in battle whether with spear he smite, or arrow from the string."[10]

Then Achilles savagely severs the poor boy's neck with his sword, heaves him by the foot into the Scamander, and calls to the fishes of the river to eat the white fat of Lycaon. Just as here the cruelty and the sympathy each ring true, and do not mix or interfere with one another, so did the Greeks and Romans keep all their sadnesses and gladnesses unmingled and entire. Instinctive good they did not reckon sin; nor had they any such desire to save the credit of the universe as to make them insist, as so many of *us* insist, that what immediately appears as evil must be "good in the making," or something equally ingenious. Good was good, and bad just bad, for the earlier Greeks. They neither denied the ills of nature,—Walt Whitman's verse, "What is called good is perfect and what is called bad is just as perfect," would have been mere silliness to them,—nor did they, in order to escape from those ills, invent "another and a better world" of the imagination, in which, along with the ills, the innocent goods of sense would also find no place. This integrity of the instinctive reactions, this freedom from all moral sophistry and strain, gives a pathetic dignity to ancient pagan feeling. And this quality Whitman's outpourings have not got. His optimism is too voluntary and defiant; his gospel has a touch of bravado and an affected twist,[11] and this diminishes its effect on many readers who yet are well disposed towards optimism, and on the whole quite willing to admit that in important respects Whitman is of the genuine lineage of the prophets.

If, then, we give the name of healthy-mindedness to the tendency which looks on all things and sees that they are good, we find that we must distinguish between a more involuntary and a more voluntary or systematic way of being healthy-minded. In its involuntary variety, healthy-mindedness is a way of feeling happy about things immediately. In a systematical variety, it is an abstract way of conceiving things as good. Every abstract way of conceiving things selects some one aspect of them as their essence for the time being, and disregards the other aspects. Systematic healthy-mindedness, conceiving good as the essential and universal aspect of being, deliberately excludes evil from its field of vision; and although, when thus nakedly stated, this might seem a difficult feat to perform for one who is intellectually sincere with himself and honest about facts, a little reflection shows that the situation is too complex to lie open to so simple a criticism.

In the first place, happiness, like every other emotional state, has blindness and insensibility to opposing facts given it as its instinctive weapon for self-protection against disturbance. When happiness is actually in possession, the thought of evil can no more acquire the feeling of reality than the thought of good can gain reality when melancholy rules. To the man actively happy, from whatever cause, evil simply cannot then and there be believed in. He must ignore it; and to the bystander he may then seem perversely to shut his eyes to it and hush it up.

But more than this: the hushing of it up may, in a perfectly candid and honest mind, grow into a deliberate religious policy, or *parti pris*. Much of what we call evil is due entirely to the way men take the phenomenon. It can so often be converted into a bracing and tonic good by a simple change of the sufferer's inner attitude from one of fear to one of fight; its sting so often departs and turns into a relish when, after vainly seeking to shun it, we agree to face about and bear it cheerfully, that a man is simply bound in honor, with reference to many of the facts that seem at first to disconcert his peace, to adopt this way of escape. Refuse to admit their badness; despise their power; ignore their presence; turn your attention the other way; and so far as you yourself are concerned at any rate, though the facts may still exist, their evil character exists no longer. Since you make them evil or good by your own thoughts about them, it is the ruling of your thoughts which proves to be your principal concern.

The deliberate adoption of an optimistic turn of mind thus makes its entrance into philosophy. And once in, it is hard to trace its lawful bounds. Not only does the human instinct for happiness, bent on self-protection by ignoring, keep working in its favor, but higher inner ideals have weighty words to say. The attitude of unhappiness is not only painful, it is mean and ugly. What can be more base and unworthy than the pining, puling, mumping mood, no matter by what outward ills it may have been engendered? What is more injurious to others? What less helpful as a way out of the difficulty? It but fastens and perpetuates the trouble which occasioned it, and increases the total evil of the situation. At all costs, then, we ought to reduce the sway of that mood; we ought to scout it in ourselves and others, and never show it tolerance. But it is impossible to carry on this discipline in the subjective sphere without zealously emphasizing the brighter and minimizing the darker aspects of the objective sphere of things at the same time. And thus our resolution not to indulge in misery, beginning at a comparatively small point within ourselves, may not stop until it has brought the entire frame of reality under a systematic conception optimistic enough to be congenial with its needs.

In all this I say nothing of any mystical insight or persuasion that the total frame of things absolutely must be good. Such mystical persuasion plays an enormous part in the history of the religious consciousness, and we must look at it later with some care. But we need not go so far at present. More ordinary non-mystical conditions of rapture suffice for my immediate contention. All invasive moral states and passionate enthusiasms make one feelingless to evil in some direction. The common penalties cease to deter the patriot, the usual prudences are flung by the lover to the winds. When the passion is extreme, suffering may actually be gloried in, provided it be for the ideal cause, death may lose its sting, the grave its victory. In these states, the ordinary contrast of good and ill seems to be swallowed up in a higher denomination, an omnipotent excitement which engulfs the evil, and which the human being welcomes as the crowning experience of his life. This, he says, is truly to live, and I exult in the heroic opportunity and adventure.

Notes

1 C. HILTY: Glück, dritter Theil, 1900, p. 18.

2 The Soul; its Sorrows and its Aspirations, 3d edition, 1852, pp. 89, 91.

3 I once heard a lady describe the pleasure it gave her to think that she "could always cuddle up to God."

4 JOHN WEISS: Life of Theodore Parker, i. 152, 32.

5 STARBUCK: Psychology of Religion, pp. 305, 306.

6 "I know not to what physical laws philosophers will some day refer the feelings of melancholy. For myself, I find that they are the most voluptuous of all sensations," writes Saint Pierre, and accordingly he devotes a series of sections of his work on Nature to the Plaisirs de la Ruine, Plaisirs des Tombeaux, Ruines de la Nature, Plaisirs de la Solitude—each of them more optimistic than the last.

This finding of a luxury in woe is very common during adolescence. The truth-telling Marie Bashkirtseff expresses it well:—

"In this depression and dreadful uninterrupted suffering, I don't condemn life. On the contrary, I like it and find it good. Can you believe it? I find everything good and pleasant, even my tears, my grief. I enjoy weeping, I enjoy my despair. I enjoy being exasperated and sad. I feel as if these were so many diversions, and I love life in spite of them all. I want to live on. It would be cruel to have me die when I am so accommodating. I cry, I grieve, and at the same time I am pleased—no, not exactly that—I know not how to express it. But everything in life pleases me. I find everything agreeable, and in the very midst of my prayers for happiness, I find myself happy at being miserable. It is not I who undergo all this—my body weeps and cries; but something inside of me which is above me is glad of it all." Journal de Marie Bashkirtseff, i. 67.

7 R. M. BUCKE: Cosmic Consciousness, pp. 182–186, abridged.

8 I refer to The Conservator, edited by Horace Traubel, and published monthly at Philadelphia.

9 Song of Myself, 32.

10 Iliad, XXI., E. Myers's translation.

11 "God is afraid of me!" remarked such a titanic-optimistic friend in my presence one morning when he was feeling particularly hearty and cannibalistic. The defiance of the phrase showed that a Christian education in humility still rankled in his breast.

Walt Whitman: A Study

JOHN ALDINGTON SYMONDS

THE INSCRIPTION prefixed to *Leaves of Grass*, opens thus:

Small is the theme of the following Chant, yet the greatest—namely
One's Self—that wondrous thing, a simple, separate person.

In all his writings, Whitman has kept personality steadily in view,
as the leading motive of his poetic and prophetic utterance. He
regards wealth, material prosperity, culture, as nothing in comparison with vigorous manhood and womanhood. "The greatest
city is that which has the greatest man or woman." "Nothing en-
dures but personal qualities." "The greater the reform needed, the
greater the personality you need to accomplish it." Nations, consequently, rise or fall, according to the quality of the persons who
constitute them. Human beings are nothing, possess nothing, enjoy
nothing, except through, and by their self, their personality. To
prove this, to demonstrate what an incomparably precious thing
a free and healthy personality, self-centered, self-reliant, self-effec-
tuated, is for the owner of it, how it transcends every other possession which riches or learning can confer, becomes the first object
of his teaching. Secondly, he aims at showing that nations only
thrive and are strong by the character, the grit, the well-developed
personality, of their inhabitants. Nothing can preserve a nation in
prosperity, or perpetuate its fame, except the spiritual elements
it has developed, as distinguished from brute force or accumulated
capital.

This is the point of view from which he says:

will effuse Egotism, and show it underlying all—and I will be
the bard of personality.

Through a want of sympathy and intelligence, people have long
time sneered or cavilled at this proclamation of egotism. We must

strive to comprehend that Whitman does not thereby mean selfishness.

In one of his sublimest flights of the imagination Whitman describes the evolution of man out of primordial elements. He has absorbed the results of modern scientific speculation regarding planetary development and the gradual emergence of life through its successive stages on our globe. The picture is dashed in with broad touches from "the huge first Nothing" to the emergence of a conscious human soul.

I am an acme of things accomplished, and I am an encloser of
     things to be.

Afar down I see the huge first Nothing—I know I was even there;
I waited unseen and always, and slept through the lethargic mist,
And took my time, and took no harm from the fetid carbon.

Long I was hugged close—long and long.

Immense have been the preparations for me,
Faithful and friendly the arms that have helped me.

Cycles ferried my cradle, rowing and rowing like cheerful boatmen;
For room to me stars kept aside in their own rings;
They sent influences to look after what was to hold me.
Before I was born out of my mother, generations guided me,
My embryo has never been torpid—nothing could overlay it.
For it the nebula cohered to an orb,
The long, low strata piled to rest it on,
Vast vegetables give it sustenance,
Monstrous sauroids transported it in their mouths, and deposited
     it with care.

All forces have been steadily employed to complete and delight me;
Now on this spot I stand with my robust soul.

This passage will serve as a transition from the theme of cosmic enthusiasm to what Whitman considered the main motive of his prophecy. A man's self, his personality, being an indestructible integer of the universe, it follows that each one of us contains within himself sympathies with nature and sensibilities that link him to the world he lives in.

I do not doubt but the majesty and beauty of the world are latent
    in any iota of the world;
I do not doubt I am limitless, and that the universes are limitless—
    in vain I try to think how limitless.

So then, the method of self-effectuation, the training and per-
fecting of personality, consists in the effort to "tally nature," as Walt
somewhat quaintly phrases it. The true man is one:

Who includes diversity, and is Nature,
Who is the amplitude of the earth, and the coarseness and sexuality
    of the earth, and the great charity of the earth, and the equili-
    brium also,
Who has not looked forth from the windows, the eyes for nothing,
    or whose brain held audiences with messengers for nothing;

Who, out of the theory of the earth, and of his or her body, under-
    stands by subtle analogies all other theories,
The theory of a city, a poem, and of the large politics of These
    States.

This is the new meaning given to that much-belauded and dis-
paraged Greek phrase, to live according to Nature. Whitman
applies it in a very particular sense:

Now I see the secret of the making of the best persons,
It is to grow in the open air, and to eat and sleep with the earth.

You must test all the products of the human mind by comparison with things in the world around you, see how far they agree
with what you find in nature, whether they are applicable to the
"broadcast doings of the night and day":

Now I re-examine philosophies and religions,
They may prove well in lecture-rooms, and yet not prove at all
    under the spacious clouds, and along the landscape and flowing
    currents.
Here is realization;
Here is a man tallied—he realizes here what he has in him;
The animals, the past, the future, light, space, majesty, love, if
    they are vacant of you, you are vacant of them.

He who has imbued himself with nature, and is at harmony
with the world, is the proper judge, and critic, and sayer of words.

To the would-be poet Whitman cries:

Can your performance face the open fields and the seaside?
Will it absorb into me as I absorb food, air—to appear again in
my strength, gait, face?

To the student of his own works he says:

If you would understand me, go to the heights or watershore;
The nearest gnat is an explanation, and a drop or motion of waves
a key;
The maul, the oar, the hand-saw, second my words.

No shuttered room or school can commune with me,
But roughs and little children know me better than they.
The young mechanic is closest to me—he knows me well.

The real poems, the real words, are not what people say, but
things in the world, actualities, emotions, whereof words are but
the shadows and grey phantoms:

Human bodies are words, myriads of words;
Air, soil, water, fire—these are words;
The workmanship of souls is by the inaudible words of the earth;
I swear there is no greatness or power that does not emulate those
of the earth.

Logic and sermons never convince:
The damp of the night drives deeper into my soul;
The real poems (what we call poems being merely pictures).
The poems of the privacy of the night, and of men like me.

Practising what he preaches, Whitman avers that he never com-
posed except in the open air, and says of his own poems:

I have read these leaves to myself in the open air—I have tried them
by trees, stars, rivers.

In the prelude of one of his solemn diatribes upon the cosmic
unity which connects and enfolds all creatures and all things, he
represents himself alone at night beside the sea, beneath the stars,
and then:

I think a thought of the clef of the universe, and of the future.

This conception of the intimate relation which exists between human personality and the external world, penetrates the whole of Whitman's work. To cull further instances would be superfluous. But, in order to understand it and to appreciate its application, three pieces ought to be attentively studied. These are: *The Song of the Open Road, To Working Men (A Song of Occupation), To the Sayers of Words (A Song of the Rolling Earth)*.

The great facts, then, are the universe and personality. The world and man. Each self alone, and for itself the measure of the world; trained and taught by nature more than by churches and traditions; by experience of life, by conduct and emotion, more than by creeds and formulas. Whitman insists upon the independence and the arrogance of the self, what the Greeks called *avtápkela*, what the Germans call Selbstständigkeit. He will even sacrifice some points of conduct and morality for this spinal quality of self-reliance. Revolt against opinion, rebellion against law, indulgence in untamed proclivities, are even justified in certain cases:

I am not the poet of goodness only—I do not decline to be the
    poet of wickedness also.
What blurt is this about virtue and about vice?
Evil propels me, and reform of evil propels me—I stand indifferent;
My gait is no fault finder's or rejecter's gait;
I moisten the root of all that has grown.

To enforce his doctrine of personality, Whitman insists that everything which is, exists for the individual. All doctrines, politics, civilizations, poems, art, music, are for him. Religions have grown like leaves of grass from the individual soul. Without you, without me, without human personalities, where would all these things be?

Whoever you are! you are he or she for whom the earth is solid
    and liquid,
You are he or she for whom the sun or moon hang in the sky,
For none more than you are the present and the past,
For none more than you is immortality.
Each man to himself, and each woman to herself, such is the word
    of the past and present, and the word of immortality;
No one can acquire for another—not one!
No one can grow for another—not one!

In like manner, it is only through ourselves, by what each one is and has become, that we enjoy or suffer, enter into our natural heritage or are defrauded of our birthright. Consider, then, of what vast importance it is for all of us to maintain our personality in health and vigour, to abstain from habits that warp or degrade, to encourage the nobler and sweeter elements of our nature. Though Whitman proclaims himself the "poet of wickedness," he is well aware that wrong conduct, perversity, meanness, uncleanliness, are deleterious to self. "The murder is to the murderer, and comes back most to him; the theft is to the thief, the love is to the lover, the gift is to the giver, and comes back most to him; it cannot fail." Whatsoever a man soweth, that shall he also reap. The doer must suffer for his deed. There is no act that has not everlasting consequences to the agent. Each soul dresses the doom of its own action and emotion. We find no immortality in Whitman's gospel of egotism.

Charity and personal force are the only investments worth anything. No specification is necessary—all that a male or female does that is vigorous, benevolent, clean, is so much profit to him or her, in the unshakable order of the universe, and through the whole scope of it forever.

The young man who composedly perilled his life and lost it, has done exceedingly well for himself, without doubt.
He who never perilled his life, but retains it to old age in riches and ease, has probably achieved nothing for himself worth mentioning.

Terrible is the doom of those who, by neglecting their health of body and soul, by shutting up their minds to natural influences, by truckling to superstitions and serving false gods, injure their own self. They have lost the greatest joy of living:

O the joy of a manly self-hood!
Personality—to be servile to none—to defer to none—not to any tyrant, known or unknown,
To walk with erect carriage, a step springy and elastic,
To look with calm gaze, or with flashing eye,
To speak with a full sonorous voice, out of a broad chest,
To confront with your personality all the other personalities of the earth.

The supremest of joys will be missed by those who do not respect self as their sole and indefeasible possession.

But what meaning does Whitman attach to this word Personality? How does he envisage that phenomenon of self, which is the one thing certain for each separate individual who thinks and feels, and which he has therefore selected as the main motive of his prophecy?

Personality presents itself to him, as to average man or woman, under the double aspect of soul and body, and furthermore as differentiated by sex. He appears to have believed that in this life the soul is inextricably connected with the body, so that whatever is done in the mind redounds to the advantage or disadvantage of the soul. At the same time the fleshly body is destined to dissolution. It is pronounced to be "excrementitious," whereas the principle of self-hood is indestructible, and the soul may be transformed, but can never perish.

During this life, at any rate, the body constitutes a man and forms the channel of communication between his soul and outer things.[1]

I too had received identity by my Body:
That I was, I knew was of my body—and what I should be, I knew should be of my body.

The body was therefore a mystic value for Whitman, not merely because of its exceeding beauty and delightfulness, but also because it is verily the temple of the divinest of all the things we know, the human soul.

If I worship one thing more than another, it shall be the spread of my own body, or any part of it.
If anything is sacred, the human body is sacred.
And the glory and sweet of a man, is the token of manhood untainted;
And in man or woman, a clean, strong, firm-fibred body, is beautiful as the most beautiful face.

---

1 In conversation with Mr. J. W. Wallace at Camden, in the year 1891, Whitman spoke of "my favourite theory of physiological development underlying all."

The paramount importance of pure and wholesome manhood or womanhood becomes apparent when we reflect that:

All comes by the body—only health puts you rapport with the
universe.

Again, though the actual form of flesh which clothes us in this life be excrementitious, still the body in some higher sense is not doomed to die.

Of your real body, and any man's or woman's real body,
Item for item, it will elude the hands of the corpse-cleaners, and
pass to fitting spheres,
Carrying what has accrued to it from the moment of birth to the
moment of death.

Behold! the body includes and is the meaning, the main concern—
and includes and is the soul;
Whoever you are! how superior and how divine is your body, or
any part of it.

Think of the soul;
I swear to you that body of yours gives proportions to your soul
somehow to live in other spheres;
I do not know how, but I know it is so.

No wonder, then, if Whitman, feeling thus, exclaims at times that the distinction between soul and body, so far as the individual is concerned, vanishes away.

I have said that the soul is not more than the body,
And I have said that the body is not more than the soul;
And nothing, not God, is greater to one than one's self is.

We may not ask what is Whitman's ideal of human personality. Where does he find the best type of self, the manliest man, the most womanly woman? The answer to this question is not far to seek, when we bear in mind what we already know about his preference for open life and nature. His hero is sure to be some "nonchalant and natural person"; not a man of culture or a bookworm, but one who has been born with a fine physique, capable of subduing the external world to his own purpose, and delighting in his labour; a man of healthy instincts and strong passions, vividly enjoying the boon pleasures of life, and keenly responding to the beauty and the wonder of the world.

The boy I love, the same becomes a man, not through derived
    power, but in his own right,
Wicked, rather than virtuous out of conformity or fear,
Fond of his sweetheart, relishing well his steak,
Unrequited love, or a slight, cutting him worse than sharp steel
    cuts,
First-rate to ride, to fight, to hit the bull's eye, to sail a skiff, to
    sing a song, to play on the banjo
Preferring scars, and the beard, and faces pitted with smallpox,
    over all latherers,
And those well tanned to those that keep out of the sun.

This theme is repeated with endless variations. The ground-thought recurs over and over again, and will be found to dominate all his theory of the state politic . . . Such men Whitman calls "athletes," and the women he demands for the back-bone of a nation must equally be "athletic." He is convinced that in such personalities the soul reaches its maximum of magnetic attraction and persuasiveness.

Here rises the fluid and attaching character;
The fluid and attaching character is the freshness and sweetness
    of man and woman;

Toward the fluid and attaching character exudes the sweat of the
    love of young and old;
From it falls distilled the charm that mocks beauty and attainments;
Toward it heaves the shuddering longing ache of contact.

I and mine do not convince by arguments, similes, rhymes;
We convince by our presence.

"To effuse magnetism," to attract and persuade by merely being vigorous and sound and free, is the crown and glory of a perfected personality.

Do you not see how it would serve to have such a body and soul, that when you enter the crowd, an atmosphere of desire and command enters with you, and every one is impressed with your personality?

❊   ❊   ❊   ❊

The transition from Personality to Sex offers no difficulty. Sex, the passions, the affections, love, are clearly the main things in life.

In his treatment of Love, Whitman distinguishes two broad kinds of human affection; the one being the ordinary sexual relation, the other comradeship or an impassioned relation between man and man. The former he describes as "amativeness," the latter as "adhesiveness." There is no reason why both forms of emotion should not co-exist in the same person. Indeed, Whitman makes it plain that a completely endowed individuality, one who, as Horace might have said, is "entirely rounded and without ragged edges," will be highly susceptible of both. The exact bearing of amativeness and adhesiveness upon one another, and upon the spiritual nature of the individual, has been fully expressed in the following poem:

Fast-anchored eternal O love! O woman I love!
O bride! O wife! More resistless than I can tell, the thought of you!
Then separate, as disembodied or another born,
Ethereal, the last athletic reality, my consolation,
I ascend, I float in the regions of your love, O man,
O sharer of my roving life.

Since this is the most condensed and weighty of Whitman's utterances upon the subject of love, every word in it may be supposed to have been carefully considered. It is not therefore insignificant to notice that, in the edition of 1860-61, "primeval" stood for "fast-anchored" in the first line, and the "purest born" for "or another born" in the third line.

The section of his complete works which deals exclusively with sexual love, is entitled *Children of Adam*. The frankness and the rankness of the pieces composing this chapter called down a storm of insults, calumnies, unpopularity, on Whitman. Yet the attitude which he assumed as poet and prophet demanded this frankness, while the spirit of his treatment deprived the subject-matter of its rankness.

His originality consisted, I have said, in giving the idealism of poetry and powerful emotion to the blank results of modern science. Now it is in the very nature of science to consider nothing as "common or unclean," to accept all the facts presented to its vision with indifference, caring for nothing in the process of analysis except the proof of reality, the elucidation of truth. Science, in her wise impartiality, regards morbid phenomena, disease and decay, crime and aberration, as worthy of attention, upon the same lines as healthy and normal products. She knows that pathology is an indispensable adjunct to the study of organic structure.

Sharing the scientific spirit in his quality of poet, Whitman was not called to celebrate what is unhealthy and abnormal in humanity. That is the proper subject for the laboratory. The poet's function is to stimulate and to invigorate. It is his duty to insist upon what is wholesome, the things in life which conduce to organic growth, the natural instincts and normal appetites upon which the continuation of the species, the energy of the individual, the welfare of the family, the fabric of the commonwealth, eventually rest. Feeling thus, and being penetrated with the scientific spirit, Whitman was justified in claiming the whole of healthy manhood and womanhood for his province. To exclude sex from his account of human nature would have been absurd; for it is precisely sex by which men and women are differentiated; sex which brings them into mutual relations of amativeness; sex which determines the preservation and the future of the species. The inspiration which prompted him, first among modern poets, to penetrate the blank results of science with imagination and emotion, led him inevitably to a frank treatment of sexual relations. Each portion of the healthy body had for a thinker of his type to be considered "sweet and clean." He could not shrink from the facts of paternity and maternity, these being the most important for both men and women, and through them for society at large. For him "the parts and poems of the body" are not "of the body only, but of the soul"—indeed "these are the soul." Following the impulse which forced him to insist upon a vigorous and healthy personality or self as the fundamental integer of human life, he proceeded to impress upon his nation the paramount duty of maintaining a robust and healthy breed. Scientific pathology may be left to deal with abnormalities and diseases. The social conscience is sufficiently, if dimly, acquainted with those evils. For the poet, who has accepted the scientific point of view, it is enough to indicate their wrongness. But he enjoys the privilege of proclaiming the beauty and the goodness of functions and organs which constitute the central reality of human life. To recognize the dignity of sex, to teach personalities, both male and female, that they have the right to take a pride in it, and that this pride is their duty, was for a poet of Whitman's stamp a prime consideration. Those mediaeval lies regarding sexual sinfulness, those foolish panegyrics of chaste abstinence, those base insinuations of foul-minded priests, had to be swept away—not by polemic or vituperation, but by a plain proclamation of the truth which had been veiled from sight so long. Delicacy in matters of sex had become indelicacy by a false habit of envisaging the fact. All falsehood is inconsistent with science and injurious to the best interests of society.

Having entered upon this region with the objects I have hinted at—a recognition of fundamental truths, an acceptance of scientific as opposed to the theological principles, a deep sense of personality, and a conviction that the maintenance of the breed at its highest level of efficiency is a prime condition of national well-being—Whitman naturally treated the ordinary sexual relations with a breadth and simplicity which appear to more sophisticated minds as brutal. He does not shrink from images and descriptions, from metaphors and phrases, as closely borrowed from the facts of sex as are his pictures of the outer world, or his transcripts from the occupations of mankind. Sex, being for him so serious and excellent a thing, has the right to equal freedom of speech with sunrise or sun-setting, the stars in their courses, the woods and fields, the industries of carpenter or typesetter, the courage of soldiers, the inevitable fact of death. Therefore he speaks plainly about many things which hitherto were tacitly ignored in poetry, or were touched upon by seekers after obscene literary effects. It is not inconsequent that he should have been accused of indecency, because the things he talked of had long been held to be indecent. Wishing to remove the stigma of indecency and obscenity, which he rightly considered due to conventionally imported prejudices, he had to face the misconstruction of those who could not comprehend his real intention.

Whitman thought and wrote habitually, not with people of culture, refined tastes, literary and social traditions in view, but for the needs and aspirations of what he called "the divine average." He aimed at depicting robust and sane humanity in his verse. He wanted to brace character, and to create through his art-work a type applicable to all sorts and conditions of men, irrespective of their previous differentiation by specific temperament or class-association. For this reason, his treatment of the sexual relations will be felt by some persons not only to be crudely frank in detail, but also to lack delicacy in its general outlines. The overwhelming attractions of sex, swaying the physique of men and women, are broadly insisted upon. The intercourse established in matrimony is regarded not so much as an intellectual and moral union, but as an association for mutual assistance in the labours of life, and for the production of noble human specimens. It is an Adamic hygienic view of marriage, satisfying the instincts of the primeval man. Take this passage, in which he describes the qualities of the helpmate for his typical male:

Without shame the man I like knows and avows the deliciousness
    of his sex,
Without shame the woman I like knows and avows hers.
Now I will dismiss myself from impassive women,
I will go stay with her who waits for me, and with those women
    that are warm-blooded and sufficient for me;
I see that they understand me, and do not deny me:
I see that they are worthy of me—I will be the robust husband
    of these women.

They are not one jot less than I am,
They are tanned in the face by shining suns and blowing winds,
Their flesh has the old divine suppleness and strength,
They know how to swim, row, ride, wrestle, shoot, run, strike,
    retreat, advance, resist, defend themselves,
They are ultimate in their own right—they are calm, clear, well-
    possessed of themselves . . .

It is obvious, from this slightly humorous, but pregnant passage, that Whitman abandoned those dregs of mediaeval sentimentalism and platonism, which, filtering through the middle-class minds of an unchivalrous modern age, have resulted in commonplace notions about "the weaker and the fairer sex," "woman's mission to console and elevate," the "protection rendered by the stronger to the frailer," "the feminine ornament of our homes"—notions and phrases which the active-minded and able-bodied woman of the present day repudiates, and from the thraldom of which she is rapidly working out her way to freedom. Whitman, to use a phrase from Clough, looked upon love as "fellow-service." He recognized the woman's right to share alike with man in labour and in privilege. And it was not for nothing, as appears from some sentences in the quotation, that he spoke in another place about "the athletic American matron."

A theory of sexual relations, so primitive, so archetypal, so based and planted on the primal needs and instincts, must of necessity lack much of delicacy and fine gradations. It is, however, bracing to return to this from the psychological studies of the modern French school, from such silly and nauseous lucubrations as Bourget's *Physiologie de l'Amour Moderne*, from all that stifling literature of *l'Amour Coupable*, which lands us at last in nothing better than what Whitman calls "the sly settee and the unwholesome adulterous couple."

There is an Aeschylean largeness, a Lucretian energy, in Whitman's *Children of Adam*. Sex is once again recognized, not in its aspect of the boudoir, the alcove, the brothel; but as the bass-note of the world, the universal Pan, unseen, yet omnipresent, felt by all, responded to by all, without which the whole vast symphony of things would have for man no value. By subtle associations, he connects the life of nature, in dewy forests and night-winds, in scents of fruits and pungent plants, in crushed herbs, and the rustling of rain-drenched foliage against our faces, with impressions of the sexual imagination. He finds the choicest images to shadow forth the acts of sex.

The hairy wild bee that murmurs and hankers up and down— that gripes the full-grown lady-flower, curves upon her with amorous firm legs, takes his will of her, and holds himself tremulous and tight till he is satisfied.

That is audacious, in spite of its consummate style, a critic will exclaim. But the same critic, being accustomed by habit to the exercise, reads with equanimity the long-drawn paragraphs and chapters which lay bare the latest secrets of the "sly settee." The boudoir, the alcove, the brothel, have come to be recognized as legitimate subjects for analytical art. Even Bourget, even Catulle Mendès, are accepted and acclaimed. From these taints of the city and civilization Whitman calls us away. He says in passing:

Have you seen the fool that corrupted his own live body? or the
    fool that corrupted her own live body?
For they do not conceal themselves, and cannot conceal themselves.

Here and there he returns to this point and repeats the warning. He insists upon the truth that sins against the body, self-contamination, uncleanly lusts and refinements of sensuality, carrying their own punishments. But he knows that their analysis in literature, except for the professional pathologist and psychiatrist, is harmful to the manhood of the nation; whereas the rehabilitation of healthy and legitimate functions restores the natural man to a sense of his own dignity and responsibility. Nor does Whitman neglect that superflux of sense, which also claims a part in human life, that phallic ecstasy of which the pagan poets sang. A much-criticized piece from *Children of Adam* puts the matter very plainly. It is called *Native Moments*, and need not be enlarged upon. Were we not expressly told by him that it is useless to extract a coherent system from his utterances, we might be puzzled to explain the logical connection of that poem with the rest of the section. I take it that he recognized the right and the necessity of "native moments" in that free play of the normal senses which he is upholding. Only, the ground-thought which penetrate the whole of his work upon this topic, the pervading essence whereof will remain longest with those who have imbibed its spirit, are expressed in lines like these:

If any thing is sacred, the human body is sacred,
And the glory and sweet of a man is the token of manhood
    untainted;
And in man or woman, a clean, strong, firm-fibred body is beautiful
    as the most beautiful face.

If Aeschylus could come again, he would recognize Whitman's treatment of Aphrodite as akin to these lines of his own:

Love throbs in holy heaven to wound the earth;
And love still prompts the land to yearn for bridals
The rain that falls in rivers from the sky,
Impregnates earth, and she brings forth her men
The flocks and herds and life of teeming Ceres;
The bloom of forests by dews hymeneal
Is perfected: in all which things I rule.

If we are to have sex handled openly in literature—and I do not see why we should not have it, or how we are to avoid it— surely it is to be better to be in the company of poets like Aeschylus and Whitman, who place human love among the large and universal mysteries of nature, than to dwell with theologians who confound its simple truth with sinfulness, or with self-dubbed "psychologues" who dabble in its morbid pruriencies.

Walt Whitman: Lover and Comrade

PAUL LAUTER

WALT WHITMAN's relations with his reader were both personal and didactic: he wished to invite comradeship and also to inculcate certain precepts. Revelation of hard won personal insight and assertion of moral and metaphysical "truths" intersect to provide Whitman's poetry with its distinctive quality. It would therefore seriously distort Whitman to view his work solely as the product of either motive; however it is useful to distinguish and to explore the psychological and programmatic impulses and their connections, if for no other reason than to clear the ground for an integrated reading of *Leaves of Grass*. The primary purpose of this paper is to organize the rich background material—for clarification of Whitman's relations with and attitudes toward real men and women, and as a kind of prologue to a study of the imaginative comradeship he established with the readers of his book.

I

Whitman idealized women as madonnas, pure and wise beyond the ken of men, but from earliest childhood he was terribly insecure in the presence of girls. George Whitman commented on Walt's youth: ". . . I am confident I never knew Walt to fall in love with young girls or even to show them marked attention. He did not seem to affect the girls."[1] Shyness toward women, originating partly in his feeling that social situations inevitably implied "sex," precluded any lasting heterosexual relationship. Brought up among lower-class working people, Whitman was further inhibited by his ignorance of "polite" society, from which he was excluded until after he had achieved a type of fame. For these reasons he never "fit" into the mixed-company drawing-room, always preferring the men's smoker,[2] or, if forced to join "society," adopting the pose he himself pathetically described:

You ought to be here with me a day or so—(likely one day would be enough *for you*, as there is no city excitement or fashions—no sogering & no balls or theatres—but quite a lot of *gals*, & some real nice ones—I take an old man's liberty of *kissing them all* (especially the handsome ones) when I go around where they are—[3]

Whitman could, as Professor G. W. Allen has pointed out, hold up his end in conversation—but only in small groups of intimate friends.[4] Whitman's letters to Peter Doyle, a man whose opinions he knew were close to his own, make apparent his ill-defined sense of social inferiority and permit us to understand the often crude over-compensation of the "free old hawk."[5]

I talked too, indeed went like a house afire. It was good exercise—for the fun of the thing. I also made love to the women, and flatter myself that I created at least one impression—wretch and gay deceiver that I am. The truth is Peter, that I am here at the present time mainly in the midst of female women, some of them young and jolly, and meet them most every evening in company, and the way in which this aged party comes up to scratch and cuts the youthful parties and fills their hearts with envy is absolutely a caution. You would be astonished, my son, to see the brass and coolness and the capacity of flirtation and carrying on with the girls—I would never have believed it of myself. Brought here by destiny, surrounded in this way and, as I in self defense would modestly state, sought for, seized upon and ravenously devoured by these creatures—and so nice and smart some of them are, and handsome too—there is nothing left for me, is there, but to go in. Of course, young man, you understand it is all on the square. My going in amounts to just talking and joking and having a devil of a jolly time carrying on—that's all. They are all as good girls as ever lived.[6]

The bluff exaggeration, the self-doubt, the quick apology for implying sexual contacts, the obvious inexperience and naivety are all perfectly typical of Whitman.

Although he could not cope with women, Whitman continued to believe them the more perfect sex: "Charley I think sometimes to be a woman is greater than to be a man—is more eligible to greatness, not the ostensible article, but the real one."[7] This persistent view springs from a deep reservoir of typically Victorian sentimentality:

> We know that humanity is by no means perfect—even the "better half" of humanity. But if goodness, charity, faith, and love reside not in the breasts of females, they reside not on earth. The man who attacks the good name of "the sex," attacks the last resort of the finer virtues which adorn his nature. Retired from the stern conflicts of the world—from the chaffering, grosser strife—women seem to be selected by Providence, as the depositories of the germs of the truest Truth and the fairest Beautiful. In their souls is preserved the ark of the covenant of purity.[8]

Indeed, Whitman's woman is so extraordinary that she will assume all the functions usually reserved for man beside retaining her own divine duties: "A woman is to be able to ride, swim, run, resist, advance, [re?]fuse, shoot, defend herself, sail a boat, hunt, rebel,—just as much as a man."[9] In his insistence upon woman's equality Whitman reaches the pitch of fervor to say nothing of the heights of bombast, usually reserved by feminists for themselves: "Why should there be these modesties and prohibitions keeps [sic] women from strong actual life—from going about there with men."[10]

He was not satisfied, however, with American femininity; even the frontier women, in whom he placed his hopes, could not fit his requirements:

> I am not so well satisfied with what I see of the women of the prairie cities. . . The ladies . . . are all fashionably drest, and have the look of "gentility" in face, manner and action, but they do *not* have, either in physique or the mentality appropriate to them, any high native originality of spirit or body, (as the men certainly have, appropriate to them.)[11]

Whitman's ideal would have to emulate his paternal great grandmother, his paragon of womanhood:

> Sarah White, my great grandmother Whitman, lived to be 90 years old,—she was a large, strong woman, chewed tobacco, opium &c . . . She would sit with her feet up before the fire,

just like a man—was every way decided and masculine in her behavior.[12]

She smoked tobacco, rode on horseback like a man, managed the most vicious horse, and, becoming a widow in later life, went forth every day over her farm-lands, frequently in the saddle, directing the labor of her slaves, with language in which, on exciting occasions, oaths were not spared.[13]

But such a woman is little more than a man who has mysteriously acquired the ability to bear children. Thus Whitman's ideal evolves from his desire to reduce as far as possible the barrier between the sexes,[14] the barrier which so continuously troubled him.

Maintaining such an impossible standard, and burdened by his fear of sexuality, Whitman could hardly have been expected to find the perfect mate for himself. Invariably he turned to the one female on whom he could depend, with whom he could feel secure, for as he loved to relate, " '. . . George like me is the son of my mother.' "[15] Whitman was indeed close to his mother: " 'We have been great chums; always next to each other.' "[16] Until she died he wrote to her at least once or twice a week whenever he was away from home, her home. Their letters are gossipy and intimate, discussing people's health, the vegetables he eats, his new shirts, her household difficulties, mutual friends (mostly older, motherly women).[17] In an early story Whitman makes much of his hero's correspondence with his mother, announcing that "strange as it may seem to most men, she was also his confidential friend."[18] His eternal dream was to build a small shanty in which he and she could peacefully live out their lives together. Mrs. Whitman seems always to have provided warmth and sympathy for Walt, a sense of contact and belongingness. In the intense depression subsequent to his paralysis she remained a rare spark of happiness:

> I have tacked your picture up on the wall at the foot of the bed—the one I like—it looks as natural as can be—& is quite company for me—as I am alone a good deal. . . .[19]

In Whitman's early stories the mother is invariably a sweet, put-upon woman, who strives to protect her son from the injustices of an unfriendly world.[20]

Louisa Whitman thus provided the pattern for all mothers;

other mothers, in turn, served Whitman as substitutes for his own beloved. "He delighted in the company of old fashioned women; mothers of large families preferred. . . ."[21] Whitman sought out motherly women like Abby Price for comfort and warmth, to them he could write and talk about his little daily chores and annoyances, obtaining in return the affection and assurances of maternal love he required. Whitman's need for maternal love also induced him to glorify the mother:

> Mothers always make a special appeal to W. "I know of nothing more beautiful, inspiring, significant: a hale old woman, full of cheer as of years, who has raised a brood of hearty children. . . ."[22]

Of the angelic sex, mothers are the Thrones, Powers, and Dominions: "Mothers precede all. Put in a poem the sentiment of women (mothers) as preceding all the rest. Let this lead the poem of women."[23] As an individual led him to the group, so the group leads him to the abstraction—motherhood the crowning achievement of woman: " 'The best part of any man is his mother. . . . But any mother of any baby has a right to be proud.' "[24] The overwhelming force of this mother-love produces a kind of superficial mother-cult:

> Behold a woman!
> She looks out from her quaker cap, her face is clearer and more
>   beautiful than the sky.
> She sits in an armchair under the shaded porch of the farmhouse,
> The sun just shines on her old white head. . . .
> The melodious character of the earth,
> The finish beyond which philosophy cannot go and does not
>   wish to go,
> The justified mother of men.[25]

This passionate attachment to the mother Whitman elsewhere transmuted into much more effective images of the sea. But while in poems like "Out of the Cradle Endlessly Rocking" a poetic asset, his devotion proved a social liability, for it was still another element inhibiting normal relations with women.

Whitman seems, in fact, to have attempted to establish some type of alliance from time to time during his life; but all attempts, if they really developed, were unsatisfying and transient. The information we have about his love life is scattered, fragmentary, and contradictory. For example, a certain "Ellen Eyre" is purported to have written the following to Whitman on March 25, 1862.

I fear you took me last night for a female privateer. It is time I was sailing under my true colors,—but then today I assume you cared nothing piratical though I would have joyfully made your heart a captive. . . . I trust you will think well enough of me soon to renew the pleasure you afforded me last p.m. and I therefore write to remind you that this is a sensible head as well as a sympathetic heart, both of which would gladly evolve with warmth for your diversion and comfort. You have already my whereabouts and hours. It shall only depend on you to make them yours and me the happiest of women.[26]

While "Ellen Eyre" seems to have existed—"Frank Sweeney . . . (is the one I told the whole story to about Ellen Eyre)"[27]— the original of the letter has never been found. Moreover, the "affair," if such indeed it was, must have ended almost as it began, for the unanimous testimony of Whitman's Washington and New York friends was that he was never "bothered up by a woman."[28] Other similarly mysterious amours—Will Wallace's "frenchy,"[29] the girl whose story Whitman never quite tells Traubel,[30] the imaginary southern belle—crop up from time to time, but the conflicting evidence indicates only rare attempts and invariable failures. Whitman's "love affairs" have been exaggerated by sentimentalist critics who wish to find a broken heart behind every poem, and excessively minimized by some psychological analysts who wish to establish his homosexuality. But the very ambiguity and obviously attenuated nature of any relationships verify only Whitman's wish to establish some sort of tie with a woman and his inability to do so on any full and permanent basis.

In spite of this failing, or perhaps because of it, Whitman considered marriage the ideal refuge for a lonesome spirit: ". . . Whitman upheld the modern theory of marriage as being the ideal relationship between sexes."[31] Thus in real life he would not abide "free love"[32]—relations with women were difficult enough, but relations without the comforting sanction of marriage were unthinkable. Besides, marriage offered particularly attractive prospects:

Whatever may be the care and mishaps of married life, it is probably undeniable that "if there's bliss to be found on earth," (a questionable find!) it must be in the domestic circle. . . . How many blissful hours must be spent by fathers, in the blessedness of mere *presence* of affectionate children! How much of happiness is going on—(a cheerful thought that almost cancels the sad evidence of misery we see towering on every side!)—that is dreamed of by no mortal mind—seen by no mortal eye—except the few participants in it . . .[33]

Those who do not marry "at best live single and imperfect lives, losing the healthy, beautifying power which God intended them to find in the family relations, isolated units in a world whose essence is association."[34] And Whitman recognized himself as one of those "isolated units," although he hid behind the generalized "authors":

Of all the calamities of authors—of all the infelicities of genius— it strikes us that their domestic difficulties are the worst. Take all else from a man and leave him a good and faithful wife and he can never be called unhappy no matter what may be the fluctuations of fortune. But take that comfort, consolation and safeguard away and he becomes "poor" indeed—a vessel without a rudder, beaten here and there, at the mercy of the wind and waves.[35]

Despite his loneliness, despite the bliss which he thought marriage afforded, Whitman remained a bachelor, sometimes fighting hard to continue single. Each time the possibility of marriage arose, his fear of intimacy with women overcame his expressed program and very probable desire. The heaviest seige laid against his bachelorship was that of Anne Gilchrist, a refined, educated, upper-class Englishwoman whom Rossetti had introduced to *Leaves of Grass* in 1869. Mrs. Gilchrist, like a number of other women, loved with an undisguised passion the virile, athletic poet she discovered in *Leaves.* Assuming equivalence of Whitman and his eidolon, she wrote to him in the same spirit she found in the poems:

In May, 1869, came the voice over the Atlantic to me—O, the voice of my Mate: it must be so—my love rises up out of the very depths of the grief & tramples upon despair. I can wait—

any time, a lifetime, many lifetimes—I can suffer, I can dare, I can learn, grow, toil, but nothing in life or death can tear out of my heart the passionate belief that one day I shall hear that voice say to me, "My Mate. The one I so much want. Bride, Wife, indissoluble eternal!" It is not happiness I plead with God for—it is the very life of my Soul, my love is its life, Dear Walt. It is a sweet & precious thing, this love; it clings so close, so close to the Soul and Body, all so tenderly dear, so beautiful, so sacred; it yearns with such passion to soothe and comfort & fill thee with sweet tender joy; it aspires as grandly, as gloriously as thy own soul. Strong to soar—soft & tender of nestle and caress. If God were to say to me, "See—he that you love you shall not be given to in this life—he is going to set sail on the unknown sea—will you go with him?" never yet has bride sprung into her husband's arms with the joy with which I would take thy hand & spring from the shore.[36]

A month later she wrote: "I am yet young enough to bear thee children, my darling."[37]

Whitman must have been flattered by the homage offered him, and titillated by the boost to his manly ego. But as pleased as parts of the letters may have made him, the suggestion of permanent ties, responsibilities, and worst, social and sexual intercourse, horrified him. As much as he would have liked to believe he was the man Mrs. Gilchrist thought him, he could not; he immediately recognized that the situation could end only pathetically. At first he hoped that by not writing, by closing his eyes to the siren, she might go away. But Mrs. Gilchrist persisted, and her second letter apparently convinced Whitman that he would have to face the threat. Thus on November 3, 1871 he replied in a letter which pathetically reveals his inability to share, and perhaps even to appreciate, the nature and the depths of Mrs. Gilchrist's passion:

I wish to give it [writing to her] a day, a sort of Sabbath, or holy day, apart to itself, under serene and propitious influences, confident that I could then write you a letter which would do you good, and me too. But I must at least show without further delay that I am not insensible to your love. I too send you my love. And do you feel no disappointment because I now write so briefly. My book is my best letter, my response, my truest explanation of all. In it I have put my body and spirit. You understand this better and fuller than anyone else. And I too fully and clearly understand the loving letter that it evoked. Enough that there surely exists so beautiful and delicate a relation, accepted by both of us with joy.[38]

Mrs. Gilchrist, however, could not recognize that the "mate" of the poems did not exist, and she continued to implore Whitman to call her to him. But the "mate," growing desperate, and hoping to friendship on a less personal level, replied:

DEAR FRIEND

Your late letter has just reached me—& I write at once to at least say specifically that both your letter of Sept. 6 and that of Oct. 15 safely reached me—this that comes today being the third.

Again I will say that I am sure I appreciate & accept your letters, & all they stand for, as fully as even you, dear friend, could wish—& as lovingly & *bona fide*.[39]

And thus the correspondence dragged on, Mrs. Gilchrist writing animated, passionate love letters, and Whitman replying only rarely, and then with the impersonal notes that became his trademark. When she finally came to the United States, despite his desperate efforts to head her off, she was, inevitably, disappointed. She found her Walt a sick, shy old man, who was not and never could have been the phallic wonder of the poems.

In spurning Mrs. Gilchrist (and her attempt must stand for the others), Whitman denied many of the principles he had affirmed for his program, for he rejected a healthy mother of three, a potential wife and companion, and above all the sexual fulfillment he insisted upon. But it was not unusual for Whitman to fear and repudiate in personal life what he emphasized so strongly in theory, for "program" served frequently to compensate for shortcomings of personality—even if we were ignorant of Whitman's difficulties with women, we might suspect his virility because of the very way in which, even outside "program" poems, he overemphasized it. Moreover, Whitman's "program" was by no means necessarily a program for Whitman (though in later life he began to assume it was). He himself hardly recognized that the "Children of Adam" poems were, in their ritualistic, mechanical, and abstract way, love bleats. When they were reacted to in kind, he became confused and unresponsive. Receiving the following letter, he had scrawled " ? insane asylum" across the envelope:

. . . Know Walt Whitman that thou hast a child for me! [Just what Whitman had been claiming] A noble perfect manchild. I charge you my love not to give it to another woman. The world demands it! It is not for you and me, *is our child*, but for the world. My womb is clean and pure. It is ready for thy child my love. Angels guard the vestibule until thou comest to deposit our and the world's precious treasure. Then oh! how lovingly will I cherish and guard it, our child my love. Thine the pleasure my love. Mine the sweet burden and pain. Mine the sacrifice. Mine to have the stinging rebuke, the shame, I am willing. My motives are pure and holy. Our boy my love! Do you not already love him? He must be begotten on a mountain top, in the open air. Not in *lust*, not in mere gratification of sensual passion, but in holy ennobling pure strong deep glorious passionate broad universal love. I charge you to prepare my love.

I love you, I love you, come, come, Write.[40]

I said to W.: "Why did you write ' ? insane asylum' there?" He asked: "Isn't it crazy?" "No: it's Leaves of Grass." "What do you mean?" "Why—it sounds like somebody who's taking you at your word." He said: "I've had more than one notion of the letter: I suppose the fact that certain things are unexpected, unusual, makes it hard to get them in their proper perspective: the process of adjustment is a severe one." I said: "You should have been the last man in the world to write 'insane' on that envelope." Then I added: "But the question mark saves you . . . . You might as well have written 'insane' across Children of Adam and the Song of Myself." He said: "Many people do." "Yes," I replied: "they do—but you don't." He assented by a nod of his head: "I suppose you are right."[41]

Whitman recognized the force of sexual drives, even if he did not (or could not) accede to them: "There are certain propensities and passions inherent in our nature which will have vent in one shape or another, despite all the combined legislative wisdom of communities."[42] This was not detached, scientific observation, but was based upon his experiences with his own highly sexed nature. Sex, in fact, became central in Whitman's apprehension of life:

"I look at the girls—at the childless women—at the old maids,
as you speak of them: they lack something: they are not completed: something yet remains undone. They are not quite full—
not quite entire: the woman who has denied the best of herself—the woman who has discredited the animal want, the eager
physical hunger, the wish of that which though we will not
allow it to be freely spoken of is still the basis of all that
makes life worth while and advances the horizon of discovery.
Sex: sex: sex: whether you sing or make a machine, or go to
the North Pole, or love your mother, or build a house, or black
shoes, or anything—anything at all—it's sex, sex, sex: sex is root
of it all: sex—the coming together of men and women: sex:
sex."[43]

Such carnal incantation vibrates somewhere between mysticism
and fustian, the poles of his sexual poems.[44]

On a deeply personal level this crucial bodily function becomes
the source of mystical experience. Klaus Mann and Schyberg both
point out that in his private life Whitman's "eroticism merges with
his religious emotion"[45] in a way not unusual among mystics:
". . . sensual enchantment is transformed into metaphysical divina-
tion: the delirium of the mortal flesh mysteriously contains and
guarantees the immortality of the soul."[46] A sexual experience
(albeit autoerotic) precipitates the central mystical revelation of
"Song of Myself":

I mind how once we lay such a transparent summer morning,
How you settled your head athwart my hips and gently turn'd
   over upon me,
And parted my shirt from my bosom-bone, and plunged your
   tongue to my bare-stript heart,
And reach'd till you felt my beard, and reach'd till you held
   my feet.
Swiftly arose and spread around me the peace and knowledge
   that pass all the argument of the earth,
And I know that the hand of God is the promise of my own,
And I know that the spirit of God is the brother of my own,
And that all the men ever born are also my brothers, and the
   women my sisters and lovers,
And that a kelson of the creation is love, . . .[47]

More theoretically, Whitman rejected, on the one hand, repression, which led to "disease and depletion," "morbidity," "inefficient maturity," and "snickering pruriency"; and, on the other, the "sexual Voluptuousness" of wit.[48] He celebrated neither the forbidden nor the sentimental. Taboos are silly, sensuality disgusting; the only proper attitude is open and hygienic,[49] for procreation is the end of sex, procreation by which man attain the divine function of creativity. Whitman shows little interest in sentimental literature,[50] but is fascinated by Lucretius' book (IV) on love, particularly with his detailing of the best positions for conception.[51]

"The time will come when the whole affair of sex—copulation, reproduction—will be treated with the respect to which it is entitled. Instead of meaning shame and being apologized for it will mean purity and will be glorified."[52]

Sex equals "copulation" and "reproduction"; hardly romantic.

This didactic Whitman dipped more toward fustian in his celebration of sex—however functional it might be. *Franklin Evans* (his early "temperance" novel) indicates that glorification of sex was rooted largely in wish-fulfillment: the novel is like an adolescent day-dream, with its voluptuous and varied love affairs—its moralizing seems intrusive among the creations of a highly sexed, but frustrated temperament. Similarly, the sexual advances of his Adamic poems were claims on those faceless, athletic women beyond his range of experience who in imagination would accept and complete him. Wooing took two stages: the ritual of virility, shaking the plumes of manliness; the sexual advance and consummation itself. Nothing of "sentimental" love-making, of affection, of social responsibility interfered with the mating ceremony—the male displayed, boasted of his prowess, and conquered. Strides the poet into the bower as Adam:

Lusty, phallic, with potent original loins, perfectly sweet,
I, chanter of Adamic songs,
Through the new garden the West, the great cities calling,
Deliriate, thus prelude what is generated, offering these, offering
    myself. . . .[53]

"Know," he calls, "I am a man, attracting, at any time, her I but look upon, or touch with the tips of my fingers."[54] Then he closes:

I draw you close to me, you women,
I cannot let you go, I would do you good,
I am for you, and you are for me . . . .

It is I, you women, I make my way,
I am stern, acrid, large, undissuadable, but I love you,
I do not hurt you any more than is necessary for you,

I pour the stuff to start sons and daughters fit for these States,
    I press with slow rude muscle,
I brace myself effectually, I listen to no entreaties,
I dare not withdraw till I deposit what has so long accumulated
    within me.[55]

"Healthy" functionality undercuts sensuality, passion, even "love"—
despite the almost ludicrous "but I love you." Still however manly
his asserted program, Whitman's attitudes toward heterosexual
relations remain essentially adolescent.

Beneath the clamor of virility, puberty whispers on in his
poems: the overwhelming discovery of the body and sex; the high-
pitched celebration; the dreams of glory and myriad conquests; the
idealization and generalization of women; and the escape from the
binding mores of society. Suddenly there bursts upon the boy's
serenity the new world of sex:

The no-form'd stings that sights, people, objects sting me with,
The hubb'd sting of myself, stinging me as much as it ever can
    any one,
The sensitive, orbic, underlapp'd brothers, that only privileged
    feelers may be intimate where they are,
The curious roamer the hand roaming all over the body, the
    bashful withdrawing of flesh where the fingers soothingly
    pause and edge themselves,
The limpid liquid within the young man,
The vex'd corrosion so pensive and so painful,
The torment, the irritable tide that will not be at rest,
The like of the same I feel, the like of the same in others,
The young man that flushes and flushes, the young woman that
    flushes and flushes,
The young man that wakes deep at night, the hot hand seeking
    to repress what would master him,

The mystic amorous night, the strange half-welcome pang,
visions, sweats,
The pulse pounding through palms and trembling encircling fingers, the young man all color'd, red, ashamed, angry. . . .[56]

The body is freshly discovered and celebrated:

O my body! . . .
Head, neck, hair, ears, drop and tympan of the ears,
Eyes, eye-fringes, iris of the eye, eyebrows, and the waking or
sleeping of the lids. . . .[57]

And so caressingly down. Dreams—ever a new Female, ever a new
success:

O to be yielded to you whoever you are, and you to be yielded
to me in defiance of the world!
O to return to Paradise! O bashful and feminine!
O to draw you to me, to plant on you for the first time the lips
of a determin'd man.[58]

The man of the world, hearty, magnetic, freely scattering his seed,
but also the shamefaced boy—vision and reality:

O hotcheek'd and blushing! O foolish hectic!
O for pity's sake, no one must see me now! my clothes were
stolen while I was abed,
Now I am thrust forth, where shall I run?

• • •

I feel ashamed to go naked about the world,
And I am curious to know where my feet stand—and what is
this flooding me, childhood or manhood—and the hunger
that crosses the bridge between.[59]

The woman is never Jane or Jill, never a special lover, but always
a woman, women, "whoever you are." Love must be universal:

By "love" as I have used the term. . . I do not mean the sickly
sentimentality which is so favorite a theme with novelists and
magazine writers. What I would inculcate is that healthy, cheerful feeling of kindness and good will, and affectionate tender-

ness, a warm-heartedness, the germs of which are plentifully
sown by God in each human breast . . .[60]

And sex must be impersonal:

That I infuse you with grits and jets of life,
I am not to be scorned:—I Compell;
It is quite indifferent to me who [you] are.[61]

I will go stay with her who waits for me, and with those women
    that are warm-blooded and sufficient for me,
I see that they understand me and do not deny me,
I see that they are worthy of me, I will be the robust husband
    of these women.[62]

No wonder the author of *Lady Chatterley's Lover*, the champion
of personal intimacy, cried out against "A Woman Waits for Me":

He might as well have said: "The femaleness waits for my
maleness." Oh, beautiful generalization and abstraction! Oh,
biological function.
"Athletic mothers of the States—" Muscles and wombs. They
needn't have had faces at all.[63]

Faceless as she is, the woman who waits "contains all, nothing is
lacking."[64] Perfect, naked, entirely responsive she (or they, it is the
same) is the forever-fleeting ideal of adolescent dream:

They are tann'd in the face by shining suns and blowing winds,
Their flesh has the old divine suppleness and strength . . .[65]

Together the poet and his ideal will escape to a mountain's
heights:

O that you and I escape from the rest and go utterly off, free
    and lawless,
Two hawks in the air, two fishes swimming in the sea not more
    lawless than we. . . .[66]

To escape utterly from others' anchors and holds!
To drive free! to love free! to dash reckless and dangerous!
To court destruction with taunts, with invitations![67]

But it was only from himself that Whitman had to escape, and only into his poems that he could.

As a record of adolescent love the "Children of Adam" poems are remarkable, in fact almost unique in our literature. Frequently flatulent and bombastic, they never contain the tenderness we have come to associate with mature love; that tenderness, the attitude of the lover, Whitman reserves for his poems to men. As an intellectual, programmatic construct. ". . . a Cluster of Poems the same *to the passion of woman-love* as the *Calmus-Leaves* are to adhesiveness, manly love,"[68] they fail because Whitman did not know and could not fully imagine the same passion for women that he did for men. But the very adolescent braggadocio serves as a perhaps too-imitative correlative to what the poems are: unconscious disclosures of a frustrated, yearning, oversexed boy. And as revelations of what they seek to hide these poems are as fascinating, if not always meritorious, as any other part of *Leaves*.

II

Alarmed and frustrated by women, Whitman turned to men for companionship and love. In notes for a proposed lecture, "To women," he confirmed his dissatisfaction with heterosexual relations and his need for man friends:

> I desire to say to you, and let you ponder well upon it, the fact that under present arrangements the love and comradeship of a woman, of his wife, however welcome, however complete, does not and cannot satisfy the grandest requirements of a man's soul for love and comradeship.—The man he loves, he often loves with more passionate attachment than he can bestow on any woman, even his wife.—Is it that the growth of love needs the free air—the seasons, perhaps more wildness more rudeness? Why is the love of women so invalid? so transient?[69]

To women he could offer the compassion and interest of a friend; to men alone the passion and devoted intensity of a lover. To Whitman came the terrible realization that what he had to have was not merely the respect or admiration, not only the friendship, but the love of those to whom he was drawn; that the meeting of eyes could not be casual, and that a smile must have the personal, secret meaning of lovers.[70]

Whitman called this emotion "adhesiveness," which he defined as "love, that fuses, ties and aggregates, making the races comrades, and fraternizing all."[71] But this was a programmatic interpretation of a far more immediate and throbbing passion. One of the phrenologists, from whom Whitman borrowed the term, indicated its carnal overtones:

> Those in whom it is large [i.e. the organ of adhesiveness], feel an involuntary impulse to embrace, and cling to any object which is capable of expressing fondness.[72]

Another showed its extreme emotional force:

> Those who have adhes. *very large*, or predominant, instinctively recognize it in each other; soon become mutually and strongly attached; desire to cling around the objects of their love; take more interest and delight in the exercise of friendship than in anything else; . . . dread an interruption of friendship as the greatest of calamities. . . Their friends may be *few*, but will be *dear*, . . . their social intercourse delightful beyond description; their separation painful, in the extreme; their loss, agonizing, almost beyond endurance; and the interruption of friendship, a frequent source of partial derangement.[73]

A kind of physicality and all but overwhelming power similarly characterized Whitman's "adhesive" passions.

Touch was all important to him:[74] bodily contact with men not only satisfied his need to "feel" reality, but consummated his worship of the male physique. He was throughout his life impelled to hug and kiss his men friends. To Harry Stafford he wrote: "Dear son, how I wish you could come in now, even if but for an hour & take off your coat, & sit down on my lap."[75] And Traubel relates a tender moment with Whitman:

> W. said: "Come, kiss me for good night." He was still lying down. I reached over him and we kissed. He took my hand—pressed it fervently. "I am in luck. Are you? I guess God just sent us for each other."[76]

This physicality was by no means solely a sublimation of sexual desires, but was motivated also by the drive for the warmth of human contact, which requires satisfaction as much as hunger or thirst.[77] Moreover, for a man as feminine in his perceptions as Whitman, it was a way of showing his affection. Thus in the famous scene of the twenty-eight men bathers, Whitman projects himself into the watching woman.[78] Physical contact also provided Whitman with one of his basic symbols of man for man love: the lovers with their arms thrown about each other's necks or waists.

Besides physical contact, Whitman searched in his relations with men for a substitute to replace his own rejected father,[79] adopted "sons" through whom he would perpetuate himself, but above all for companions and lovers. In view of Whitman's passion for marriage and a family, one can understand his attempts to surmount his inability to have real sons by "adopting" as his own the young soldiers, horse-car drivers, farmers, he everywhere met. To these he was a spiritual and intellectual father, introducing them to literature, guiding their taste and attitudes. In another way he was a mother (really the more natural role for him), buying their clothes, nursing them, cooking for them. And in return he received affection of sons for a father:

> . . . i hope the day may come wen i can do for yo some gud in return, for father yo donte know how i do love you i donte know wy it is i am more attached yo than en ny one that i was acquainted with.[80]

Or from another of his boys:

> You will allow me to call you Father wont you. I do not know that I told you that both my parents were dead but it is true and now Walt you will be a second Father to me won't you. for my love for you is hardly less than my love for my natural parent I have never before met with a man that I could love as I do you Still there is nothing strange about it for "to know you is to love you" And how any person could know you and not love you is a wonder to me.[81]

Thus Whitman not only satisfied his latent paternalism, but entered a wedge against oblivion, for through his "sons," as in his *Leaves*, he could gratify his need for self-perpetuation.

But filial affection was not sufficient unto Whitman's "adhesiveness." That he required a fuller, more intense response than "sons" could supply is indicated by his relations with Peter Doyle. They met abruptly, informally, mutually attracted:

"We fell to each other at once. I was a conductor. The night was very stormy,—he had been over to see Burroughs before he came down to take the car—the storm was awful. Walt had his blanket—it was thrown round his shoulders—he seemed like an old sea-captain. He was the only passenger, it was a lonely night, so I thought I would go in and talk with him. Something in me made me do it and something in him drew me that way. He used to say there was something in me had the same effect on him. Anyway, I went into the car. We were familiar at once—I put my hand on his knee—we understood. He did not get out at the end of the trip—in fact he went all the way back with me.[82]

They rode together frequently, drawing closer as, in the months that followed, Whitman adopted Doyle. Separation, as the phrenologists predicted, brought agony to Walt and letters to Doyle:

I think of you very often, dearest comrade, and with more calmness than when I was there. I find it first rate to think of you Pete, and to know that you are there all right and that I shall return and we will be together again. I don't know what I should do if I hadn't you to think of and look forward to.[83]

More than father-son affection or mere abstract Platonic attachment, this is passionate, perturbed love, love that is terribly dependent—but, at last, mutual:

Pete there was something in that hour from 10 to 11 o'clock (parting though it was) that has left me pleasure and comfort for good—I never dreamed that you made so much of having me with you, nor that you could feel so downcast at losing me. I foolishly thought it was all on the other side. But all I will say further on the subject is, I now see clearly, that was all wrong.[84]

Thus Whitman's attachments developed in passionate perturbation, but never, so far as one can tell, in carnality.

Rather, these friendships permitted him, like many others whose instincts force them toward their own sex, to channel his impulses into socially commendable outlets, particularly into charitable work among men.[85] He himself recognized the inner compulsion which drove him to work in the hospitals as something akin to that passionate manly love which possessed him:

> Then came the War. "I was no spring chicken then." His consecration "was no youthful enthusiasm—no mere ebullition of spirit—but deliberate, radical, fundamental." Here he paused, turned his face towards me, passed his fingers, spread, over his heart. "Deliberate? more than that: it was necessary: I went from the call of something within—something, I cannot explain what—something I could not disregard." Whether for good or bad he "could not pause to weight it." "There's something in the human critter that only needs to be budged to reveal itself: not always observed: it is a folded leaf: not absent because we fail to see it: the right man comes—the right hour; the leaf is lifted.[86]

This need joined with Whitman's compassion to direct him toward his hospital activities (which, incidentally, began in New York long before the Civil War). In such work he could practice his principle of sympathy, which in his program required action to relieve misery, and at the same time sublimate the smouldering yearning for lovers that might otherwise have consumed him.

In his hospital labors Whitman played out his more feminine impulses. He realized that his own place was that of sympathetic companion rather than trumpeting prophet and leader:

> Arous'd and angry, I'd thought to beat the alarum, and urge relentless war,
> But soon my fingers fail'd me, my face droop'd and I resign'd myself,
> To sit by the wounded and soothe them, or silently watch the dead.[87]

He gave up the male role of leader and soldier and assumed the for him more suitably feminine robe of nurse. For as Burroughs saw,

With all his rank masculinity, there was a curious feminine undertone in . . . his voice, the delicate texture of his skin, the gentleness of his touch and ways, the attraction he had for children and common people.[88]

Whitman himself did recognize his femininity, insisting that he took after the women in his family, and claiming that " 'Leaves of Grass is essentially a woman's book,' " that its " 'cry is the cry . . . of the woman sex. . . .' "[89] From this female perspective, he formulated what Bychowski calls a "truly feminine cult of manliness and the phallos."[90]

The expression of a perfect made man appears not only in his face—but in his limbs—the motion of his hands and arms and all his joints—his walk—the carriage of his neck—and the fleck of his waist and hips. Dress does not hide him. The quality he has and the clean strong sweet supple nature he has strike through cotton and woolen—To see him walk conveys the impression of hearing a beautiful poem.—To see his back and the back of his neck and shoulderside is a spectacle. Great is the body![91]

Again and again in the poems Whitman revels in the delight of a man's supple body:

The negro holds firmly the reins of his four horses, the block swags underneath on its tied-over chain,
The negro that drives the long dray of the stoneyard, steady and tall he stands pois'd on one leg on the string piece,
His blue shirt exposes his ample neck and breast and loosens over his hip-band,
His glance is calm and commanding, he tosses the slouch of his hat away from his forehead,
The sun falls on his crispy hair and mustache, falls on the black of his polish'd and perfect limbs.[92]

Whitman was conscious of the ambiguity, perhaps of the perverseness on which this feminine ardor bordered. His irrational outbursts against Symonds' innocuous questions about "Calamus" indicate his testiness on the subject when, after the fires had burnt out, he could sense their darker implications:

I said to W.: "That's a humble letter enough: I don't see anything in that to get excited about. He don't ask you to answer the old question. In fact, he rather apologizes for having asked it." W. fired up. "Who is excited? As to that question, he does ask it again and again: asks it, asks it, asks it." I laughed at his vehemence: "Well, suppose he does. It does no harm. Besides, you've got nothing to hide. I think your silence might lead him to suppose there was a nigger in the woodpile." "Oh nonsense! But for thirty years my enemies and friends have been asking me questions about the Leaves: I'm tired of not answering questions."[93]

Such self-doubt is registered more directly in the poems. Mourning his lost love, the poet admits "I am ashamed—but it is useless—I am what I am," and asks, "I wonder if other men ever have the like, out of like feelings?"[94] But these terrible doubts could for him be answered only by the affection, the presence of "my lovers, my dear friends." For in his lonely life it was to these young men that Whitman had to turn for consolation and love.

Pathetically, his special friends never really fathomed Whitman's ardor, appeared in fact confused and bashful before it. His correspondence with Tom Sawyer reads like a pitious mirror-image of the Anne Gilchrist affair. Here Whitman was the active, passionate one:

Dear comrade, you must not forget me, for I never shall you. My love you have in life or death forever. I don't know how you feel about it, but it is the wish of my heart to have your friendship, and also that if you should come safe out of this war, we should come together again in some place where we could make our living, and be true comrades and never be separated while life lasts—and take Lew Brown too, and never separate from him, or if things are not so to be—if you get these lines, my dear, darling comrade, and anything should go wrong, so that we do not meet again here on earth, it seems to me (the way I feel now) that my soul could never be entirely happy, even in the world to come, without you, dear comrade. [What I say is pretty strong talk I suppose but it is I mean exactly what I say am writing have written] And if it is God's will, I hope we shall yet [live] meet, as I say, if you [could] feel as I do about it—and if it is destined that we shall not, you have my love none the less, whatever should keep you from me,

no matter how many years. God bless you, Tom, and preserve
you through the perils of the fight.[95]

Whitman continued to write, asking repeatedly why Sawyer did
not answer. Finally, a note from Tom, probably written for him
by some more literate member of his outfit:

> Dear Brother
> As you have given me permission, I have taken the liberty
> to address you as above. And I assure you I fully reciprocate
> your friendship as expressed in your letter and it will afford me
> great pleasure to meet you after the war will have terminated
> or sooner if circumstances will permit.[96]

How this letter must have torn Whitman; how ironical that he
would one day reply to Mrs. Gilchrist: "I too send you my love."
Later, however, Sawyer replied, apparently in his own person:

> Dear Brother I hardly know what to say to you in this letter
> for it is my first one to you but it will not be my last I should
> have written to you before but I am not a great hand at writtin
> and I have ben very buisy firming my tent for this winter and
> I hope you will forgive me and in the future I will do better
> and I hope we may meet again in this world and now as it is
> getting very late you must ecuse this short letter this time—and
> I hope to here from soon I send you my love and best wishes.[97]

This was the best Whitman could expect from his shy, uneducated
boys; clearly a passionate nature could little be satisfied by such
replies.[98]
    Howevermuch love Whitman showered on his young men, he
could never obtain full reciprocation, full satisfaction of his yearning for the one perfect comrade: "Why is it a sense comes always
crushing on me, as of one happiness I have missed in life? and
one friend and companion I have never made?"[99] Not finding in
life his desired ideal, Whitman had to turn to the unknown audience of his poems for final love and consummation:

> Poemet embodying the idea I wander along my life hardly ever
> meeting comrades. . . . For I have not met them Therefore
> I have put my passionate love of comrades in my poems.[100]

Thus in "Calamus" Whitman opens the face of love to his reader.

The "Calamus" group, although not strictly ordered, incorporates many of the characteristics of traditional sonnet sequences. The poet cannot write without his lover near him. His lover answers his doubts, contents him with his lot merely by his presence, and shows him that the root of all philosophy is love. The poet wishes to be remembered only as a lover and a celebrator of love, discounting other kinds of fame as superficial.[101] Always qualifying these love lyrics, however, is the fact that they are directed to men, for the kind of love essential to such poetry Whitman could experience only in relations with men. It is therefore necessary for the poet to lead us away from the trodden paths and the prying eyes—the Calamus emotion avoids public display. Whereas he would stride off with his women defying society to do its worst, with his men, secretly and shyly, he slips out to where he can permit the smouldering fires to flame. He does not any longer "compell," but warns:

> Whoever you are holding me now in hand,
> Without one thing all will be useless,
> I give you fair warning before you attempt me further,
> I am not what you supposed, but far different.[102]

Still behind the admonition is the desirous lover tenderly beckoning the new person to join him at the pond side where grow the "Calamus" roots of manly love: "Passing stranger! you do not know how longingly I look upon you."[103]

From this remote backwater emerges Whitman's Democracy, the Democracy of comrades, expanded from the intimate "Calamus" love to the adhesive join of the coming republic:

> Come, I will make the continent indissoluble,
> I will make the most splendid race the sun ever shone upon,
> I will make divine magnetic lands,
>   With the love of comrades,
>
>   With the life-long love of comrades.
> I will plant companionship thick as trees along all the rivers of
>   America, and along the shores of the great lakes, and all
>   over the prairies,

I will make inseparable cities with their arms about each other's
    necks,
By the love of comrades,
    By the manly love of comrades.

For you, these from me, O Democracy, to serve you ma femme!
For you, for you I am trilling these songs.[104]

It was not only for Democracy, however, that Whitman trilled,
but for Walt Whitman—had he sung nothing but ditties like this
last, he would never have survived his adulators. For us Whitman's
most affecting Leaves are those in which he does not try to convert
love to program, those which spring directly from his troubled
breast:

Scented herbage of my breast,
Leaves from you I glean, I write, to be perused best afterwards,
Tomb-leaves, body-leaves growing up above me above death,

● ● ●

You are often more bitter than I can bear, you burn and sting me,
Yet you are beautiful to me you faint-tinged roots, you make
    me think of death,
Death is beautiful from you, (what indeed is finally beautiful
    except death and love?)
O I think it is not for life I am chanting here my chants of
    lovers, I think it must be for death . . . .[105]

Baffling, balking life is cast aside as the "usual adjustments and
pleasures," while "adhesiveness" merges with death, with delicious
desirable death. For only in death and beyond death can Whitman
embrace the ideally responsive comerado, the reader who will
wholly accept and complete his song:

When you read these I that was visible am become invisible,
Now it is you, compact, visible, realizing my poems, seeking me,
Fancying how happy you were if I could be with you and become
    your comrade;
Be it as if I were with you. (Be not too certain but I am now
with you.)[106]

Notes

1 *In Re Walt Whitman,* ed. Horace Traubel, R. M. Bucke, and T. B. Harned (Philadelphia, 1893), p. 34.

2 He wrote to Nelly O'Connor (11/15/63): "I find my New York boys the same gay-hearted joyous fellows, full of friendship & determined to have pleasure. We have been together quite a good deal. They have given me little supper parties, Men only. With drinks &c. of course we have great times."

Manuscript in the Henry W. and Albert A. Berg Collection of The New York Public Library.

3 Letter to John R. Johnston, Jr., 2/18/?, in Berg Collection.

4 Gay Wilson Allen, *The Solitary Singer* (New York, 1955), p. 403.

5 See *Calamus, Letters to Peter Doyle,* ed. R. M. Bucke (Boston, 1897), pp. 47-48. Cf. Allen, *Solitary Singer,* p. 403.

6 *Calamus,* p. 49.

7 Letter to Charles W. Eldridge, 11/17/63, The Oscar Lion Collection of Walt Whitman, Reserve Division, New York Public Library. Quoted by Allen, *Solitary Singer,* p. 305.

8 *The Gathering of the Forces,* ed. Cleveland Rodgers and John Black (New York, 1920), II, 88–89.

9 "Sketches on Womanhood" (ms. version of lines from "A Woman Waits For Me"), in Barrett Collection, University of Virginia Library.

10 Ms. in Harned Collection of The Library of Congress, Box #3. Printed in *Walt Whitman's Workshop,* ed. Clifton J. Furness (Cambridge, 1928), p. 63.

11 "Specimen Days," *Complete Prose Works* (Philadelphia, 1892), p. 153.

12 "A Family Record," ms. in Berg Collection.

13 "Specimen Days," p. 12. "Quoted" by Whitman from John Burrough's *Notes.*

14 Carpenter and Bucke recognized this and, thinking a third sex actually possible, tried to justify it. Their primary example, of course, was Whitman himself, whose "bisexuality" seemed to them to presage the eventual desired fusion. See Edward Carpenter, *Days With Walt Whitman* (London, 1906), and R. M. Bucke (with H. L. Traubel and T. B. Harned), "Introduction" to the *Complete Writings of Walt Whitman* ed. Bucke, Harned, and Traubel (New York, 1902), vol. I, and also scattered comments elsewhere in Bucke's writings.

15 Traubel, *With Walt Whitman in Camden* (New York, 1914), III, 541.

16 *Ibid.,* III, 525.

17 See *Letters Written By Walt Whitman to His Mother* (New York, 1936).

18 "The Shadow and Light of a Young Man's Soul," *Uncollected Poetry and Prose,* ed. Emory Holloway (Garden City, 1921), I, 229–234. Hereafter abbreviated as *UPP.*

19 Letter of 2/7/73 printed in *In Re,* p. 77.

20 See plot outlines in Notebook "C," Library of Congress Walt Whitman Collection, Box 15; also "Young Grimes," *UPP,* I, 2–3,

21 William Eldridge to J. H. Johnston, 5/29/02, in Berg Collection. Quoted by Allen, *Solitary Singer,* p. 370.

22 Traubel, *With Walt Whitman in Camden* (Boston, 1906), I, 332.

23 *Complete Writings,* X, 24.

24 Traubel, *Walt Whitman in Camden,* I, 11.

25 "Faces," 5: 9–12, 15–17. The texts in this paper are those of the "Inclusive" edition of *Leaves of Grass,* ed. Emory Holloway (Garden City, 1948) unless otherwise indicated.

26 Typescript in The Oscar Lion Collection of Walt Whitman, Reserve Division, New York Public Library. Printed in Allen, *Solitary Singer,* p. 279; cf. p. 571, note 60.

27 In ms. notebook in Library of Congress Collection. Quoted by Louis Untermeyer in *The Poetry and Prose of Walt Whitman* (New York, 1948), p. 53. Cf Emory Holloway, "Whitman Pursued," *American Literature,* XXVII, 1–11 (March, 1955).

28. Peter Doyle's words as recorded by Bucke in *Calamus,* p. 25.

29 Will Wallace to Whitman: "I am surprised at your frenchy leaving you in such a deplorable state, but you are not alone. I had to dismiss mine to save the reputation of the hospital and your humble servant." Transcription of original in Bucke Collection by Emory Holloway, reproduced in G. L. Sixbey, "Whitman's Middle Years," Unpublished Doctoral Thesis, Yale University, 1941, p. 209.

30 "Some day when I feel more like it than I do now I will tell you about her." Whitman to Traubel, *Walt Whitman In Camden,* I, 389.

31 Ellen H. Calder, "Personal Recollection of Walt Whitman," *Atlantic Monthly,* XCIX, 830 (June, 1907).

32 See *UPP,* II, 7, f.n., and Calder, "Recollection," p. 829.

33 *The Gathering of the Forces,* II, 216–217.

34 *New York Dissected,* ed. Emory Holloway and Ralph Adimari (New York, 1936), p. 96.

35 *UPP,* II, 19.

36 *The Letters of Anne Gilchrist and Walt Whitman,* ed. Thomas B. Harned (New York, 1918), p. 60–61.

37 *Ibid.,* p. 66.

38 *Ibid.,* p. 67.

39. Located in University of Pennsylvania Library, quoted by Allen, *Solitary Singer,* p. 439.

40 Printed in Traubel, *With Walt Whitman in Camden,* ed. Sculley Bradley (Philadelphia, 1958), IV, 313.

41 *Ibid.,* IV, 313–314.

42 *UPP,* II, 7, f.n.

43 Traubel, *Walt Whitman in Camden,* III, 452–453.

44 See, e.g., "I Sing the Body Electric," 5: 1–9.

45 Frederick Schyberg, *Walt Whitman,* trans. Evie Allison Allen (New York, 1951), p. 162.

46 Klaus Mann, "The Present Greatness of Walt Whitman," *Decision,* I, 23 (April, 1941).

47 "Song of Myself," 5: 6–14.

48 "A Memorandum at a Venture," *Prose Works,* pp. 302–303.

49 See Traubel, *With Walt Whitman in Camden* (New York, 1908), II, 152.

50 *UPP,* I, 48.

51 See unpublished notebook in Library of Congress Collection, Box 15A.

52 Traubel, *Walt Whitman in Camden,* II, 151–152.

53 "Ages and Ages Returning At Intervals," 11. 3–6.

54 "One Hour To Madness and Joy," 1. 8 of 1860 version, "Inclusive" Edition, p. 589.

55 "A Woman Waits For Me," 11. 20–23, 26–30.

56 Spontaneous Me," 11. 23–34.

57 "I Sing the Body Electric," 9: 1, 5–6.

58 "One Hour To Madness and Joy," 11. 7–9.

59 1855 reading of part of section one of "The Sleepers"; "Inclusive" edition, p. 683.

60 *UPP,* I, 48.

61 *UPP,* II. 72.

62 "A Woman Waits For Me," 11. 12–14.

63 D. H. Lawrence, "Whitman," *Studies in Classic American Literature* (Garden City, 1953), pp. 179–180.

64 "A Woman Waits For Me," 11. 12–14.

65 *Ibid.,* 11. 16–17.

66 "From Pent-Up Aching Rivers," 11. 29–30.

67 "One Hour To Madness and Joy," 11. 17–19.

68 *Complete Writings,* IX, 150.

69 Ms. in Harned Collection of The Library of Congress, Box #3. Printed in *Walt Whitman's Workshop,* pp. 63–64.

70 I do not suggest that Whitman had any overt homosexual experiences; there is no evidence whatever to indicate that he was, in our sense of the word, a "homosexual." I do assert, however, that he sought from men the kind of day to day warmth and intimacy usually found by a man in relations with a woman. The debate about Whitman's sexual nature has been considerably muddled by failure to distinguish between urge and practise and by the application of twentieth-century psychological abstractions to nineteenth-century realities.

71 "Democratic Vistas," *Prose Works,* p. 220.

72 George Combe, *A System of Phrenology* (Boston, 1835), p. 143.

73 *Phrenology: Proved, Illustrated, and Applied* (New York:Fowler and Wells, 1856), pp. 65–66; the book by Whitman's first publishers.

74 ". . . I guess I am mainly sensitive to the wonderfulness & perhaps

spirituality of things *in their physical & concrete* expression—& have celebrated all that." Letter to William O'Connor, 4/18/88, in Berg Collection.

75 Letter of 6/19/77 in Berg Collection.

76 *Walt Whitman in Camden*, II, 82.

77 "One might naively assume that the need for companionship is a product of acculturation. But, according to Sullivan, it is not. Animals manifest gregarious traits. Furthermore, people have a need for physical contact, a need to touch one another and to be physically close. But this need for physical closeness is *not* in itself a sexual phenomenon." Patrick Mullahy, "A Theory of Interpersonal Relations and the Evolution of Personality," in Harry Stack Sullivan, *Conceptions of Modern Psychiatry* (Washington, 1947), p. 120.

78 "Song of Myself," 11: 9–15.

79 His relations with Walter Whitman were always strained. In the early stories, desperately autobiographical in meaning, the sensitive, artistic son is frequently pitted against a harsh, tyrannical father-figure. Walt was in effect adopted by some of his early preceptors in the newspaper trade.

80 W. E. Vandermark, 12/16/63, in "Soldier's Letters to Me During the War (Some Since)," Whitman's scrapbook of letters; located in Berg Collection.

81 Elijah D. Fox, 11/10/65, in the Oscar Lion Collection of Walt Whitman, Reserve Division, New York Public Library.

82 *Calamus.* p. 23. "Adventures of this kind are frequent," William D. O'Connor commented, explaining Whitman's attractiveness to plain, unlettered men. *The Good Gray Poet* (New York, 1866), p. 9.

83 *Calamus*, pp. 36-37.

84 *Ibid.*, p. 61.

85 See Eustace Chesser, *Sexual Behavior—Normal and Abnormal* (New York, 1949), who suggests that "non-practicing homosexuals sometimes seek to find outlets for the sexuality in non-sexual spheres by taking up work, often of a voluntary kind, among their own sex," p. 158.

86 Traubel, *Walt Whitman in Camden*, III, 204. Note the image of the folded leaf, crucial in the "Calamus" poems.

87 "The Wound Dresser," 11. 4–6.

88 John Burroughs, *Whitman: A Study* (Boston, 1896), p. 49.

89 Traubel, *Walt Whitman in Camden*, II, 331.

90 Gustav Bychowski, "Walt Whitman: A Study in Sublimation," *Psychoanalysis and the Social Sciences*, ed. G. Roheim (New York, 1951), I, 240.

91 *Walt Whitman's Workshop*, p. 62.

92 "Song of Myself," 13: 1–5; cf. 12: 3–8. Contrast Whitman's descriptions of the male and female forms in "I Sing the Body Electric." The woman's body is never really described, while the man's is detailed with loving tenderness.

93 Traubel, *Walt Whitman in Camden*, I, 204. With this should be compared a note Whitman wrote to himself, presumably sometime in 1870:

"Depress the adhesive nature/ It is in excess—making life in torment/ Ah this diseased, feverish disproportionate adhesiveness." In The Library of Congress Whitman Collection, Notebook 9, "Lincoln Material," on a page with a clipping dated March, 1870. Printed in *UPP*, II, 96.

94 "Hours Continuing Long, Sore and Heavy-Hearted," 11. 6–7.

95 Draft of letter in the Berg Collection. Material in brackets is crossed out in the original. Quoted by Allen, *Solitary Singer*, p. 298.

96 In Berg Collection. Printed in Allen, *Solitary Singer*, p. 299.

97 In Berg Collection. Sawyer's letter to Lew Brown shows, like this letter, his illiteracy and poor hand. The previous letter is perfect in construction and penmanship and therefore almost certainly not written directly by him.

98 Whitman expressed in his letter to Sawyer another of his favorite desires—to set up housekeeping with his boys. To Doyle he wrote: "My darling, if you are not well when I come back I will get a good room or two in some quiet place, and we will live together and devote ourselves altogether to the job of curing you, and making you stronger and healthier than ever." *Calamus*, p. 55.

99 *UUP*, I, 112, f.n.

100 Printed in Allen, *Solitary Singer*, p. 504.

101 "I Saw In Louisiana A Live-Oak Growing"; "Of The Terrible doubt of Appearances"; "The Base of All Metaphysics"; "Recorders Ages Hence"; "When I Heard At The Close Of The Day."

102 "Whoever You Are Holding Me Now In Hand," 11. 1–4.

103 "To A Stranger," 1. 1.

104 "For You O Democracy."

105 "Scented Herbage Of My Breast," 11. 1–3, 9–12.

106 "Full Of Life Now," 11. 5–8.

A Selected Bibliography

Adelson, S. L. Lincoln's health. *Harper Hospital Bulletin (Detroit)*, 18:117-119, 1960.

Asselineau, Roger. *The Evolution of Walt Whitman: The Creation of a Personality.* Cambridge, Mass.: Harvard University Press, 1960.

Bertz, Eduard. Walt Whitman Ein Charakterbild. *Jahrbuch für sexuelle Zwischenstrifen,* 7:155-289, 1907.

————.*Der Yankee-Heiland: Ein Beitrag zur Modernen Religionsgeschichte.* Dresden: Carl Reissner, 1906.

————. Zwei Gedichte aus 'Calamus.' *Jahrbuch für sexuelle Zwischenstrifen,* 22:55-58, 1922.

Bett, W. R. Walt Whitman. The invert who sought to redeem democracy, in *The Infirmities of Genius.* New York: Philosophical Library, 1952. Pp. 45-56.

Briggs, Arthur E. *Walt Whitman. Thinker and Artist.* New York: Philosophical Library, 1952.

Bragman, Louis J. Walt Whitman, hospital attendant and medical critic. *Medical Life,* 39:606-615, 1932.

Bychowski, Gustav. Walt Whitman: a study in sublimation. In Roheim, Géza (Ed.), *Psychoanalysis and the Social Sciences,* Vol. III. New York: International Universities Press, 1951. Pp. 223-261.

Carpenter, Edward. *Some Friends of Walt Whitman; A Study in Sex-Psychology.* Pub. No. 13: The British Society for the Study of Sex Psychology. London: Athenenaeum Press, 1924.

Catel, Jean. *Walt Whitman: la Naissance du Poète.* Paris: Les Éditions Rieder, 1929.

Clark, L. Pierce. *Lincoln: A Psycho-Biography.* New York: Charles Scribner's Sons, 1933.

Crenshaw, Ollinger. Psychological background of the election of 1860 in the South. *North Carolina Historical Review,* 19:260-280, 1942.

Fiedler, Leslie A. Images of Walt Whitman, in *An End to Innocence.* Boston: Beacon Press, 1952. Pp. 152-173.

Hartley, L. Conrad. *The Spirit of Walt Whitman. A Psychological Study in Blank Verse.* Manchester, England: J. L. Cornish, Ltd., 1908.

Hesseltine, William B. *Civil War Prisons—A Study in War Psychology.* Columbus, Ohio: 1930

Holloway, Emory. Walt Whitman's love affairs. *Dial,* 69:473-483, 1920.

———. *Whitman: An Interpretation in Narrative.* New York: Alfred A. Knopf, 1926.

Hungerford, Edward. Walt Whitman and his chart of bumps. *American Literature,* 2:350-384, 1931.

Miller, James E., Jr. 'Song of Myself' as inverted mystical experience. *PMLA,* 70:636-661, 1955.

Reardon, William, & Foxen, John. Civil War theater: the propaganda play. *Civil War History,* 1:281-293, 1955.

Rhodes, S. A. The influence of Walt Whitman on André Gide. *Romantic Review,* 31:156-171, 1940.

Rivers, W. C. *Walt Whitman's Anomaly.* London: George Allen, 1913.

Schlaf, Johannes. *Walt Whitman Homosexueller, Kritische Revision einer Whitman-Abhandlung von Dr. Eduard Bertz.* Minden: Brun's Verlag, 1906.

Schyberg, Frederick. *Walt Whitman.* New York: Columbia University Press, 1951.

Wilson, George W. John Wilkes Booth: father murderer. *American Imago,* 1:49-60, 1940.

Mitchell College Library
New London, Conn.

TE DUE

5